Narrative Identity

Evangelical Missiological Society Monograph Series

Anthony Casey, Allen Yeh, Mark Kreitzer, and Edward L. Smither

SERIES EDITORS

———————————————

A Project of the Evangelical Missiological Society

www.emsweb.org

"I very much enjoyed reading Trevor Castor's excellent work. I believe it makes a new, creative, excellent contribution to missiology. I myself have written, edited, and published in this area . . . and found myself drawn in by Castor's research and analysis. That is, he had something new to say; it was not hard to literally read every page. I would not say that about everything I read along these lines."

—**David Greenlee**, Operation Mobilization

"This book brings a fresh perspective on how people self-identify, a dynamic process that is both individual and collective. As such, it questions the popular paradigm of people group thinking in missions and deems it cultural determinism and static. Fascinating narratives of Pashtuns in the USA illustrate how immigrants navigate the 'system.' They must fit into the American way of life and simultaneously keep in touch with family back home. It is well worth the read."

—**Warren Larson**, Columbia International University

"Castor takes on some key immigration and anthropological issues—identity, acculturation, life histories—regarding the Pashtun, and presents the analysis of these as they relate to the Pashtun with a critical eye and significant nuance."

—**Steven J. Ybarrola**, Asbury Theological Seminary

"The dissertation makes a substantial contribution to the field of study. It attempts to show how understandings of identity are moving away from the 'essentialist' and 'constructivist' impasse to a more relational view of how identity is to be understood. The methodology is clearly set out and there is a good review of literature. Castor has discussed well the different factors involved in the emergence of transnational identity."

—**Michael Nazir-Ali**, Oxford Centre for Training, Research, Advocacy and Dialogue

"This book explores identity formation across countries and through social media at the intersection of personal, sociocultural, and global narratives. Historical and theoretical background is skillfully juxtaposed with real-life analysis to question stereotypes and popular missiological concepts. Through its contents and model, the book constitutes an invaluable resource in understanding people and communities within our current world of widespread transmigration."

—**Moyra Dale**, Australian College of Theology

"Castor's new book is groundbreaking on several levels. His application of a narrative identity framework informs the active debates in the fast-changing field of identity studies. Furthermore, Castor's focus on Pashtun immigrants in the USA offers compelling new insights into digital-age communication contributions to identity formation. Moreover, his consideration of people group identity represents a challenge to one of the theoretical icons of mission studies. This is a must-read book."

—**Peter G. Riddell**, Australian College of Theology

Narrative Identity

Transnational Practices of Pashtun Immigrants
in the United States of America

Trevor Castor

PICKWICK *Publications* · Eugene, Oregon

NARRATIVE IDENTITY
Transnational Practices of Pashtun Immigrants in the United States of America

Evangelical Missiological Society Monograph Series 9

Pickwick Publications
An Imprint of Wipf and Stock Publishers
199 W. 8th Ave., Suite 3
Eugene, OR 97401

www.wipfandstock.com

PAPERBACK ISBN: 978-1-6667-0036-7
HARDCOVER ISBN: 978-1-6667-0037-4
EBOOK ISBN: 978-1-6667-0038-1

Cataloguing-in-Publication data:

Names: Castor, Trevor, author.

Title: Narrative identity : transnational practices of Pashtun immigrants in the United States of America / by Trevor Castor.

Description: Eugene, OR: Pickwick Publications, 2021 | Evangelical Missiological Society Monograph Series 9 | Includes bibliographical references.

Identifiers: ISBN 978-1-6667-0036-7 (paperback) | ISBN 978-1-6667-0037-4 (hardcover) | ISBN 978-1-6667-0038-1 (ebook)

Subjects: LCSH: Pushtuns—Ethnic identity. | Pushtuns—Social life and customs. | Minorities—United States—Cross-cultural studies.

Classification: DS354.58 C37 2021 (print) | DS354.58 (ebook)

10/20/21

To my wife and best friend Katie—one who is utterly unique and beyond classification. I now understand what you meant thirteen years ago concerning the *identity* of an oak tree.

Contents

List of Figures | xi
Preface | xiii
Acknowledgments | xxi

1. **Shifting Identity** | 1
   Identity According to the OED   4
   Shifting Identity from the Soul to Rational Self   6
   From Rational to Intuitive   11
   Conclusion   14

2. **Shifting Pashtun Identity in Ethnography** | 16
   Essentialist Views of the Pashtun   16
   Constructivist Shift   21
   More Recent Studies   25
   Conclusion   28

3. **Shifting Fields in Immigrant Research** | 30
   Acculturation Theory   31
   Transnationalism   36
   Computer Mediated Communication   37
   Context of Virtual Spaces   38
   Imagined Virtual Communities   39
   Deterritorialization or Reterritorialization   41
   Conclusion   42

4. Narrative Identity | 44

   Inner and Outer Role of Narratives   46

   Epistemological Public Narratives   50

   The Medium of Digital Media Discourse   53

   Essentialist and Nominalist Frameworks   53

   Epistemology of Fear   55

   Fear of Muslims in American Media   57

   "Us" versus "Them" in National News Media   60

   Media Double Standard   61

   Evangelical "Us" Versus "Them"   65

   Evangelical's Use of the Essentialist Framework   68

   Diverse Communities of Interpretation rather than
      "Us" and "Them"   71

   Diverse Groups of Protestant Reformation   72

   Conclusion   76

5. Transnational Pashtun Narratives | 80

   Propaganda Narratives   80

   Pre-9/11 U.S. Pashtun Propaganda of "Us"   82

   Propaganda through Textbooks   84

   Post-Cold War, "Us" becomes "Them"   87

   Recent Pashtun Public Narratives   91

   Pashtun in the News Media   92

   Conclusion   95

6. Narrative Identity of Sayyid Qutb (1906–1966) | 97

   Competing Global Narratives in Childhood   97

   Competing Sociocultural Narratives in Childhood   99

   Synthesizing Islam and Modernism through Education   103

   Competing Narratives of Tribalism and Nationalism   107

   The Need for Social Justice   108

   A Vision to become an Intellectual   110

   Conflicting Narratives for Egypt   111

   Qutb's Visit to America   113

   Qutb's Return to Egypt   115

   The Impact of Imprisonment on Qutb's Identity   116

Milestones: A Re-imagined Islamic Identity   117
Competing Narratives of Jahiliyyah and Islamic Identity   119
Divine Shari'ah and Jihad   122
Conclusion   124

7. Three Young Men from Kabul | 126
Competing Narratives of Rural Afghanistan and Kabul   128
Competing Narratives of America and Kabul   130
Public Narratives of Christianity and Islam and the Impact
    of Acculturation   131
Lack of Meaningful Work   134
Transnationalism through Computer Mediated Communication   135
Conclusion   137

8. Life History of Alan | 140
Transnational Narratives through Film   141
Returning to Kabul   142
Joining the Fight to Rebuild Afghanistan   144
Good Days Killing Bad Guys and Bad Days Losing Good Guys   147
Jihad in the Context of Global Narratives   151
Alan on being Pashtun   153
The Move to America: Loss of Close Relationships
    and Meaningful Work   155
Reshaping Boundaries of Identity in America   156
Conclusion   159

9. Life History of Miriam | 161
Miriam's Grandfather: Ahmad Wazir   161
Inherited Honor through Ahmad Wazir   164
Miriam's Parents Fazal and Nazima   166
Nazima's People (Mountain People)   167
Fazal's People   170
Seeking Asylum in America   171
Moving to America   173
High School Freshman at Seventeen Years Old   174
Green Card Denied   176
Transnational Family Dynamics in Pakistan   178

Nazima Returns to Pakistan   180

Miriam's Role as a Financial Provider   181

Analysis of Miriam's Narrative Identity   184

Problematic Social Media Posts   184

Conclusion through the Lens of the Taliban   185

10. **Concluding with a Reflexive Challenge
to People Group Identity** | 189

The 1974 Lausanne Congress   190

Popularizing the Model   194

Missiology not Shifting   197

From Analytical Tool to the Biblical Model   200

Identity or Identification   207

Conclusion   211

Bibliography | 221

Figures

Figure 1: Google Ngram Identity | 2

Figure 2: Berry's Model of Acculturation Strategies | 35

Preface

THE PASHTUN ARE PERHAPS one of the most feared and least understood people in the world. For centuries, they have been accustomed to war, ethnic, tribal, and religious violence. Ongoing war in the Pashtun regions of Afghanistan and Pakistan generates a considerable amount of negative media attention in the West, raising concerns for both Pashtun immigrants and their societies of settlement. Some American media reports speculate that the Pashtun are prone to radicalization due to their ethnic and religious identity.[1] While there is no research on Pashtun immigrants lending credibility to the media claims, the arrests of multiple Pashtun immigrants in the United States and Europe for terrorist activity between 2009–2019 raises concerns.

Using qualitative research methods, including ethnography and life history interviews, this work discusses the context and factors that impact identity formation for Pashtun immigrants in the United States. Particular attention is given to the role of transnational relationships, computer-mediated communication, and public narrative discourses concerning Islam and the Pashtun people. I argue that identity is best understood as relationally constituted at the convergence of individual and sociocultural narratives that provide a sense of continuity or self-sameness between past experiences, present circumstances, and an imagined future. Narrative identity moves beyond the binary framework of cultural essentialism or constructivism. It is through narratives, drawn from the collective or social memory and imagination, that the symbolic systems of cultural domains are often organized, learned, and expressed as a collective framework or suitable way in which to live and view the world. Yet, it is the individual's interpretation, drawn from one's own remembered experience, that gives these collective symbols and cultural domains power. While individuals story their experience, they do so in the contexts of shared sociocultural experiences which

1. Elliot et al., "For Times Square Suspect"; Kaylan, "Immigration, Terror and Assimilation"; News Week, "Pashtuns May Bring The Afghan War Home To America."

xiii

are also storied. It is therefore important to approach identity at the point of narrative convergence between the individual and the collective without privileging one over the other. The role of shared sociocultural discourse in identity formation is particularly concerning for Pashtun immigrants whose Muslim faith and ethnic background is regularly discussed in the context of religious and ethnic violence.

Purpose and Background of the Study

This research discusses the context and factors that impact the process of identity formation of Pashtun immigrants living in the United States. Particular attention is given to the role of transnational relationships and public narrative discourses concerning Islam and the Pashtun people.

Chapter 1 discusses how recent events have spurred significant interest in identity research across academic disciplines. Despite a significant upsurge in academic writing and public discourse, there is little conformity concerning the meaning of the term identity. Often the word is used in research without defining the term due to an assumption that the term itself has a self-defining quality. This line of reasoning is reinforced when identity becomes an affix to another word that a person may consider important to their sense of self (e.g., national identity, racial identity, ethnic identity, religious identity, etc.). Rather than add to the confusion, chapter one explores the history of the term and the development of identity studies within social sciences in order to clarify what is meant by identity.

Chapter 2 demonstrates through a literature review how the Pashtun informed the significant paradigm shift in social science away from cultural essentialism toward the postmodern constructivist approaches. Some of the earliest identity theories in the social sciences come from nineteenth-century ethnographies where identity is often framed within a cultural or ethnic framework. Conceptualizing identity as ethnicity, particularly among collective societies, dominates the literature throughout the nineteenth and much of the twentieth century and the Pashtun are no exception to the ethnic identity framework. However, in the mid-twentieth century, researchers make a noticeable shift in their depictions of the Pashtun that impacts the entire field of anthropology.

Chapter 3 focuses on the development of acculturation theory and the emerging trends of transnationalism, computer mediated communication, and social media. The constructivist view of identity places the emphasis primarily on the individual to self-ascribe an identity and to find others who will confirm their ascription. The dynamic view of identity places prominence on the ways in which the immigrant cultures change or acculturate in their new context. The transnational practice of maintaining multiple social networks across national and geographical boundaries adds new layers of complexity to the acculturation process, particularly when it comes to immigrant understandings of collective belonging.

Chapter 4 proposes a way to move beyond the binary categories of determinism and constructivism towards an approach that aims to neither give culture too much power nor deny its influence. This balance can be achieved through a narrative identity framework. Narrative identity acknowledges that while an individual does construct their identity, they do so relationally, and through a limited repertoire of canonized stories. These narratives are shaped and, in some cases, even controlled through public discourse. Given the role of American media in forming epistemological assumptions about Islam and Muslims, current public discourses concerning Muslim immigrants are also explored in this chapter.

Chapter 5 looks specifically at American public discourse on the Pashtun in the context of war propaganda. The section shows the underlying political power structures often associated with Pashtun immigrants. These public narratives may prove to be problematic for Pashtun immigrant identity formation. The negative representation of the Pashtun in America and the negative portrayal of America in Pakistan may lead to feelings of not belonging in either place. The historic and ongoing tension between nation-states of origin and settlement may be a potential strain on the identity formation of Pashtun immigrants considering it is negotiated at the intersection of two competing sociocultural narratives.

Chapter 6 is a historical case study on Sayyid Qutb that illustrates the process of narrative identity formation. Using well-known historical figures to demonstrate theories of identity is well documented in social science. While not Pashtun, Qutb's ideas have had a profound influence among the Pashtun. Approaching Qutb's theological ideas through the lens of his life history demonstrates the potential consequences when an individual is unable to reconcile competing public and personal sociocultural identity narratives.

Chapters 7, 8, and 9 are the life history narratives of Pashtun immigrants living in the United States. Their stories will provide insight to the impact of transnationalism, computer mediated communication, and the role of sociocultural narratives in identity formation.

Chapter 10 is a reflexive conclusion and challenge to the missiological paradigm of People Group Identity. Prior to this research, much of my understanding concerning culture and identity came from this missiological model of identity. This chapter discusses how this research led me to reconsider the validity of my initial assumptions regarding identity formation.

Methodology

The development of a cultural document for the Pashtun immigrant community is achieved through qualitative research using multi-sited ethnographic methods.[2] Multi-sited ethnography is primarily interested in the ways cultural artifacts and meanings shift depending on the context. The approach lends credibility to the development of a community beyond a specific locale by tracing the cultural negotiation across multiple interconnected sites.

> As groups migrate, regroup in new locations, reconstruct their histories, and reconfigure their ethnic projects, the *ethno* in ethnography takes on a slippery, non-localized quality, to which the descriptive practices of anthropology will have to respond.[3]

For this research, three sites serve as the primary fields for data collection. The first site is a mid-sized city in the southeastern United States. The second is the computer mediated communication of research participants through social media. The Internet is a virtual social field where diaspora groups often maintain connections with their country of origin and develop social networks where collective identity is negotiated. The third site includes public narratives of Islam and the Pashtun in American media. It is necessary for a modern ethnography to explore the sociocultural narratives concerning the people being researched in order to articulate the context through which identity is shaped.[4]

Life History

Data collection will include life-history research, semi-structured interviews, and participant observation. Life-history research considers the complexity of individual experiences and draws on these to inform broader application and meaning.[5] This qualitative approach can provide a good basis for understanding a culture, especially when little research

2. Marcus, "Ethnography in/of the World System."
3. Appadurai, *Modernity at Large*, 48.
4. Marcus, "Ethnography in/of the World System."
5. Cole and Knowles, *Lives in Context.*

exists on a social group.[6] While a life history typically involves only one person's experience, there are broader implications. "To understand some of the complexities, complications, and confusions within the life of just one member of a community is to gain insights into the collective."[7] In other words, there is a symbiotic relationship between individual identity formation and the larger collective.

In addition to providing insight into group dynamics, life-history is an effective means to understand the influential historical processes.[8] Suggesting an individual focus of ethnography will likely be met with accusations of exporting Western individualism to non-Western communal societies. There is, however, a difference in individuality and individualism. Individuality is "an ideological neutral concept" whereas "individualism is a dogmatic posture which privileges the individual over society."[9]

This study presents the life history narratives of five individuals. Given the small number of participants, it is imperative to recognize the difference between cultural patterns and idiosyncrasies.[10] This is achieved by cross-checking data analysis with other semi-structured interviews and participant observation of the broader Pashtun immigrant community.

Semi-Structured Interviews

The semi-structured interview is less an interview and more a conversation. In fact, "skilled ethnographers often gather most of their data through participant observation and many casual, friendly conversations."[11] In contrast to a casual conversation, the ethnographic interview has a purpose. The interviews are focused on gaining insight and testing cultural inferences gathered from the life-history interviews. Because of the importance of gender segregation in the Pashtun culture, my semi-structured interviews with women were not conducted in private. Neither were the interviews with Miriam, whose life history is presented in chapter nine. While there is precedence in ethnographic research of the Pashtun for male researchers to successfully work through their spouses to obtain the female perspectives, this was not necessary for this study.[12] I conducted

6. Langness, *Life History in Anthropological Science.*
7. Cole and Knowles, *Lives in Context*, 11.
8. Erikson, *Life History.*
9. Cohen, *Self Consciousness*, 168.
10. Langness, *Life History in Anthropological Science.*
11. Spradley, *Ethnographic Interview*, 58.
12. Ahmed, *Pukhtun Economy and Society*; Lindholm, *Generosity and Jealousy.*

the interviews with Miriam along with my wife's assistance. Miriam and her family granted my wife and me the privilege of being in their home without strict adherence to gender segregation.

Participant Observation

Participant observation is considered to be the "bedrock" of ethnographic research.[13] It is through participant observation that the information provided in semi-structured and life history interviews takes shape. These methods combined provide an effective research method for documenting acculturation patterns for transnationals:

> Participant observation and ethnographic interviewing allow researchers to document how persons simultaneously maintain and shed cultural repertoires and identities, interact within a location and across its boundaries, and act in ways that are in concert with or contradict their values over time.[14]

I have engaged in participant observation of the Muslim community over the past twelve years. Locations include three local mosques, various workplaces, and multiple homes. Throughout this project, I strived to immerse myself as much as possible into the daily lives of research participants in order to understand the importance and meaning of cultural practices.[15] The goal of participant observation is not simply to observe cultural patterns and behaviors but rather to provide a "thick description."[16] A digital recorder was used for life history narratives. Acknowledging that transcription is an interpretive process, all the interviews were personally transcribed.[17] In order for the voices of the research participants to be the primary source, the only edits offered are for the sake of readability.[18]

Limitations of the Study

Life history and semi-structured interviews were conducted in English, not Pashto. The use of a second language has the potential to distort

---

13. Agar, *Professional Stranger,* 117.

14. Levitt and Schiller, "Conceptualizing Simultaneity," 192.

15. Emerson et al., *Writing Ethnographic Fieldnotes.*

16. Geertz, *Interpretation of Cultures,* 10.

17. Emerson et al., *Ethnographic Fieldnotes.*

18. Blauner, "Problems of Editing First-Person."

research findings.[19] In order to minimize this distortion, participants were asked to tell stories on more than one occasion to clarify and confirm my understanding.

Acculturation is defined as a change that happens in either or both groups that come into continuous contact.[20] For this study, changes in American communities as a result of continuous contact is not assessed. Furthermore, while transnationalism impacts both the society of settlement and origin, the primary focus of this project is Pashtun immigrants in the United States; therefore, interviews with the participant's social networks in their home countries were not pursued.

19. Spradley, *Ethnographic Interview.*

20. Redfield et al., "Memorandum for the Study of Acculturation," 149–52.

Acknowledgments

I WOULD HAVE NEVER attempted this project without the encouragement of my professors and now colleagues at Columbia International University (CIU). I want to thank Dr. Joel Williams for being the first one to encourage me to pursue a doctorate. I would also like to express my gratitude to my friends in the College of Intercultural Studies at CIU, especially deans Dr. Mike Barnett and Dr. Ed Smither. I am thankful for the support these deans provided for me to do this research. Finally, I want to thank my mentor, Dr. Warren Larson, for instilling a passion within me to understand the Muslim community. The faculty and staff at CIU have been a constant encouragement to me throughout my doctoral research. I also want to acknowledge the students at CIU whose passion for learning inspired my research. I am particularly grateful for my grad assistant Abigail Kraus for her editorial assistance.

I want to thank my doctoral advisors, Dr. Peter Riddell, Dr. Steve Johnson, and Dr. Moyra Dale. Thank you, Dr. Riddell, for continually encouraging me during times of self-doubt. Thank you, Dr. Johnson, for patiently listening to me and helping me fine-tune my ideas. While Dr. Dale was not able to remain on my committee for health reasons, I want to thank her for inspiring me toward ethnographic methodology and narrative analysis. Her insights in these research methodologies were invaluable to me.

I am also incredibly grateful to my family and friends. To my wife and children, thank you for your support over the past six years. I would have never been able to accomplish this work without each of you. Thank you, Katie, for teaching me how to be fully present with people and hear their story. I appreciate that you have taken a genuine interest in my research topic and that you are always willing to process ideas with me. Thank you, Benjamin, Chloe, and Anna, for patiently enduring what likely seemed to be endless conversations between your parents on topics you did not always understand. Benjamin, you taught me to see identity like a Rubik's Cube. Focusing one side of the puzzle is insufficient and may even limit your ability to complete the puzzle. Chloe, your ability to see the best in people encourages me to look beyond what is immediately observable and see people in context and with charity. Anna, your capacity to bring peace amidst chaos blesses our family beyond measure and is a constant reminder that we need other people in our lives. I hope and pray that the three of you continue to know and experience the love and grace of God and that you are continually an instrument of that love and grace toward others.

Thank you to my parents, Rick and Della. Not only would I not be alive if it were not for you, but I also would not be the person I am today. Thanks to my brother J. R. and his family, as well as my weekly guys' group. Joe and Chicken, you are the foundation for the concept of *close friendships* discussed in this work. No one can do life alone! I cannot imagine my life without my family and friends. If any of you ever read the following pages, you will understand why.

Finally, I want to thank the Muslim community that allowed me to enter into their lives for the sake of research. I acknowledge that I can never fully explain my experiences with you over the past decade. This thesis is my humble attempt to put to words what is not entirely capable of being understood apart from experiencing it.

1

Shifting Identity

THE TERM IDENTITY IS frequently used but rarely defined in public discourse; and, in some cases, the same could be said for academic writing as well. There seems to be considerable confusion regarding the meaning of identity yet there is hardly a more popular word. Phillip Gleason highlighted this phenomenon in his 1983 essay on the semantic history of identity. He suggested that though the word was being used constantly in discussions and in writing, most people, if pressed would have a difficult time defining what exactly they meant. The lack of precision and consistency coupled with the popular and clichéd usage of the term extinguished any analytical value for Gleason. He concluded his study by suggesting "that a good deal of what passes for discussion of identity is little more than portentous incoherence."[1]

Despite the lack of clarity and questionable analytical value of the term identity, interest both on the academic and popular level continued throughout the twentieth century and into the twenty-first. In 1999, James Fearon conducted a similar study as Gleason's and observed that in the fifteen years not much had changed:

> Overwhelmingly, academic users of the word 'identity' feel no need to explain its meaning to readers. The readers' understanding is simply taken for granted, even when 'identity' is the author's primary dependent or independent variable.[2]

Fearon's observation is particularly troubling considering the rapid expansion of publications containing the term identity since the mid-twentieth century. The following Google Ngram chart shows the dramatic increase in book publications containing the word identity leading into the twenty-first century.

1. Gleason, "Identifying Identity," 931.
2. Fearon, "What is Identity," 4.

1

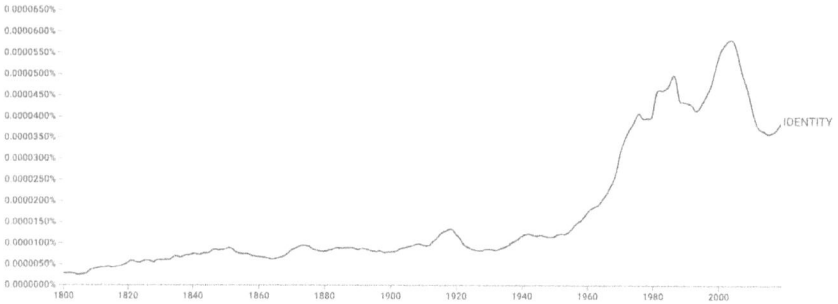

Note the dramatic increase following the end of WWII.

The number of academic dissertations on identity has dramatically increased as well. A brief survey of the ProQuest dissertation database shows that in 1983, the year Gleason wrote his essay on identity, there were 181 dissertations published with the term identity in the abstract.[3] The same search in 2013 reveals 3,325 dissertations, an increase of 1,737 percent in thirty years. Granted, these numbers must be considered alongside the overall growth of dissertations in social science in order to see whether there is any correlation. In comparison, in 1983 there were 9,599 dissertations published on social science. In 2013, the same search reveals 34,382 published dissertations. That is a 258 percent increase in published dissertations in social science in thirty years. This is a significant increase; however, it does not account for the 1,737 percent increase in dissertations with the term identity mentioned in the abstract.

The increase in academic publications is by no means a suggestion that the term identity is more understood. It is indeed possible, as some researchers have suggested, that the rapid semantic expansion only further contributes to the ambiguity.[4] "If identity is everywhere it is nowhere."[5] In other words, if identity has come to mean so many different things to so many different people, is there any analytical value to the term? This is a genuine concern considering the sheer volume of identity studies in social science as well as the recent upsurge in popular discourse.

In addition to publications, there is a significant increase in media discourse concerning identity. It is fair to say that the popular meaning of the term is no less elusive than the academic usage. In 2015, Dictionary.com awarded the term identity the "Word of the Year" prize. The rationale

---

3. ProQuest database accessed June 1, 2017.

4. Gleason, "Identifying Identity," 910–31.

5. Brubaker and Cooper, "Beyond Identity," 1.

for the award was attributed to the ongoing expansion and fluidity of the term, particularly in the areas of usage surrounding issues of gender, sexuality, and race. This makes sense considering that 2015 could be described as a watershed year for these topics in American popular media. A few clear examples that year include the public transgender transition of Bruce Jenner to Caitlyn Jenner, the Supreme Court ruling that legalized gay marriage in all fifty of the United States, and the racially motivated slaying of nine black church members by a self-proclaimed white supremacist in Charleston, South Carolina. Needless to say, 2015 sparked much debate concerning the topic of identity.

However, it should not come as a surprise that the recent increased interest in identity surrounds controversy. This phenomenon was observed by Erik Erikson nearly seventy years ago when the topic of identity was first popularized in social science: "We begin to conceptualize matters of identity at the very time in history when they become a problem."[6] Erikson's observation comes from the mid-twentieth century during the initial surge in identity discourse. The "problem" of identity at this point in history is primarily related to the post-WWII increase in immigration. Many of these immigrants, having left their homelands and families, found themselves in the midst of what Erikson called an identity crisis. He argued that the rise of national identity provided a new foundation for those who had lost their heritage. The conceptualization of a national identity, in the words of Erikson, was an attempt "to make a super-identity out of all the identities imported by its constituent immigrants."[7] Erikson's words concerning the issues related to immigrant identity continue to be relevant today and are potentially even more debated as identity politics. Immigrant and national identity discussions are at least partially responsible for the recent revival of the term in addition to the aforementioned topics of gender, sexuality, and race.

Regardless of which "problem" initially spurred the recent movement to reconceptualize identity, there is a common underlying debate regarding whether or not identity is fixed or fluid and housed individually or collectively. In order to address these issues, the chapter will briefly discuss how the term identity has shifted since the sixteenth century to current usages in social science. Early uses of the term and the relationship among the disciplines of Theology and Philosophy provides a helpful framework to comprehend the ongoing debate. Understanding the underlying presuppositions of these positions and exploring the origin of the term identity

6. Erikson, *Childhood and Society*, 282.

7. Erikson, *Childhood and Society*, 282.

will clarify the discussion regardless of what prefix is added to the term (i.e., ethnic, national, gender, racial, sexual, religious, etc.).

Identity According to the OED

According to the 2017 Oxford English Dictionary, the English word *identity* appears in the sixteenth century. Of the four references listed, three of the works are theological and the fourth is Henry Billingsley's 1570 translation of Euclid's *Elements of Geometry* (300 BCE). These works include an obsolete spelling of the word "idemptitie" which comes from the Latin *idem* (same) + the suffix *tās* (meaning quality or condition). This meaning is confirmed in the theological texts which are primarily concerned with the doctrine of transubstantiation or sameness of substance concerning Christ's body and the eucharist. Both Catholics and Protestants employ the term differently in order to condemn or defend the doctrine.

One Catholic author, Nicholas Saunders, accuses Protestant reformer Alexander Nowell of twisting the scripture in order to make the Catholic doctrine of transubstantiation unintelligible by conceptualizing the identity of the eucharist as a similitude or metaphor meaning likeness of Christ's body rather than sameness:

> How long will you continue in falsifying the holy Scriptures, M. Nowell? When shall a man find you to deal uprightly? Where is it written, *I am bread?* Where sayeth Christ those words? Verily if he had said them, yet you may know, he meant himself to be bread only by a similitude or Metaphor: as it was expounded before in the words, *I am the true vine . . .* The verb *sum, I am,* being joined with two natures clean distant doth always signify a like condition or property, and no identity of substance.[8]

According to Saunders, Nowell intentionally conflated the metaphorical "I am" statements in John's Gospel with Christ's words in Luke's Gospel "this is my body" in order to show the impossibility of transubstantiation since it would require a change in Christ's substance rather than a change in the substance of bread (Luke 22:19). This is not to suggest that Saunders rightly understood Nowell or vice versa. Rather, it is simply to demonstrate the debate as to whether or not the English word identity means sameness or likeness can be traced back to the sixteenth century.

---

8. Saunders, *Supper of Our Lord*, 4:249.

Queer literary theorists have recently suggested that Billingsley's translation of Euclid did not have the meaning of sameness but rather likeness or similarity:

> Rather than think of "identity" in the sense of identity politics, however, we invoke the earliest use of "idemptitie" recorded in the OED: and Henry Billingsley's Euclid translation of 1570, idemptitie refers to a proportionality, likeness, or similarity that is more of an approximation than a substantialization ("identity").[9]

In order to address this claim, it is necessary to consider the entire reference from Billingsley's English translation Euclid:

> As in proportion are compared together two quantities, and proportion is nothing else but the respect and comparison of the one to the other, and these quantities are the terms of the proportion: so in proportionality are compared together two proportions. And proportionality is nothing else, but the respect and comparison of the one of them to the other. And these two proportions are the terms of this proportionality. He calleth it the similitude, that is, the likeness or idemptitie of proportions: As if ye will compare the proportion of the line A containing 2, to the line B containing 1, to the proportion of the line C containing 6, to the line D containing 3, either proportion is dupla. This likeness, idemptitie, or equality of proportion is called proportionality.[10]

Billingsley is commenting on Euclid's definition of proportionality. Considering ancient Greek mathematics were not interested in measurements but rather comparisons, one can see how Goldberg and Menon came to define identity as likeness rather than sameness.[11] However, suggesting Billingsley's use of the term idemptitie meant likeness may not be so clear when taking into consideration that algebraic operations had a significant influence in Billingsley's translation of Euclid. According to Antonio Malet, "a purely numerical understanding of the terms compared in ratios was achieved by the end of the 16th century."[12] Therefore, Billingsley's use of the term identity should not be read through the lens of an ancient Greek geometrical framework of comparison but rather a sixteenth-century framework of arithmetic

9. Goldberg and Menon, "Queering History," 1610.
10. Euclid, *Elements of Geometrie*, 5:128.
11. Goldberg and Menon, "Queering History," 1610.
12. Malet, "Changing Notions of Proportionality," 204.

where identity would have had a meaning of numerical sameness. This debate over whether or not the term identity should be used in Euclid's theory of proportionality is explained by eighteenth-century Mathematician Isaac Barrow: "The word similitude is too loose and ambiguous, and identity does not so well agree with things actually different compared immediately."[13] Barrow clearly sees the term identity as sameness whereas proportionality for Euclid was likeness, hence the discrepancy.

The final work listed in the OED is by Thomas Morton who uses the term more philosophically in comparing the mutability of man and immutability of God which he calls *identite* or sameness of God.[14] In discussing regeneration of those who are in Christ, Morton argues that there is no change in substance of the soul, body, or mind but rather a change in the quality and condition. Conceptualizing identity as personal sameness or personal identity is of great interest to the enlightenment philosopher John Locke. However, before discussing Locke, it is important to briefly explore early Greek philosophers' interest in identity to see how the conceptualization of personal identity shifted from the immaterial soul to the rational self.

Shifting Identity from the Soul to Rational Self

The philosophical interest in the concept of personal identity or sameness of a person across time and space can be traced back as early as the fifth century BCE:

> One of the earliest indications of interest in the problem of personal identity occurs in a scene from a play written in the fifth century BCE by the comic playwright Epicharmus. In this scene, a lender asks a debtor to pay up. The debtor replies by asking the lender whether he agrees that anything that undergoes change, such as a pile of pebbles to which one pebble has been added or removed, thereby becomes a different thing. The lender says that he agrees with that. "Well, then," says the debtor, "aren't people constantly undergoing changes?" "Yes," replies the lender. "So," says the debtor, "it follows that I'm not the same person as the one who was indebted to you and, so, I owe you nothing." The lender then hits the debtor, who protests loudly at being abused. The lender replies that the debtor's complaint is

13. Barrow, *Usefulness of Mathematical Learning*, 386.
14. Morton, *Threefolde State of Man*, 3:350.

misdirected since he—the lender—is not the same person as the one who hit him a moment before.[15]

This is an early example of a public narrative expressing an appropriate sociocultural view of identity. The scene demonstrates both the historical debate concerning whether or not identity is fixed, fluid, or somewhere in between. In addition, this account brilliantly shows the ancient relationship between individuality and collectivity regarding the constitution of identity. While the debtor's sameness or consistency of self is existentially drawn into question, he is physically reminded by another, specifically the lender, that he is in fact the same person. There seems to be a recognition of the overlap between personal and relational constitution of identity early on in identity discourse. At the very least, there is a recognition of the problem concerning the historical continuity of identity.

One way of reconciling the problem of a consistent identity amidst a lifetime of change is linking personal identity to the soul. The soul was initially introduced and popularized through the narrative works of Homer, though he does not associate the soul with identity. It would be hundreds of years later before philosophers such as Pythagoras (530 BCE) and Empedocles (450 BCE) would begin exploring the relationship between identity and the soul as a means to reconcile the problem of identity. Some have suggested these philosophers may have developed their ideas from a mystical religious movement known as Orphism, which taught that the soul persisted into eternity after death.[16] While this is certainly a possibility, the evidence regarding the relationship between the mystical cult and these early philosophers is unclear. What is certain is their interest in the soul as the solution to the problem of identity, an opinion that is widely accepted in ancient Greece.

The rise of interest and the semantic expansion of the soul during the fifth and sixth century BCE is described by the Stanford Encyclopedia of Philosophy as "remarkable;" and that by the time of Socrates's death the role of the soul is a common topic for philosophical discourse:

> [The] soul is standardly thought and spoken of, for instance, as the distinguishing mark of living things, as something that is the subject of emotional states and that is responsible for planning and practical thinking, and also as the bearer of such virtues as courage and justice.[17]

---

15. Martin and Barresi, *Rise and Fall of Soul and Self*, 4.

16. Martin and Barresi, *Rise and Fall of Soul and Self*.

17. Lorenz, "Ancient Theories of the Soul."

These early Greek philosophical theories of conceptualizing identity through the soul significantly impacted the church fathers and thus set the framework for much of Western Civilization's identity discourse.[18] While there is certainly diversity among Western philosophers regarding the soul as well as the relationship between identity and the soul, by and large, the soul served as the solution to a person's sameness or identity across changing time and space until the enlightenment.

Those who conceptualize identity as a self-sameness centered within individual cognition are influenced by Locke's theory of personal identity which he articulates *An Essay Concerning Human Understanding Book II: Ideas*. In this seminal work, Locke defines personal identity as follows:

> This being premised to find wherein personal identity consists, we must consider what *Person* stands for; which, I think, is a thinking intelligent Being, that has reason and reflection, and can consider itself as itself, the same thinking thing at different times and places; which it does only by that consciousness, which is inseparable from thinking, and, as it seems to me, essential to it: It being impossible for anyone to perceive, without perceiving that he does perceive. When we see, hear, smell, taste, feel, meditate, or will anything, we know that we do so. Thus it is always as to our present Sensations and Perceptions: And by this every one is to himself, that which he calls *self*: it not being considered in this case, whether the same *self* be continued in the same, or diverse Substances. For since consciousness always accompanies thinking, and it is that which makes every one to be what he calls *self*; and thereby distinguishes himself from all other thinking things, in this alone consists *personal identity*, i.e. the sameness of a rational Being: And as far as this consciousness can be extended backwards to any past Action or Thought, so far reaches the Identity of that *Person*; it is the same *self* now it was then; and 'tis by the same *self* with this present one that now reflects on it, that that action was done.[19] [*sic*]

Locke's definition moves identity away from the substantialist views of his predecessors who focused on the immutable and immaterial soul towards an interior relational view of memory and consciousness of a rational self over time. While there is no shortage of interpretations of Locke's theory of personal identity, there is a significant consensus that his views set the groundwork for modern empirical identity theories that are largely

---

18. Martin and Barresi, *Rise and Fall of Soul and Self.*
19. Locke, "Essay Concerning Human Understanding," 335.

dependent on the relationship between consciousness and memory in order to individually constitute the self.[20]

It is debatable whether or not the inward tradition and emphasis on continuity of consciousness and memory as the solution to the problem of sameness across changing time and space should be attributed to Locke. For example, Augustine's fourth century work *Confessions* discusses, quite profoundly, the relationship between narration and memory in the discovery of self. In *Book X*, Augustine describes his memory as a "great field, or a spacious palace, a storehouse for countless images." It is through these images that he meets himself through the recollection of past events. A process he describes as an inward journey:

> When I use my memory, I ask it to produce whatever it is that I wish to remember. Some things it produces immediately; some are forthcoming only after a delay, as though they were being brought out from some inner hiding place; others come spilling from the memory, thrusting themselves upon us when what we want is something quite different, as much as to say 'Perhaps we are what you want to remember?' These I brush aside from the picture which memory presents to me, allowing my mind to pick what he chooses, until finally that which I wish to see stands out clearly and emerges into site from its hiding place. . . . All this goes on inside me, in the vast cloisters of my memory. In it are the sky, the earth, and the sea, ready at my summons, together with everything that I have ever perceived in then by my senses, except the things which I have forgotten. In it I meet myself as well. I remember myself and what I have done, when and where I did it, and the state of my mind at the time. In my memory, too, are all the events that I remember, whether they are things that have happened to me or things that I have heard from others. From the same source I can picture to myself all kinds of different images based on either my own experience or upon what I can find credible because it tallies with my own experience. I can fit them into the general picture of the past; from them I can make a surmise of actions and events and hopes for the future; and I can contemplate them all over again as if they were actually present.[21]

In this autobiographical account, Augustine recognizes the mediating role of an individual's memory as well as the role of social memory in the recognition that he does not experience life alone. In fact, his memories

---

20. Martin and Barresi, *Rise and Fall of Soul and Self.*
21. Augustine, *Confessions,* 8.

are greatly tied to his friendships as oppose to Locke's account which Paul Ricoeur describes as "utterly singular."[22] It may be more appropriate to credit Locke with removing the social component of the inward tradition rather than the inward tradition itself.

The inward tradition, following Locke, places a heavy emphasis on the individual experience and memory. However, there is an insufficient recognition concerning the influence of the sociocultural context in which our perceptions are situated. Thus, the individual and the collective are often juxtaposed rather than interconnected. Ricoeur suggests there is an intersection between the individual and the collective:

> Does there not exist an intermediate level of reference between the poles of individual memory and collective memory, where concrete exchanges operate between the living memory of individual persons and public memory of the communities to which we belong? This is the level of our close relations, to whom we have a right to attribute the memory of a distinct kind. These close relations, these people who count for us and for whom we count, are situated along a range of varying distances in the relation between self and others.[23]

According to Ricoeur, these close relations intersect multiple boundaries of individual belonging (2004). This relational approach brings the fields of sociology and phenomenology into the same sphere allowing for a reciprocal ascription of both individual being and collective belonging through shared memories. Ricoeur's understanding of the mediatory role of close relations comes from Augustine's original emphasis on the role of true brothers.

> They are my true brothers, because whether they see good in me or evil, they love me still. To such as these I shall reveal what I am. Let them breathe a sigh of joy for what is good in me and a sigh of grief for what is bad.[24]

Ricoeur re-defines Augustine's "true brothers" as close relationships:

> My close relations are those who approve of my existence and whose existence I approve of in the reciprocity and equality of esteem. . . .What I expect of my close relations is that they approve of what I attest: that I am able to speak, act, recount, impute to myself the responsibility of my actions. . . . I include

22. Ricoeur, *Memory, History, Forgetting*, 102.

23. Ricoeur, *Memory, History, Forgetting*, 131.

24. Augustine, *Confessions*, 209.

in my close relations those who disapprove of my actions, but not my existence.[25]

In other words, for both Augustine and Ricoeur, identity has both an inner and outer component that intersects in the relationships that are ontologically significant.

From Rational to Intuitive

Augustine may have conceptualized identity as both an inner and outer process, but, it is not until the mid–twentieth century that the notion is popularized by social scientists, particularly Erik Erikson. His use of the term continues to reflect an idea of self-sameness in the tradition of Locke; however, framework becomes less rational and more intuitive.

In addition to introducing identity as an emotional process, the sociocultural context takes on significant meaning in Erikson's research. He never clearly defines the term identity though he describes it as "a subjective sense of an *invigorating sameness* and *continuity*."[26] Erickson's theory of identity developed from his work with WWII veterans who had returned from the war without a sense of being the same person that they were before leaving:

> Most of our patients, so we concluded at the time, had neither been "shellshocked" nor become malingerers, but had through the exigencies of war lost a sense of personal sameness and historical continuity. They were impaired in that central control over themselves for which, in the psychoanalytic scheme, only the "inner agency" of the ego could be held responsible. Therefore, I spoke of a loss of "ego identity." Since then, we have recognized the same central disturbance in severely conflicted young people whose sense of confusion is due, rather, to a war within themselves, and in confused rebels and destructive delinquents who war on their society.[27]

Erickson's reference to historical continuity or personal sameness is drawn into question because some of the returning soldiers were unable to reconcile their experiences with their pre-war hopes and sense of belonging. Their involvement in war left a gap or discontinuity between their pre-war and post-war conceptualization of self that was not easily reconcilable.

25. Ricoeur, *Memory, History, Forgetting*, 132.
26. Erikson, *Identity: Youth and Crisis*, 19.
27. Erikson, *Identity: Youth and Crisis*, 17.

Erikson's work with these veterans eventually develops into the theory of an *identity crisis*.

For Erickson, identity is more of a feeling or awareness than a cognitive ascent. In order to explain this feeling of identity, he references the personal experiences of William James and Sigmund Freud, two men he describes as "bearded and patriarchal founding fathers of the psychologies on which our thinking on identity is based."[28] According to Erikson, the following excerpt from the personal correspondence of James to his wife, "best described" what is meant by a "sense of identity":

> A man's character is discernible in the mental or moral attitude in which, when it came upon him, he felt himself most deeply and intensely active and alive. At such moments there is a voice inside which speaks and says: "This is the real me!" . . . although it is a mere mood or emotion to which I can give no form in words, authenticates itself to me as the deepest principle of all active and theoretical determination which I possess."[29]

Erikson continues with an excerpt from Freud's 1926 address to the Society of B'nai B'rith in Vienna to broaden identity beyond individual interiority and towards a model that incorporates socio-cultural and historical processes as well as human development:

> What bound me to Jewry was (I am ashamed to admit) neither faith nor national pride, for I have always been an unbeliever and was brought up without any religion though not without respect for what are called the "ethical" standards of human civilization. Whenever I felt an inclination to national enthusiasm I strove to suppress it as being harmful and wrong, alarmed by the warning examples of the peoples among whom we Jews live. But plenty of other things remained over to make the attraction of Jewry and Jews irresistible—many obscure emotional forces, which were the more powerful the less they could be expressed in words, as well as a clear consciousness of inner identity, the safe privacy of a common mental construction.[30]

These examples, according to Erikson, demonstrate that identity is something that reveals itself to the person rather than something to be pursued. Once identity it is revealed, you know you have it though it is somewhat indescribable. In addition, you recognize there are others who also received

28. Erikson, *Identity: Youth and Crisis*, 19.

29. Erikson, *Identity: Youth and Crisis*, 19

30. Erikson, *Identity: Youth and Crisis*, 20

a similar revelation. This is not to suggest that only a select few have an identity but rather that not everyone is aware of their identity. He argues for a shared sense of identity revelation or illumination.

Concerning those who are aware, Erikson suggests a "deep communality known only to those who share in it and expressible in words more mythical than conceptual."[31] For example, while James and Freud are keenly aware of their identity as an inner process of emotions, neither seems able to find words that can sufficiently explain or conceptualize the process. Yet both James and Freud attempt to share this inner sense of awareness with those whom they share a sense of intimacy. The personal nature of James's correspondence to his wife is apparent. However, Freud's lecture is less obvious without Erikson's commentary. He describes the context of the conference as an "address to his "brothers" by an original observer long isolated in his profession."[32] What might appear as a public lecture to the outsider, for Erikson, represented a deep communality for Freud. It is in these relationships that both James and Freud attempt to transcend their inwardly revealed identities which words cannot properly express, and move towards a communion with others who were also aware of their identity. Similar to Augustine, Erikson argues that while internally revealed, identity has an external or social component that further constitutes one's sense of identity through *close relationships*. Erikson describes those who have a healthy sense of identity as "feeling at home in one's body, a sense of 'knowing where one is going,' and an inner assuredness of anticipated recognition from those who count."[33]

Erikson builds upon this complex relationship of interiority and otherness through Freud's contemplation of his Jewish heritage. Freud's reflection demonstrates nicely the relationship between competing conceptualizations of identity in explaining that his inner "Jewry" is neither tied to nationalism nor belief, but rather a subjective sense of shared adoration of an imagined Jewish identity.[34] For Freud, there seems to be a collective consciousness of Jewishness that is deeper than religious belief or geopolitical space. His brief reference to the suffering of Jews by nationalistic movements provides insight that Freud's inner desire for Jewish belonging may be rooted in a sense of collective suffering. In other words, Freud is able to re-narrate or re-imagine what it means to be Jewish. This is an early example of social scientists challenging the positivist thinking of identity as *self-sameness*.

31. Erikson, *Identity: Youth and Crisis*, 21

32. Erikson, *Identity: Youth and Crisis*, 21

33. Erikson, *Identity: Youth and Crisis*, 165.

34. Anderson, *Imagined Communities*.

Erickson demonstrates through Freud a psychosocial construction of identity. A process that is mutually informed by both the individual life history and sociocultural history simultaneously.

The brief quote from Freud also reveals the complex relationship between personal identity and social or collective identity. When collective identity is conceptualized as shared affinities or sameness (i.e., us), a boundary of difference exists by default (i.e., them). Other collectivities may then be labeled different and a potential threat to the other.[35] The reification of one group identity may come at the expense of the suffering of another group that is determined different. This in turn may produce a deeper sense of collective identity for both the persecuted and the persecutors. This concept is further explored in chapter four.

Conclusion

In sum, Erikson's conceptualization of identity is something difficult to explain with words, yet it is very obvious to those who have it. While it is revealed internally, it is often constituted through meaningful relationships. There is a sense of communion with those who share in this inner awareness of identity. Finally, identity may be collectively constituted through a shared sense of being. For Erikson, identity is by no means fixed but rather constantly changing and located in the overlap of the individual and collective as well as the context of time and space.

Erikson concludes his discussion of James and Freud by suggesting they "serve to establish a few dimensions of identity and, at the same time, help to explain why the problem is so all-pervasive and yet so hard to grasp: for we deal with the process "located" *in the core of the individual* and yet also *in the core of his communal culture*, a process which establishes, in fact, the identity of those two identities."[36] In addition to the process being located in the overlap of the individual and society, Erickson further complicates matters by suggesting that identity "contains a complementarity of past and future both in the individual and in society: it links the actuality of a living past with that of a promising future."[37] If there is an event that disrupts this continuity, an identity crises will likely ensue. Erikson attempts to move the term identity away from its early philosophical framework of an inner rational self towards a psychosocial framework where the individual mediates their sense of identity in relationship to their sociocultural context.

35. Zizioulas, *Being as Communion*.
36. Erikson, *Identity: Youth and Crisis*, 22.
37. Erikson, *Identity: Youth and Crisis*, 310.

The mid-twentieth century shift in conceptualizing identity in the overlap of the individual life history and sociocultural history is not unique to Erikson. Anthropologists were also experiencing similar shifts concerning identity around the same time. The next chapter demonstrates a significant shift from cultural essentialism toward constructivism in the ethnographic representations of Pashtun identity.

2

Shifting Pashtun Identity in Ethnography

THIS CHAPTER DEMONSTRATES THE postmodern shift from an essentialist paradigm to the current constructivist approaches through a critical assessment of the ethnographic representations of the Pashtun. In assessing the Western descriptions of the Pashtun, it is imperative to recognize that much of the research, both past and present, takes place within a political context. The military expeditions of the Indian subcontinent's North-West Frontier, coupled with an essentialist anthropological framework prevalent at the time, resulted in some disturbing depictions of the Pashtun and the religion of Islam. Anthropologists, however, make a clear shift in the mid-twentieth century reflecting the complexity of the people and their cultural practices.

Essentialist Views of the Pashtun

Pashtun representations are, at times, reminiscent of Edward Said's Orientalism—"a way of coming to terms with the Orient that is based on the Orient's special place in European Western experience."[1] By and large, the European Western experience among the Pashtun was, and continues to be, amidst the backdrop of Western military interests. This is particularly important in assessing depictions of the Pashtun produced by military officers and historians in the nineteenth and early-twentieth century. One of the earliest British references comes from Sir John William Kaye's 1851 publication, *The War in Afghanistan*:

> They knew no happiness in anything but strife. It was their delight to live in a state of chronic warfare. Among such a people civil war has a natural tendency to perpetuate itself. Blood is always crying aloud for blood. Revenge was a virtue among

1. Said, *Orientalism*, 1.

them; the heritage of retribution passed from father to son; and murder became a solemn duty. . . . Every man was more or less a soldier or a bandit.[2]

Kaye's reference concerns the character of the Afghan people in general. However, British Judge of the Chief Court of the Punjab George Elsmie would later reference this quote as applying particularly to the Pashtun people.[3] It is not until after the 1883 Census Report on the Punjab, conducted by Sir Denzil Ibbetson, that the Pashtun are distinguished from Afghans as a particular people with a distinct language and culture. The character of the Pashtun is described in the census by Ibbetson as follows:

> The true Pathan [Pashtun; Pathan and Pukhtun are used interchangeably] is perhaps the most barbaric of the races . . . he is cruel, bloodthirsty and vindictive in the highest degree; he does not know what truth and faith is . . . there is a sort of charm about him, especially about the leading men, which almost makes one forget his treacherous nature. As the proverb says: 'The Pathan is at one moment a saint and the next a devil.' For centuries at least he has been on our frontier subject to no man. He leads a wild, free, active life in the rugged fastnesses of his mountains; and there is an air of masculine independence about him which is refreshing in a country like India. He is a bigot of the most fanatical type, exceedingly proud, and extraordinarily superstitious.[4]

This census, while impressive in its scope, reads like a nineteenth-century naturalist's field guide. The use of a classification system that is best suited for plants and animals is incapable of demonstrating the complexity of individuals and is therefore a generalization at best and a gross distortion at worst. Nevertheless, the census depiction of the Pashtun had a significant impact on subsequent representations.

Another provocative account comes from Winston Churchill's *The Story of Malakand* (1897). This description of the North-West Frontier was Churchill's first nonfiction work, though it can be argued there is a fair bit of inventing present. It is worth noting, however, that Churchill was awarded the Nobel Prize in literature in 1953 "for his mastery of historical and biographical description as well as for brilliant oratory in defending exalted human values."[5] Churchill's description of the Pashtun was no

2. Kaye, *War in Afghanistan*, 11–12.

3. Elsmie, *Characteristics of Crime and Criminals in Peshawar*, 11.

4. Rose, *Tribes and Castes of the Punjab*, 219.

5. Nobelprize.org.

doubt acclaimed as defending human values shared by fellow imperialists. However, his work offers little nuance or complexity to the lives lived, and the Pashtun are thus reduced to savage byproducts of a determining system of cultural and religious violence:

> And yet so full of contradictions is their character, that all this is without prejudice to what has been written of their family vendettas and private blood feuds. Their system of ethics, which regards treachery and violence as virtues rather than vices, has produced a code of honour so strange and inconsistent, that it is incomprehensible to a logical mind. I have been told that if a white man could grasp it fully, and were to understand their mental impulses—if he knew, when it was their honour to stand by him, and when it was their honour to betray him; when they were bound to protect and when to kill him—he might, by judging his times and opportunities, pass safely from one end of the mountains to the other. But a civilised European is as little able to accomplish this, as to appreciate the feelings of those strange creatures, which, when a drop of water is examined under a microscope, are revealed amiably gobbling each other up, and being themselves complacently devoured. . . . Those simple family virtues, which idealists usually ascribe to primitive peoples, are conspicuously absent. Their wives and their womenkind generally, have no position but that of animals. They are freely bought and sold, and are not infrequently bartered for rifles. Truth is unknown among them.[6]

Churchill's dim assessment of the Pashtun culture and its determinism on one's behavior is not the only reason for their so-called savagery. He further suggests their propensity to violence is a result of their religious adherence to Islam:

> Every influence, every motive, that provokes the spirit of murder among men, impels these mountaineers to deeds of treachery and violence. The strong aboriginal propensity to kill, inherent in all human beings, has in these valleys been preserved in unexampled strength and vigour. That religion, which above all others was founded and propagated by the sword—the tenets and principles of which are instinct with incentives to slaughter and which in three continents has produced fighting breeds of men—stimulates a wild and merciless fanaticism.[7]

6. Churchill, *Story of the Malakand Field Force*, 25–27.
7. Churchill, *Story of the Malakand Field Force*, 20.

Churchill believed the Christian faith, in light of rationalism, tempered passion and the propensity toward fanaticism and violence. Islam, on the other hand, had just the opposite effect:

> But the Mohammedan religion increases, instead of lessening, the fury of intolerance. It was originally propagated by the sword, and ever since, its votaries have been subject, above the people of all other creeds, to this form of madness. In a moment the fruits of patient toil, the prospects of material prosperity, the fear of death itself, are flung aside. The more emotional Pathans are powerless to resist. All rational considerations are forgotten. Seizing their weapons, they become Ghazis—as dangerous and as sensible as mad dogs: fit only to be treated as such. While the more generous spirits among the tribesmen become convulsed in an ecstasy of religious bloodthirstiness, poorer and more material souls derive additional impulses from the influence of others, the hopes of plunder and the joy of fighting.[8]

Churchill frames the Pashtun resistance to British imperialism as reminiscent of demonic possession. The code of honor referred to by Churchill is known as *Pashtunwali*; other pronunciations include *Pakhtunwali*, and *Pathanwali*. *Pashtunwali* code and the religion of Islam are common themes throughout much of the research conducted among the Pashtun. In some cases, *Pashtunwali* and Islam are used almost interchangeably to explain the backwards behaviors so often present in the early ethnographic works. These behaviors are often reified to encompass the well-known Pashtun identity. A tribal identity that is often suggested to be deep-rooted and clearly defined amongst all the people.

British officer Collin Davies's *The Problem of the North-West Frontier 1890–1908* gives a more nuanced account of the Pashtun than his predecessors. He suggests that the vast diversity represented in tribes as well as the geographical landscape leads to misleading generalizations about the Pashtun. According to Davies, some of the generalizations include unfair depictions such as "treacherous, pitiless, vindictive and bloodthirsty."[9] Davies gives a great deal of attention to the tribal unrest in the region and the complexities involved in trying to colonize the Pashtun, rather than simply painting them as products of religious and tribal essentialism. However, even with this emphasis on Pashtun diversity, Davies still argues for a unifying Pashtun identity under a tribal honor code:

8. Churchill, *Story of the Malakand Field Force*, 79–80.
9. Davies, *Problem of the North-West Frontier*, 48.

> *Pakhtunwali* imposes upon the tribesman three obligations, the
> non-observance of which is regarded as the deadliest of sins,
> and is followed by lasting dishonour and ostracism. He must
> grant to all fugitives the right of asylum (*nanawatai*), he must
> proffer open-handed hospitality (*melmastia*) even to his deadli-
> est enemy, and he must wipe out insult with insult (*badal*).[10]

Davies concludes that the tribal code leads to blood feuds between tribes
and even families and that it is almost impossible to find a family who does
not have a hereditary enemy.

Davies also points out a pervasive adherence to Islam, albeit also a
diverse representation. He notes that many of the Pashtun lack doctrinal
understanding, particularly the frontier tribesman who are "often ignorant
of even the fundamental tenets of their faith."[11] He further adds that while
Islam is certainly a significant part of Pashtun life, it by no means supersedes
the ethnic/political convictions of the tribe. Davies, unlike Churchill, demonstrates the diversity and complexity of the Pashtun in his recognition that
their tribal identity is far more complex than lineage or language, noting
that not all Pashtun speak Pashto. In addition, Davies suggests that not all
who claim to be Pashtun are in fact Pashtun. He notes that some claim a
Pashtun ethnicity simply as a means of obtaining a beneficial social status.
Despite Davies's emphasis on Pashtun diversity, his description of the frontier tribes falls prey to the error of his predecessors in giving Islam and the
culture a deterministic power. These essentialist or determining factors in
the frontier Pashtun identity for Davies are most notable in his comparison
of the Pashtun with the Baluch:

> We must now pass on to compare and contrast the Pathans of
> the north with the Baluch of the south. Both are Muhammad-
> ans, as a rule of the orthodox Sunni sect, recognizing one God,
> Allah, and one true Prophet, Muhammad; both are warlike
> and predatory in the extreme, possessing most of the vices and
> virtues of semi-barbarous races; and both abide by a peculiar
> code of honour, the most sacred duties of which are to recognize
> as inviolable the person of one's guest, to exact an eye for an
> eye and a tooth for a tooth, and to wipe out dishonour by the
> shedding of blood. . . . Less turbulent, less fanatical, and less
> blood-thirsty, he [the Baluch] is far easier to control than the
> Pathan. . . . A rude, perfidious savage he may be, yet one can-
> not but admire his proud bearing and resolute step, his martial

10. Davies, *Problem of the North-West Frontier*, 49.

11. Davies, *Problem of the North-West Frontier*, 51.

instincts and independent spirit, his frank, open manners and
festive temperament, his hatred of control, his love of country,
and his wonderful powers of endurance.[12]

Along with the religion and culture, Davies credits the harsh environment
as an additional factor in determining what he describes as a "race of men
who are the most expert guerilla fighters in the world."[13]

Davies is an excellent example of a budding shift in ethnographic
research that reconsiders the determinism so often perpetuated by his con-
temporaries. His work demonstrates the complexity of the frontier tribes
and makes distinctions between tribes based on their context. While he
acknowledges the danger of generalizing Pashtun culture and is critical of
those who have misrepresented them in the past, he ultimately falls prey
to the same representation that is at best overgeneralized and at worst a
misrepresentation of the frontier Pashtun tribesman.

The problem in the early depictions of the Pashtun is not the recognition of *Pashtunwali* or Islam, but rather the externally ascribed power
and rigidity these systems are given in the lives of the Pashtun. It is certainly possible that Islam and *Pashtunwali* can influence and perhaps be
utilized to shape and even drive violent behaviors. However, it is also possible that Islam and *Pashtunwali* can influence and perhaps be utilized in
peace movements. One should not assume that the Pashtun are somehow
predisposed to violence because of their ethnicity or religion; however,
one should not underestimate the prevalent cultural narratives of violence
throughout their history.

Constructivist Shift

It is not until the mid-twentieth century that there is a clear movement
away from cultural determinism and towards constructivism in regards
to Pashtun representations. This is most notable in Fredrik Barth's seminal work *Ethnic Groups and Boundaries* (1969). Barth moves away from
the ecological deterministic model, calling it a "simplistic view [in which]
geographical and social isolation have been the critical factors in sustaining
cultural diversity."[14] He argued "ethnic distinctions do not depend on an
absence of social interaction and acceptance, but are quite to the contrary

---

12. Davies, *Problem of the North-West Frontier*, 46–49.
13. Davies, *Problem of the North-West Frontier*, 179.
14. Barth, *Ethnic Groups and Boundaries*, 9.

often the very foundations on which embracing social systems are built."[15]
He believed that the same group of people would renegotiate cultural forms
in different social and geographical contexts in order to maintain a sense of
group identity amidst cultural diversity:

> Cultural features that signal the boundary may change, and the
> cultural characteristics of the members may likewise be trans-
> formed, indeed, even the organizational form of the group may
> change—yet the fact of continuing dichotomization between
> members and outsiders allows us to specify the nature of conti-
> nuity, and investigate the changing cultural form and content.[16]

This perspective allows the actors to define what cultural features or boundary markers are most significant in maintaining their sense of identity. For
Barth, the social processes which are often the impetus for shifting boundaries should be the object of investigation as they are often critical in identity
formation. The process of forming boundaries is particularly important as
groups migrate and construct new ways of defining individual and collective membership in new spaces.

Barth's research on the Pashtun is not a move away from the study of
Pashtunwali and Islam, but rather a conceptual shift in how to approach
the tribal code and religion. Barth agrees that the honor code is an identity marker—"common and distinctive to all Pathans."[17] He further details
certain aspects of Pashtun identity such as patrilineal descent and Islamic
adherence. Concerning Pashtun traditions or *Pashtunwali*, Barth lists three
institutions: *melmastia* (hospitality), *jirga* (councils), and purdah (seclusion
of women). In addition to these principles, he writes extensively on *badal*
(revenge or blood feuds), citing five case studies from the region.

The difference between Barth's approach to ethnicity is not in regards
to the existence or practice of cultural traditions, but rather the sociocultural development and employment of these traditions. For Barth, it is
the boundaries that distinguish groups rather than the content or cultural
forms and symbols contained inside the group that needed to be studied.
He did not see ethnic categories and culture as ontological but rather socially constructed:

> Ethnic categories provide an organizational vessel that may be
> given varying amounts and forms of content in different socio-
> cultural systems. They may be of great relevance to behavior, but

---

15. Barth, *Ethnic Groups and Boundaries*, 10.

16. Barth, *Ethnic Groups and Boundaries*, 14.

17. Barth, *Ethnic Groups and Boundaries*, 119.

they need not be, they may pervade all social life, or they may be
relevant only in limited sectors of activity.[18]

Barth was making the case for boundaries based on social interaction
rather than cultural traditions alone. In the most recent printing of his
seminal work (1998), Barth says in the preface that he lacked the postmodern language at the time but he was arguing for what is commonly
today known as constructivism. His work among the Pashtun showed that
the unambiguous tribal code of honor is far more malleable, complex,
contextual, and socially constructed than previous researchers asserted.
In other words, the Pashtun were far more complex than the sum of their
sociocultural practices. Barth argued that individuals can choose to maintain the status quo of *Pashtunwali* as an identity marker, reinterpret *Pashtunwali* to fit their context, or abandon it all together for another more
advantageous identity that is within reach.

The publication of Barth's work among the Pashtun was a watershed
moment in anthropology. The works that would follow Barth continue
to validate his claims and further articulate postmodern views of culture
through the lens of social interaction. Following Barth's work, there is a
substantial movement away from essentialism toward constructivism in
anthropological field work.

Anthropological inquiry of the mid-twentieth century continued to
focus on *Pashtunwali* and Islam. There is disagreement among researchers
concerning the practice of *Pashtunwali* and its relationship to Islam. What
is not disagreed upon is the ubiquity of honor code and its use as an ethnic
identity marker. Essentially, Pashtun identity and *Pashtunwali* become synonymous in much of the literature. According to James Spain, "It is virtually
impossible to find even a child—male or female—who is not keenly aware
of the main elements of Pakhtunwali."[19] The principles of *Pashtunwali*, according to Spain, are *badal* (revenge) and *melmastia* (hospitality) as the
"two great commandments of Pahktunwali."[20] Spain further includes the
following as essential parts of the Pashtun social system: *jigra* (councils),
Islamic law, *lashkar* (war party), *hujra* (community center), *purdah* (seclusion of women), and land tenure.

Similarly, Charles Lindholm refers to *Pashtunwali* in the Swat as one
of the most formal known honor codes of tribal peoples. He cites a Pashto
proverb saying, "Only the man who follows Pukhtunwali can be called a

---

18. Barth, *Ethnic Groups and Boundaries*, 14.
19. Spain, *Pathan Borderland*, 63–64.
20. Spain, *Pathan Borderland*, 66.

Pukhtun.”[21] Lindholm refers to the "pillars" of *Pashtunwali* as *badal* (revenge), *melmastia* (hospitality), and *nanawatai* (refuge).[22] Recognizing that the "pillars" listed did not exhaust the tribal code, Lindholm mentions a list of additional principles that writers most often associated with the Pashtun: "equality, respect, loyalty, pride, bravery, purdah, pursuit of romantic encounters, the worship of Allah and most importantly the unselfish love for the friend."[23] He also stresses the significance of *taburwali* (a relationship of enmity).

Lindholm explains how these contentious relationships are usually a result of inheritance disputes. The enmity usually exists between cousins, however in some cases it may be within the nuclear family structure, particularly when there is a lack of a male heir. Lindholm discusses in great detail the importance of land, patrilineal inheritance, and the difficulty this places on Pashtun widows who do not have a son. If the widow does not have a son she is encouraged to practice the Levirate custom of marrying her husband's brother thus preserving the patrilineal right to the land. The widow may choose not to marry her brother in-law and return to her father's home. However, she is prohibited from marrying another man outside of her husband's lineage in order to prevent a future contestation for land.

Lindholm suggests that the treatment of women, particularly in regards to divorce, inheritance, and purdah, demonstrates how *Pashtunwali* often takes precedence over Islam when the two are in conflict. He presents *Pashtunwali* as incredibly influential in the daily lives of those living in the Swat, however, not for the Pashtun migrant who is able to quickly "drop his tribal ways and assume a new lifestyle once he has managed to flee his native land."[24]

Akbar Ahmed, in his thorough works on the Pashtun, affirms much of the aforementioned literature concerning the principles of *Pashtunwali* and adds the principles *tarboorwali* (agnatic rivalry between first cousins) and *tor* (when the chastity of a woman has been compromised).[25] Ahmed calls the tribal code "the very core and essence of Pukhtunness and that which forms and defines a Pukhtun."[26] A significant contribution of Ahmed is his recognition of the dynamic nature of *Pashtunwali*. He suggests that the tribal code has survived and continues to thrive through "suspension,

---

21. Lindholm, *Generosity and Jealousy*, 209.

22. Lindholm, *Generosity and Jealousy*, 211.

23. Lindholm, *Generosity and Jealousy*, 211.

24. Lindholm, *Generosity and Jealousy*, 193.

25. Ahmed, *Pukhtun Economy and Society*.

26. Ahmed, *Pukhtun Economy and Society*, 7.

accommodation, and alteration of parts of it."[27] However, Ahmed maintains some views of cultural essentialism in his dichotomy of the settled and frontier lands suggesting that the tribal areas display a purer or ideal form of *Pashtunwali*. Additionally, Ahmed also fails to see any conflict between Islam and the tribal code stating, "Pathan tribal society is part of the 'larger' or 'greater' tradition of the Islamic world. To the Pathan there is no conflict between his tribal code, '*Pukhtunwali*,' and religious principles."[28]

In a more recent study on the English village of Fowlmere, Ahmed argues for cohesive group or tribal identities among the so-called individualized West.[29] He emphasizes the role of shared perceptions of change and continuity in the construction of group identity. While Ahmed recognizes the importance of individual perception, he argues that a common or shared perception is what often defines group identity. Unlike Barth, Ahmed concludes that even in Europe, group interests will often take precedent over individual or self-interests.

More Recent Studies

More recent studies continue to affirm the flexibility of *Pashtunwali* in regards to values, behaviors, and organization in light of external conflicting social constraints. They also tend to affirm Lindholm's conclusion of a dynamic relationship to Islam as well. In fact, Sayyid Shah argues that this malleable relationship between Pashtun culture and Islam is not a recent phenomenon. He states, "Only when the situation of 'Islam in crisis' was created (1939), did a small section of the Pashtoon society consider it the religious duty to forget temporarily their sense of belonging to a separate ethnicity and set out to defend Islam."[30] Aligning the Pashtun under the banner of Islam during partition proved to be a difficult task. According to Shah, the majority of the frontier Pashtun "had little interest in belonging to the larger Muslim community of the subcontinent."[31] He suggests that this was not due to a lack of Islamic devotion but rather a greater desire for a Pashtun identity. According to Shah, the people placed a higher value on traditional Pashtun traditions than Islam.

A group that was more successful in mobilizing and unifying the Pashtun politically was the Khudai Khidmatgars or KK movement—a

27. Ahmed, *Pukhtun Economy and Society*, 333.

28. Ahmed, *Millennium and Charisma among Pathans*, 6.

29. Ahmed and Mynors, "Fowlmere: Roundheads, Rambo and Rivalry," 3–8.

30. Shah, *Ethnicity, Islam and Nationalism*, 247.

31. Shah, *Ethnicity, Islam and Nationalism*, 247.

mid-twentieth-century movement of Pashtun practicing non-violent resistance to their British colonizers. Mukulika Banerjee examines the KK
movement in detail and demonstrates the dynamics between Islam and
Pashtunwali both relationally and contextually. She affirms that Islam is
an important identity marker for the Pashtun. However, she further states
that "being a Pathan is certainly not seen as equivalent to or synonymous
with being a Muslim."[32] Banerjee suggests that Islam and *Pashtunwali* are
equally influential, and attributes the success of the KK movement to the
reinterpretation of both saying,

> In order to accommodate nonviolence, the symbiosis of
> *Pukhtunwali* and Islam had to be adjusted; the notions of ji-
> had changed; martyrdom was promoted in place of conquest,
> and self-restraint in place of revenge; and customary terms
> concerning honour and sanctuary were subtly redefined or
> given different emphasis. Thus from our study of the Khudai
> Khidmatgar movement we can conclude that Pathan culture
> is not *only* or *essentially* composed of strict codes of revenge,
> blood feud and aggressive hospitality, as anthropology has
> sometimes led us to believe.[33]

The KK movement's use of *Pashtunwali* and Islam as the impetus for nonviolence shows the flexibility of both Islam and the otherwise documented
violent code of honor. Banerjee argues that the principles of *Pashtunwali* did
not need to be changed in order to accomplish this but simply redefined.

Muhammad Ayub Jan's study on identity formation and maintenance among the Malakand (ironically the same area of Churchill's study)
Pakhtuns agrees that the "features of Pakhtunwali are not static and that
its features can be interpreted, manipulated and negotiated."[34] He further
concludes that the renegotiation of the tribal code is used as a defining factor or boundary marker of identity amidst inter-ethnic and intra-ethnic
contestation. One reason for contestation is the desire for Pashtun identity
not to be absorbed into a broader Pakistani national identity where Islam is
seen as the unifying factor. For many, the consensus and contestation of the
dynamic relationship between ethnic, religious, and national identities have
created "multiple senses of belonging for Pakhtuns."[35] He argues that Pashtun identity and its markers are highly contextual and dependent on the

---

32. Banerjee, *Pathan Unarmed*, 153.

33. Banerjee, *Pathan Unarmed*, 208.

34. Jan, "Contested and Contextual Identities," 223.

35. Jan, "Contested and Contextual Identities," 215.

flexibility of *Pashtunwali*. These markers are used by individuals to signify boundaries of inclusion and exclusion.

One way the Pashtun negotiate this relationship is through the use of proverbs. Leonard Bartlotti explains that "meanings and symbols associated with the Islamic and *Pashtunwali* traditions are expressed, transformed, or manipulated by actors in the process of proverb use."[36] He further suggests that Pashtun proverbs are used to negotiate the boundaries between religion and culture as well as, "reconstruct and negotiate notions associated with Pashtunness and Muslimness, that is, with Pashtun ethnic and religious identity."[37] Bartlotti also proposes that *peghor* (taunting, verbal ostracism) be considered a behavioral expression of *Pashtunwali*, something he refers to as "verbal *pakhto.*"[38] While affirming *Pashtunwali* as a system to signal identity or belonging, Bartlotti by no means considers the honor code or its relationship with Islam to be fixed, but rather in continuous contextual negotiation.

Similarly, Amineh Ahmed posits that the customs of *gham-khadi* (sorrow and joy) celebrations—principally weddings and funerals—are becoming new additions to *Pashtunwali*.[39] Ahmed also states that "while Pukhtuns insist on a Muslim identity, Pukhto is considered separate from adherence to Islam."[40] Furthermore, Ahmed suggests a theoretical framework that views *Pashtunwali* as a "set of representations" which allows for innovation, rather than a "code (as previously defined by anthropologists) whose operations are invariant."[41]

Finally, Robert Nichols's recent study focuses on the "multiple changes and continuities that have shaped Pashtun society, in the homelands and in the diaspora."[42] Nichols focuses primarily on the effects of South Asian and Middle Eastern migration, including the transnational flow of "capital, labor and ideas."[43] He concludes that while many Pashtun migrants assimilated into their host societies, for some, Pashtun identity—including language, ethnicity, and *Pashtunwali*—remained a central theme in the diaspora community and was often used to their advantage in negotiating better treatment of migrant workers.

---

36. Bartlotti, "Negotiating Pakhto: Proverbs," 348.
37. Bartlotti, "Negotiating Pakhto: Proverbs," 348.
38. Bartlotti, "Negotiating Pakhto: Proverbs," 351.
39. Ahmed, *Sorrow and Joy among Muslim Women.*
40. Ahmed, *Sorrow and Joy among Muslim Women*, 219.
41. Ahmed, *Sorrow and Joy among Muslim Women*, 162.
42. Nichols, *History of Pashtun Migration*, xii–xiv.
43. Nichols, *History of Pashtun Migration*, 229.

Conclusion

Although globalization and modernization have changed *Pashtunwali*, the Pashtun, by and large still use it as an identity marker. This is a result, as recent studies show, of the dynamic and highly contextual nature of *Pashtunwali*, making it conducive for negotiation. Precedent literature is consistent in labeling *Pashtunwali* as an identity marker for the Pashtun. However, the dynamic nature of *Pashtunwali* results in inconsistent representations. Some principles that are most often associated with *Pashtunwali* in the literature are: *badal* (revenge), *melmastia* (hospitality), and *nanawatai* (forgiveness/asylum). Secondary principles mentioned are: *tarburwali* (enmity between first cousins), *purdah* (seclusion of women), *jirga* (tribal council), *hujra* (men's communal house), land ownership, and Islamic adherence. Some suggested additions to *Pashtunwali* include: *tor* (when the chastity of a woman has been compromised), *peghor* (taunting, verbal ostracism), and *gham-khadi* (sorrow and joy) celebrations. While some have made the patrilineal ancestry a key identity marker for the Pashtun,[44] others disagree, arguing that adherence to the tribal code is more important than patrilineal descent and that *Pashtunwali* allows for intermarriage.[45]

The relationship between *Pashtunwali* and Islam is also dynamic because Islam itself is in constant fluctuation.[46] *Pashtunwali*, however, is often used as a boundary marker, allowing for Pashtun cultural identity to take precedence over a wider religious identity. The Pashtun are repeatedly observed as being Pashtun first and Muslim second. The literature affirms that Pashtun immigrants, if they desire, should have no problem renegotiating *Pashtunwali* for their transnational context. The literature regarding the Pashtun demonstrates the complexity of identity and group collectivity and the shift from essentialism to constructivism in the field of anthropology.

The constructivist shift has not taken place in some of the works produced by the United States military. For example, in 2010, The Foreign Military Studies Office (a research organization of the U.S. Army) in partnership with the Maneuver Center of Excellence reprinted a book published in 1932 titled *Passing It On: Fighting the Pushtun on Afghanistan's Frontier* by General Andrew Skeen. The back cover of the new edition states "The terrain and enemy have not changed." Suggesting that in seventy-eight years the Pashtun have not changed is a bold claim given the

---

44. Ahmed, *Pukhtun Economy and Society*; Jan, "Contested and Contextual Identities."

45. Glatzer, "Pashtun Tribal System"; Lindholm, *Generosity and Jealousy*.

46. The fluctuation of Islam and Muslims is discussed further in ch. 4.

amount of research that suggests otherwise. The editors go on to say the following concerning the Pashtun:

> Your opponent, as a member of a 'warrior culture,' is moti-vated by loot and a tribal tradition of doing what a man should do. The most prized loot (as in Skeen's day) is a weapon. Your enemy can be lured into a well-conceived trap. But you need to understand your opponent's culture and mentality to know how to set and spring that trap. Your opponent's mentality is tempered by the Pathan code of conduct—Pashtunwali, and hundreds of years of history. His family, tribal and personal honor are the most important things in his life. His ability to protect his family and his tribe determine his worth as a man and he is willing to die for his beliefs.[47]

The above statement is reminiscent of Churchill's comments at the begin-ning of this chapter. Despite the movements away from nineteenth-century cultural determinism in ethnographic depictions of the Pashtun, some parts of the U.S. military continue to operate under a cultural framework that suggests the Pashtun are somehow immutable byproducts of a warrior cul-ture trapped in a time capsule.

The notion that some continue to espouse Pashtun culture as static is difficult to imagine given the shifts in the ethnographic literature. It is espe-cially unrealistic for the Pashtun to maintain an unaltered culture given the mass migration in the twentieth century and continued cultural production over multiple locations. The next chapter discusses the impact of migration studies and some of the emerging trends brought on by globalization and computer mediated communication that further demonstrate the complex process of conceptualizing identity.

47. Skeen, *Passing It On*, xxix.

3

Shifting Fields in Immigrant Research

THROUGHOUT THE TWENTIETH CENTURY, the discipline of anthropology underwent significant theoretical and methodological shifts.[1] Much of this was a result of postmodern literary criticism's undermining claims of researcher objectivity in ethnography. In addition, the rise of postcolonial studies drew significant attention to the political context in which field-work was often conducted and the unequal distribution of power between the researcher and informant.[2] These critical assessments resulted in the deconstruction and a continuing reconstruction of theories and methods in anthropological inquiry.

Despite anthropologists's best efforts to move away from the essentialization of culture toward a more constructivist approach, the early ethnographic representations and the wake of criticisms continue to draw into question the reliability or bias of Western depictions of non-Western cultures. Rather than abandon the method of the ethnography, researchers began to refine their methods and produce new theories of approaching cultural studies. This has led to greater reflexivity in cultural depictions as well as a keen awareness of the need for the research informant to tell *their* story. It is imperative that the informant's voice is heard rather than simply represented through the lens of the researcher. In other words, identity is to be self-ascribed.

In addition to reforming research methods, the anthropological concept of "fieldwork" took on new meanings in the mid-twentieth century. No longer would anthropologists define fieldwork in terms such as exotic, untouched, or tribal. There was a renewed interest in the study of immigrants, particularly in the United States. Certainly, the early Chicago School of Sociology pioneered this research with works like *The Polish Peasant in*

1. Clifford and Marcus, *Writing Culture*.
2. Said, *Orientalism*.

Europe and America.[3] This is considered a seminal work, showing the need and value of allowing immigrants to self-represent their lives through their autobiographical voice in life history research. While the method of life history has a long tradition in the field of anthropology, it was not until the mid-twentieth century that this method began to flourish. The study of individual immigrants was instrumental in further developing the anthropological theories of diffusion and acculturation.

Twenty-first-century trends such as globalization and mass migration led to a significant increase in the studies concerning immigrant cultural production. By and large, the research has taken on an interdisciplinary approach to the study of culture. This chapter explores some of the anthropological contributions including acculturation theory and transnationalism. In discussing the transnational framework, particular attention is given to computer mediated communication (CMC) and the Internet, particularly social media, as new fields of research for immigrant identity formation.

Acculturation Theory

While the emphasis on acculturation is relatively new in social science, the concept is ubiquitous and can be traced back throughout human history. Floyd Rudmin, in his brief historical survey, explains how acculturative awareness can be traced back as far as 2370 BC when Sumerian rulers used written codes of law in order to preserve cultural traditions. He also suggests that the biblical nation of Israel used their Levitical code of law as a means of avoiding acculturation and reifying a sense of ethnic identity by maintaining exclusive sociocultural traditions and assimilation of the sojourner.[4] However, concerns regarding acculturation are not isolated to the Ancient Near East. According to Rudmin, "The history of Western civilization is a history of acculturation."[5] To demonstrate his claim, Rudmin references Plato's policies and concerns regarding the intermixing of diverse ethnic peoples saying,

> Rather than complete cultural isolation, Plato proposed minimizing acculturation according to an implicit psychological theory that older people acculturate less than younger people. He argued that people should travel abroad only after 40 years of

3. Thomas and Znaniecki published this as a five volume set from 1918–1921.

4. Rudmin, "Critical History of the Acculturation," 3–37.

5. Rudmin, "Critical History of the Acculturation," 10.

age. He also recommended that sojourners be restricted to the port district of the city so as to minimize citizens' contacts with foreigners.[6] (2003:10)

Rudmin further explains that Plato saw the intermixing of cultures as potentially dangerous in that it would likely lead to social disorder. There is not sufficient space to address the underlying assimilation versus integration debate. However, it is important to acknowledge the political context in which recent acculturation studies are often situated.

Although man has been experiencing acculturation for millennia, the academic theory is rooted in social science. Anthropologists' initial interest in acculturation theory was to understand the effects that European contact had on indigenous peoples. J.W. Powell has the first recorded use of the word in his book *Introduction to the Study of Indian* [Native American] *Languages* (1880):

> The force of acculturation under the overwhelming presence of millions of civilized people has wrought great changes. Primitive Indian society has either been modified or supplanted, primitive religions have been changed, primitive arts lost, and, in like manner, primitive languages have not remained unmodified.[7]

Powell's use of the word acculturation remained relatively unaltered by researchers until the *Memorandum for the Study of Acculturation* offered the following definition:

> Acculturation comprehends those phenomena which result when groups of individuals having different cultures come into continuous first-hand contact, with subsequent changes in the original cultural patterns of either or both groups.[8]

The significant difference between Powell's use of the word and the definition given in the memorandum is the recognition that acculturation can mean culture change in "either or both groups." In other words, acculturation is a bidirectional process as opposed to Powell's unidirectional view. Powell was unaware or unwilling to admit that the researcher and/or the host/majority society was also changed by encountering diverse cultural practices.

While the early recognition of the bi-directional process of acculturation is not readily apparent in ethnographies produced in foreign fields, the same cannot be said for research conducted among immigrant

---

6. Rudmin, "Critical History of the Acculturation," 10.

7. Powell, *Study of Indian Languages*, 46.

8. Redfield et al., "Memorandum for the Study of Acculturation," 149.

communities in the United States by sociologists. Anthropologist Melford Spiro suggests that sociologists were producing some of the best anthropological research on acculturation.[9] Despite the clear value in research among immigrants, by and large, anthropologists continued pursuing foreign fields to study culture.

Anthropologists struggled to break free from the narrow focus on studying "untouched" cultures in natural settings. Spiro criticized fellow anthropologists for not giving more attention to the acculturation processes of American ethnic groups. He attributes the anthropological lack of interest to "professional ignorance" of the existence of American ethnic groups.[10] Spiro believed that studying ethnic groups in America is a unique opportunity to explore questions that have been for many years framed in binary terms such as nature versus nurture or determined versus constructed:

> Psychological characteristics such as attitudes, values, and emotions seem to persist despite acculturation and overt behavior—at least among those groups for whom there are data; and these characteristics are acquired in the early experience of the individual. . . . On the other hand, if early experiences are of determinative importance, why do most ethnic groups prefer social mobility to ethnic integrity, and class-over ethnic identification? This preference, to be sure, is not found in all ethnic groups . . . These differences in cultural persistence are relevant not only for the problem of early experience but for the general question of "cultural determinism" broadly conceived. If behavior is determined by one's cultural heritage, then why do ethnics (who desire acculturation) attempt to behave in accordance with norms they do not know rather than in accordance with those they have already learned? But "cultural determinism" is concerned with psychological phenomenon as well. To what extent, for example, is culture a constituent element of the self? And to what degree is ego–identity a function of group identification? Ethnic studies raise, and perhaps may solve, questions of this kind. Do the lower–class Norse resist acculturation because they perceive their cultural heritage positively and therefore do not wish to alter their self-conceptions, while other ethnic groups perceive their cultural heritage negatively and wish, therefore, to alter the consequent negative self-conceptions through acculturation? If so, how do these differential evaluations develop?

9. Spiro, "Acculturation of American Ethnic Groups," 1240.
10. Spiro, "Acculturation of American Ethnic Groups," 1241.

And if a person changes his group identification through acculturation, is there a corresponding change in his ego–identity?[11]

There is a cohesive theme of identity underlying the questions posited by
Spiro. This makes sense considering the overarching discussion specifically
relates to a person or group's sameness in the midst of significant cultural
changes.

While Spiro's questions related to identity have historically been approached in multiple ways by a variety of academic disciplines, the study of
immigrant acculturation has generated interdisciplinary cooperation between anthropologists, sociologists, and psychologists. For example, John
Berry's seminal work on acculturation draws from an interdisciplinary
framework that has dominated much of the discussion concerning immigrant identity since 1984.[12] For Berry, the primary issues of acculturation
are "cultural maintenance" and "contact participation."[13] In other words,
how much cultural or ethnic identity does an individual want to maintain
and how much does one want to participate in other cultural groups (i.e.,
his or her society of settlement or host society)? His four-quadrant model
for assessment is based on the following attitudinal dimensions:

> *Assimilation*—"Individuals do not wish to maintain their cul
> tural identity and seek daily interaction with other cultures."
>
> *Separation*—"Individuals place a value on holding on to their
> original culture, and at the same time wish to avoid interaction
> with others."
>
> *Integration*—"Interest in both maintaining one's original cul
> ture, while in daily interactions with other groups."
>
> *Marginalization*—"There is little possibility or interest in cultur
> al maintenance (often for reasons of enforced culture loss), and
> little interest in having relations with others (often for reasons of
> exclusion or discrimination)."[14]

11. Spiro, "Acculturation of American Ethnic Groups," 1250.
12. Rudmin, "Critical History of the Acculturation."
13. Berry, "Immigration, Acculturation, and Adaptation," 9.
14. Berry, "Immigration, Acculturation, and Adaptation," 9.

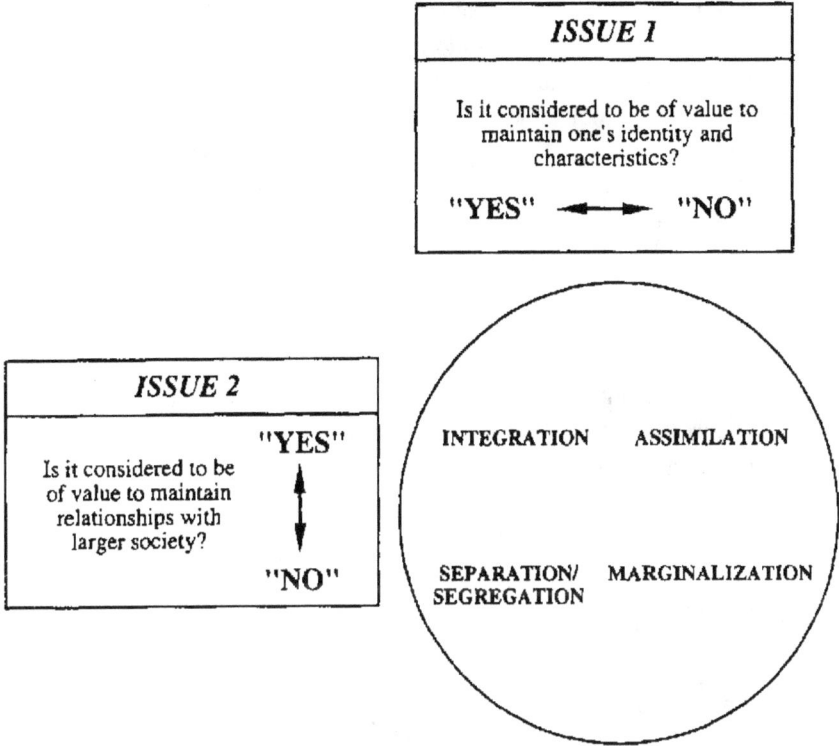

Berry's Four Quadrant Model of Acculturation Strategies.

Berry's model has been criticized for treating culture as though it can be assessed through issues that are simple matters of choice or personal preference (i.e., food, language, dress, etc.) while ignoring issues such as religion.[15] Berry considers religion as "highly normative" and therefore does not address the issue in his attitudinal scales but rather focuses only on cultural domains considered personal preference.[16] This, of course, is a disregard of precedent anthropological literature that considers a change in religious patterns significant in the analysis of acculturation.[17] Berry's assumption of religion being "highly normative" or a given is an externally ascribed assumption and a significant weakness in his acculturation model.

Berry refers to "religious conversions" and "fundamental alterations to value systems" as deeper change when compared to the superficial changes

15. Rudmin, "Psychometric Critique of Acculturation," 41–56.

16. Berry and Sam, "Accuracy in Scientific Discourse," 65–68.

17. Herskovits, *Acculturation*; Powell, *Study of Indian Languages*; Spiro, "Acculturation of Ethnic Groups."

measured by his attitudinal scale; however, he relegates these changes to the category of "group-level acculturation"[18] Berry's view of conversion begs the question of how much culture change can truly be assessed when little emphasis is put on an individual's personal religious belief? While religion may often be a unified normative expression of an ethnic group it should not be assumed. Even if there is a self-ascription of group faith, each individual may have different experiences of that faith and therefore varying interpretations of the same outward religious expressions. Though a community might have uniform texts, symbols, forms, and teachings, there is no uniform experience and therefore little, if any, uniform meaning.

An additional limitation is the static nature of Berry's model. It fails to take into account the dynamic process of individuals and their complex social networks that span the globe. This model may be more helpful in assessing immigrant identity if their interactions were limited to the society in which they have settled. However, immigrants today do not tend to cut off their societies of origin when they migrate. It is no longer sufficient to perceive an immigrant as uprooting themselves from their homeland, family, culture, and pursuing a new life in their country of settlement.[19]

Transnationalism

Attitudes toward the society of settlement and society of origin are often in constant flux because of continuing contact or transnational connection between societies of origin and settlement. This continual negotiation between two social fields requires immigrants to become proficient in negotiating ideal or desired representations of themselves. Thus, quantitative data that focuses on attitudes towards society of origin and settlement, while helpful, may be unreliable. In addition, attitudes toward a society are highly flexible and often dependent on a number of contextual factors that are difficult to assess. For example, immigrant attitudes may change depending on the political relationship between the host society and society of origin.[20] Though immigrant connections back home and complex networks of cultural contact are not new, "they have not acquired until recently the critical mass and complexity necessary to speak of an emergent social field."[21] Transnational anthropology views immigrants in light of the fact that their "daily lives depend on multiple and constant

18. Berry, "Immigration, Acculturation, and Adaptation," 17.

19. Schiller et al., "From Immigrant to Transmigrant," 48–63.

20. Bauböck, "Towards a Political Theory of Transnationalism," 700–723.

21. Portes et al., "Study of Transnationalism," 217.

interconnections across international borders and whose public identities are configured in relationship to more than one nation-state."[22] Transnationalism or transnational migration "is the process by which immigrants forge and sustain simultaneous multi-stranded social relations that link together their societies of origin and settlement."[23]

The transnational framework can focus on activities and histories of individuals or a single family and at the same time assess the impact of institutional or macro-structural effects that emerge.[24] This micro-anthropological framework is an effective and appropriate method for documenting the "transfer and retransfer of cultural customs and practices."[25] The institutional and macro-structural factors that emerge are considered alongside of individuals, keeping in mind that "a main concern guiding transnational research should be the study of the causes of transnationalism and the effects that transnational practices and discourses have on preexisting power structures, identities, and social organization."[26] It is through the experience of navigating these interconnected social fields that individuals maintain and continue to construct their identity in relationship to the broader collective. Much of this transnational interaction takes place through computer mediated communication on the Internet, and it is therefore necessary to consider this space as an additional field for assessing the process of immigrant identity formation.

Computer Mediated Communication

Immigrant use of the Internet for maintaining transnational networks is summarized well in Victoria Bernal's study on the political aspirations of the Eritrean diaspora, "The Internet is the quintessential diasporic medium, ideally suited to allowing migrants in diverse locations to connect, share information, and analyses, and coordinate their activities."[27] For much of the world, technology is quickly becoming the primary medium of communication in everyday life.[28] This is especially true of immigrants who often use this virtual space to renegotiate and or reinforce ethnic identity.[29]

22. Schiller et al., "From Immigrant to Transmigrant," 48.

23. Schiller et al., "From Immigrant to Transmigrant," 48.

24. Portes et al., "Study of Transnationalism," 217–37.

25. Faist, "Diaspora and Transnationalism," 11.

26. Smith and Guarnizo, *Transnationalism from Below*, 29.

27. Bernal, "Diaspora, Cyberspace and Political Imagination," 175.

28. Murthy, "Digital Ethnography" 837–55.

29. Alonso and Oiarzabal, *Diasporas in the New Media Age*; Brinkerhoff, *Digital*

Consequently, ethnographic methods should take a balanced approach of combining digital and physical field sites. Combining the online and offline worlds in ethnography may provide a richer account than either can provide on its own.[30] This can be achieved through participant observation of virtual spaces such as social media and ethnic forums coupled with field research in real time and space.

Immigrants often use social media and ethnic forums as a virtual vehicle to return to the homeland. This virtual transnational social space allows peoples to create and maintain an imagined community online where they achieve a sense of belonging through broadening the boundary markers of both ethnic and nationalistic identities.[31] Alonso and Oiarzabal use the terms digital diasporas and define these groups as follows:

> We define digital diasporas as the distinct online networks that diasporic people use to recreate identities, share opportunities, spread their culture, influence homeland and host-land policy, or create debate about common-interest issues by means of electronic devices.[32]

The Internet is perhaps the cheapest and most effective medium in maintaining and developing social networks across international borders. Consequently, the personal computer and the Internet are often daily resources for transnational migrants who regularly "constitute webs of exchange of information and transfers of knowledge in the physical world as well as in the digital world."[33] This in turn supports the rise of deterritorialized imagined communities that are rooted in a variety of identifications (i.e., ethnic, political, religious, etc.).

Context of Virtual Spaces

This virtual transnational social space not only provides a medium for the exchange of information but also a "forum for re-negotiating and reinforcing diaspora identity."[34] This space, however, is not monolithic. While early studies focused on anonymous multi-user sites such as chat rooms, forums, and bulletin boards, more recent studies focusing on less anonymous online

Diasporas.

30. Murthy, "Digital Ethnography" 837–55.
31. Bernal, "Diaspora, Cyberspace and Political Imagination," 161–79.
32. Alonso and Oiarzabal, *Diasporas in the New Media Age*, 11.
33. Alonso and Oiarzabal, *Diasporas in the New Media Age*, 6.
34. Brinkerhoff, *Digital Diasporas*, 235.

environments found "online self-presentations varied according to the nature of the settings."[35] Therefore, the context of the Internet space being investigated must be taken into consideration. For example, Internet forums are often non-hierarchical, non-coercive, and anonymous public discussions, allowing its members to experiment with non-traditional values and discuss topics that might otherwise be culturally taboo.[36] Anonymity allows for these ideas to be discussed without fear of institutional or social repercussions. Facebook, however, does not provide complete anonymity, and research shows that self-presentations in this setting are influenced by what is socially acceptable. In fact, a Facebook identity may be better understood as a socially desirable identity than an actual one that is embodied offline.[37]

The Internet also provides a global public sphere where unequal power relationships can be both marginalized and magnified.[38] For example, gender and age can easily be disguised in a virtual setting, providing a platform for women and youth that they might not be allotted in some public spaces. The unequal power relationship of income level and education, however, cannot be so easily disguised. The mere fact that an individual has access to the Internet shares something about their social status. This "digital divide" must be taken into account when researching transnational virtual social space.[39]

Additionally, this "virtual space is a realm in which physical space, both proximity and distance, is of no importance."[40] It is in this digital social space that diaspora groups may attempt to renegotiate distinctive socio-cultural features and the basic value orientations that serve as ethnic and nationalistic boundary markers, essentially reconstructing and reinforcing a transnational identity.[41]

Imagined Virtual Communities

The Internet also provides a social space where co-dispersed communities can create new social networks in their society of settlement while simultaneously maintaining existing social networks in their society of origin. This allows immigrants to create "sustain and recreate diasporas

35. Zhao et al., "Identity Construction on Facebook," 1817.

36. Brinkerhoff, Digital Diasporas.

37. Zhao et al., "Identity Construction on Facebook," 1816–36.

38 Benitez, "Transnational Dimensions of the Digital Divide," 181–99.

39 Benitez, "Transnational Dimensions of the Digital Divide," 181–99.

40. Sökefeld, "Alevism Online," 111.

41. Sökefeld, "Alevism Online."

as globally imagined communities."[42] Although these communities are in cyberspace, they are more than simply virtual. Unlike many other virtual communities, the digital diaspora online networks are often based on face-to-face relationships.[43] They are, in fact, real communities making use of a virtual space.

Most researchers conclude that the majority of online social networks are used to reinforce existing relationships, serving as a tool to strengthen offline relationships in an online setting.[44] This is often the case regarding online social media as opposed to online forums and gaming. Certainly, this is true for diaspora groups who typically "have an existing real network of relationships and grounded community before they use the Internet to connect with one another and build their digital communities."[45] For example, Abdisalam Issa-Salwe differentiates virtual Somali diaspora communities from typical virtual communities stating,

> Generally, the shared identity born of the virtual community is temporal. However, a group of Somalis using CMC [computer mediated communication] may create a virtual community, which also has another relationship: that of a specific group identity—one, in turn, backed by the real world (or offline relationships).[46]

Issa-Salwe's research demonstrates how the activities and discussions of the virtual Somali community impacts the actual Somali community in real time and space. The Internet serves as the vehicle for both a reinforcement of the cultural homogeneity and the fragmentation of Somali society through these sociocultural divisions.

These digital communities use a variety of computer-mediated-communications—including blogs, forums, and YouTube—to define their virtual community. These communities are not limited to reinforcing only ethnic identity. Some studies demonstrate the use of CMC to reinforce or re-construct national identities as well. For example, after surveying a Moroccan diaspora Internet forum—*Yabiladi*—one study concluded that Moroccan immigrants use the Internet "as a vehicle for strengthening national feelings and forging a sense of belonging to a national community of

42. Alonso and Oiarzabal, *Diasporas in the New Media Age*, 9.

43. Alonso and Oiarzabal *Diasporas in the New Media Age*; Brinkerhoff, *Digital Diasporas*.

44. Perez-Latre et al., "Social Networks, Media, and Audiences," 63–74.

45. Banerjee and German, "Migration and Transculturation in the Digital Age," 23–35.

46. Issa-Salwe, "Internet and the Somali Diaspora," 56.

Moroccan Muslims scattered around the world."[47] It was suggested in the same study that the Internet served as a place for the Moroccan diaspora to cope with feelings of displacement and reconstruction of a transnational collective identity. Similarly, research conducted on a group of Sierra Leoneans revealed a creation of a "virtual nation—any community that communicates in cyberspace, whose collective discourse and/or actions are aimed towards the building, binding, maintenance, rebuilding or rebinding a nation."[48] The Sierra Leoneans, through use of an online ethnic forum, *Leonenet*, were able to effectively use virtual space to impact geographically bound Sierra Leone. After more than a decade of civil war, government institutions of Sierra Leone were ineffective at best and nonexistent at worst. Consequently, the diaspora used online social space to generate, negotiate, and maintain ideas about Sierra Leonean identity until the government structures were reinstituted and capable of carrying the ideas generated online forward. In other words, the Sierra Leonean diaspora played a significant role in the rebuilding of a nation by first building a virtual nation.

Deterritorialization or Reterritorialization

These virtual nations provide a sense of virtual return for many migrants. While the Internet is in essence deterritorialized and often disembodied, this is not the case for virtual transnational communities. Their virtual space is often "anchored in offline contexts rather than self-contained, disembodied universe."[49] Certainly, this was the case with the Iranian migrants who used virtual space to negotiate Iranianness and at the same time forming "mobile and dynamic, yet sustained, emotional connections to two distant and bounded nation-states."[50] Negative media representations of Iran in the mainstream media and a disillusionment of an American-Iranian identification led many to create a transnational identity online that is embodied in memory, shaped by offline experiences, and although virtual, rooted in the geographically bounded territories of Iran and the United States. This idea of a transnational online identity is quite common for many immigrants as they attempt to re-territorialize their living space, often blending the countries of origin and settlement.[51]

47. Loukili, "Moroccan Diaspora, Internet and National Imagination," 7.

48. Tynes, "Nation-building and the Diaspora on Leonenet," 501–2.

49. Van den Bos and Nell, "Territorial Bounds to Virtual Space," 216.

50. Alinejad, "Mapping Homelands through Virtual Spaces," 59.

51. Bustamante, "Tidelike Diasporas in Brazil," 170–89.

Indeed, some will argue that transnationalism and digital diasporas are reducing boundaries and moving society towards a global identity in a borderless world. Victoria Bernal, however, argues just the opposite. Her research among the Eritrean diaspora community shows an expansion of boundaries, suggesting "what might have once been outside the margins (of the nation) is now more effectively included within a larger framework of imagined community."[52] She further suggests, because of the transnational nature and influence of diaspora groups online, that they be conceptualized as "offshore citizenry or extension of the nation."[53]

The Internet allows immigrants to transcend geographical boundaries and reinforce or re-construct collective belonging through an instantaneous transfer of ideas. Some scholars suggest that rather than dissolving geographical boundaries these transnational practices in virtual space often reinforce territoriality and may even broaden it beyond locality.[54] Understanding the offline context of these online interactions is essential in assessing factors for transnational identity formation.[55]

Conclusion

Research is consistent in stating that identity is negotiated online, however, not enough research has focused on the relationship between these online and offline worlds. Considering digital diaspora groups are often anchored in the real world, this study involves a balanced combination of physical and digital ethnography. In addition, the impact of transnational practices on acculturation is assessed through observing and evaluating displayed collective boundaries to signal belonging.[56] The primary difference between Barth's ethnic boundaries and the emergence of transnationalism is the latter focuses on the continued social interaction between societies of origin and settlement. Barth's primary focus is on the distinctive cultural features that form an ethnic boundary and thereby affirm a self-ascribed identity amidst inter-ethnic contact. In contrast, transnational practices of the twenty-first century demand that boundaries affirm a self-ascribed identity in both inter-ethnic and intra-ethnic social fields simultaneously.

52. Bernal, "Diaspora, Cyberspace and Political Imagination," 163.

53. Bernal, "Diaspora, Cyberspace and Political Imagination," 163.

54. Van den Bos and Nall, "Territorial Bounds"; Bernal, "Diaspora, Cyberspace and Political Imagination."

55. Wilson and Peterson, "Anthropology of Online Communities," 449–56.

56. Barth, *Ethnic Groups and Boundaries*.

Transnationalism and the Internet provides a storehouse of new narratives for identity formation across geographical boundaries. These multiple narratives are available on the local and global scale. When considering the identity formation of a Pashtun immigrant, it is imperative to take into consideration how an individual integrates their individual story with broader sociocultural and global narratives. The inner and outer role of narratives in identity formation is discussed in the next chapter.

4

Narrative Identity

THE RISE OF MASS migrations and the Internet have blurred disciplinary boundary lines concerning identity studies. This phenomenon reveals some common threads of approaching identity from various academic disciplines. One significant intersection is in the field of narrative identity. This chapter explores how individuals narrate their identity within the broader context of sociocultural narratives. Narrative identity is an interdisciplinary approach that acknowledges the overlap between individual or personal identity and a collective identity rather than placing them in opposition. In addition, this approach moves away from the dichotomy of essentialism and constructivism and towards a model that affirms and limits both perspectives. While individuals construct a sense of being, they do so relationally and from a limited repertoire of narratives influenced by their sociocultural context. Identity is therefore best understood as relationally constituted at the intersection of individual and sociocultural narratives that provide a sense of continuity or self-sameness between past experiences, present circumstances, and an imagined future.

This approach neither gives sociocultural factors too much power nor denies their influence in limiting, as well as shaping the available narratives through public discourse. We must recognize that even the inner process of emotions is informed by our sociocultural context. We learn what feelings are as well as the appropriate expressions of these emotions through a cultural lens. Clifford Geertz explains,

> The point is that in man neither regnant fields nor mental sets can be formed with sufficient precision in the absence of guidance from symbolic models of emotion. In order to make up our minds we must know how we feel about things; and to know how we feel about things we need the public images of sentiment that only ritual, myth, and art can provide.[1]

---

1. Geertz, *Interpretation of Cultures*, 81–82.

Geertz's recognition of the overlap of individual emotions with already present sociocultural forms may lead some to attribute a deterministic power to culture. However, we must keep in mind that culture is not static and neither are the forms and symbols that are representative of a particular culture. In addition, Anthony Cohen reminds us that the meaning and power of forms and symbols are dependent on an individual's interpretations. This cognitive process must not be taken for granted lest we give culture an unwarranted privilege over the individual:

> Cultural forms, such as language, ritual and other symbolic constructions, are made meaningful and substantial by people's interpretations of them. They are given life by being made meaningful. We may well regard these symbols as being compelling: the flag, the tomb, the soldier's slouch hat, the mateship and the booze. But the power they exercise lies in providing us the means by which to think. The assumption that under normal circumstances they can make us think in specifiable ways is mistaken. It privileges culture over thinking selves, instead of seeing it as the product of thinking selves.[2]

Cohen suggests this is not an elevation of individual cognition above social and cultural structures but rather the linking of individual mediation of these collective forms and symbols. The problem is not in the acknowledgment of a group, culture, or context but rather failing "to distinguish between the appearance and the reality of an interpretation common to different individuals."[3]

Shared cultural forms do not necessarily imply a shared meaning. Cultural meaning is profoundly influenced through personal experience. While the forms may be the same, the experiences likely vary and thus the meanings may vary as well. For example, a group of Muslims participating in the same rituals at the same mosque may each have different experiences of faith and, therefore, varying interpretations of the same outward religious expressions. This is particularly the case when a mosque is made up primarily of immigrants whose past experiences include a variety of local expressions. In these mosques, it is not uncommon to hear religious debates ranging from significant theological issues such as what it means to be Muslim or how a particular teaching in the Qur'an should be interpreted to less important matters such as how high to hold your hands when performing *salat* (ritual prayers).

2. Cohen, *Self Consciousness*, 166–67.
3. Cohen, *Self Consciousness*, 17.

The interdependence of religious experience, alongside uniform texts, symbols, and forms is not unique to Islam. The same could be said of any faith community. My own faith tradition of Anglicanism for example is bound by articles of faith, creeds, and liturgy, and yet there remains significant internal debate regarding how to live out the faith. This may be, as Cohen suggests, because meanings and power of the shared forms and symbols come from the individual interpretations which are informed by experience. However, we must also acknowledge that whether or not an individual lends power or gives meaning to these forms, will not change the fact that they do exist independent of individual interpretation. In fact, it is often the case that practicing a religious form will shape the individual's interpretive process. In other words, there is a tension between the individual and the collective experience. Paul DiMaggio suggests that the collective experience is communicated in the form of "narratives or stories repeatedly invoked in public discourse."[4]

Inner and Outer Role of Narratives

The tension between the individual and collective identity lies in the negotiation of public or collective narratives with personal ones. Margaret Sommers addresses this tension by suggesting that narratives have both an ontological and epistemological role in our lives. Stories are ontological in that they help us to understand who we are and epistemological in that they help us to understand how we should live. She further argues that these narratives are both social and interpersonal. The social role of narratives is most often perpetuated though social or public discourse. These public narratives, according to Sommers, may range from a micro-scale such as the family to a macro-scale that represents local or even global institutions. For Sommers, narrative identity is best understood at the intersection of relationships, time, and space. It is at this contextual intersection that individual and social identity is undergoing constant construction. "Identity-formation takes shape within these relational settings of contested but patterned relations among narratives, people, and institutions."[5]

It is through narratives, drawn from the collective or social memory and imagination, that the symbolic systems of cultural domains are often organized, learned, and expressed as a collective framework or suitable way in which to live and view the world. Yet, it is the individual's interpretation, drawn from one's own remembered experience, that gives these collective

4. DiMaggio, "Culture and Cognition," 273.
5. Sommers, "Narrative Constitution of Identity," 626.

symbols and cultural domains power. While individuals story their experience, they do so in the contexts of shared sociocultural experiences which are also storied. Alasdair MacIntyre explains,

> For the story of my life is always embedded in the story of those communities from which I derive my identity. I am born with a past; and to try to cut myself off from that past, in the individualist mode, is to deform my present relationships. The possession of an historical identity and the possession of a social identity coincide. Notice that rebellion against my identity is always one possible mode of expressing it. Notice also that the fact that the self has to find its moral identity in and through its membership in communities such as those of the family, the neighborhood, the city, and the tribe does not entail that the self has to accept the moral limitations of the particularity of those forms of community.[6]

The medium for identity formation as well as the overlap between the internal and external processes are the narratives that inform one another. It is important therefore to approach identity at the point of narrative convergence between the individual and the collective without privileging one over the other. Stories have the unique ability to demonstrate this convergence in that they allow for multiple interpretations without significantly altering a story.[7]

It is through the interaction of personal and public narratives that the self and the collective are simultaneously constituted. According to Jerome Bruner there is "an emerging consensus" among researchers that the self is "constructed through interaction with the world rather than just being there immutably, that it is a product of transaction and discourse."[8] These inner and outer processes are continually informing one another and helping us know ourselves and others through the stories lived and told. We tend to understand our past experiences, present circumstances, and future hopes in a storied sequence alongside the stories of significant others. This gives us a sense of accountability to others in that we are a part of their story and they are a part of ours as well.

These narratives are embedded within a sociocultural context that constrains the individual understanding of the self and others as an interpretative process. Paul Ricoeur suggests that narratives are a "privileged mediation" for interpreting the self:

6. MacIntyre, *After Virtue*, 221.
7. Bruner, "Culture and Mind," 29–45.
8. Bruner, "Narrative Model of Self-Construction," 146.

> The self does not know itself immediately, but only indirectly, through the detour of cultural signs of all sorts, which articulate the self and symbolic mediations that already articulate action, among them the narratives of daily life. Narrative mediation underlines this remarkable aspect about knowledge of the self as being an interpretation.[9]

The self as an interpretation requires a framework that recognizes the interaction and mutual constitution of personal and collective identity through narratives. While individuals story their experiences, they do so in the context of culture. These stories are not picked at random from an unlimited repertoire; rather, they are drawn from a canonized cultural collection that is highly dependent upon what is a socially acceptable way of being.

We see and interpret the world and the self through personal narratives that are informed and in some cases constrained by the broader context of sociocultural and global narratives. Life stories, while individually constituted, must fit into the cultural context as acceptable representations of self in light of a collective or shared discourse. Bruner suggests that the self is the "offspring" of these inner and outer narratives in a community of other selves that are situated in a shared sociocultural canon of narratives.[10] For Bruner, narratives are the medium through which the inner-self is constituted and outer-culture is legitimized:

> We internalize our culture's demands, make them our own as it were, but we then somehow legitimize them by externalizing them into an institutionalized, super organic world "beyond" us. . . . The impact of culture on mind is through the conventionalization of experience into shared ordinariness, a conventionalization that makes place as well for rendering deviations from shared ordinariness into a comprehensible and manageable form, even to "disguise" them artfully.[11]

Narratives are the medium through which this ordinariness, as well as acceptable deviations from ordinariness, are communicated. Bruner suggests stories are a particularly effective medium to reframe the strange as ordinary and that this elasticity of the narrative form makes it a particularly advantageous medium for mediating individual and collective identity. Even the process of individual narrative deviation, in a sense, acknowledges a cultural canonicity of stories from which the individual is deviating.[12]

---

9. Ricoeur, "Narrative Identity," 80.
10. Bruner, "Narrative Model of Self-Construction," 159.
11. Bruner, "Culture and Mind," 35.
12. Bruner, "Culture and Mind," 29–45.

In order to maintain a sense of self continuity amidst constant change, individuals must remain flexible in their interpretation of self in order to avoid an identity crisis when they experience something that does not fit easily into their current narrative. According to Bruner,

> The more fixed one's self-concept, the more difficult it is to manage change. 'Staying loose' makes repair and negotiation possible. Not so surprising, then, that turning points are so characteristic of the autobiographies we finally write or tell.[13]

These turning points are significant in that they link the past, present, and future, as well as illustrate how individuals tailor stories to fit their reality. This is particularly true when an individual is facing a crisis, real or imagined, that motivates them to re-construct a narrative self that is better able to integrate an experience that meshes well with their past experiences and future hopes.

It is through narratives that individuals construct the past, present, and a potential future by plotting themselves within a story or potential story that stems from the sociocultural cannon. Therefore, the story must be both a personally and culturally consistent and acceptable way to live. If, however, there is no current acceptable narrative, and an individual is sufficiently motivated, they may deviate from the culturally canonized script. The dynamic nature of narratives means that individuals may transcend the available cultural repertoire by creating new narratives or simply re-interpreting old ones. New stories may initially be rejected; on the other hand, they may eventually become canonical public narratives. The ability to re-narrate canonical scripts is according to Bruner, "what makes the innovative storyteller such a powerful figure in culture."[14] They are powerful because they are able to influence people to see the world in a new way through re-narrating canonical scripts or inventing entirely new scripts that become canonical. The individual potential to transcend sociocultural narratives for more suitable stories destabilizes the narrative framework and thereby avoids slipping into cultural essentialism. That said, the sociocultural context and epistemological role of public narratives must not be underestimated.

13. Bruner, "Narrative Model of Self-Construction," 157.
14. Bruner, "Narrative Model of Self-Construction," 12.

Epistemological Public Narratives

Epistemological narratives frame how we see and interpret the world. This sociocultural framework is often storied. Nigel Rapport succinctly explains this dual role of narratives:

> Narratives represent a primary embodiment of our understanding of the world, of experience, and ultimately of ourselves: the typical way in which experience is framed and schematized and orderly worlds constructed. Narrative is the form of human consciousness, the form of our conscious experiencing. Carried variously in languages of words, images, gestures, behavioural routines, buildings, therefore, human narratives are ubiquitous. They are found in myths, fables, epics, novellas, histories, tragedies, dramas, comedies, litigations, dreams, mimes, memories, paintings, films, photographs, stained-glass windows, comics, newspapers and conversations. Rendering experience in terms of narrative is an instrument for making meaning which dominates much of life.[15]

In other words, stories give us an understanding about the world and ourselves; they tell us and others who we are, where we've come from, and where we are going. MacIntyre suggests that stories are a universal experience:

> Man is, in his actions and practice, as well as in his fictions, essentially a story-telling animal. He is not essentially, but becomes through his history, a teller of stories that aspire to truth. But the key question for men is not about their own authorship; I can only answer the question 'What am I to do?' if I can answer the prior question 'Of what story or stories do I find myself a part?' We enter human society, that is, with one or more imputed characters—roles into which we have been drafted—and we have to learn what they are in order to be able to understand how others respond to us and how our responses to them are apt to be construed. It is through hearing stories about wicked stepmothers, lost children, good but misguided kings, wolves that suckle twin boys, youngest sons who receive no inheritance but must make their own way in the world and eldest sons who waste their inheritance on riotous living and go into exile to live with the swine, that children learn or mislearn both what a child and what a parent is, what the cast of characters may be in the drama into which they have been born and what the ways of the world are. Deprive children of stories and you leave

15. Rapport, "Narrative as Fieldwork Technique," 76.

them unscripted, anxious stutterers in their actions as in their words. Hence there is no way to give us an understanding of any society, including our own, except through the stock of stories which constitute its initial dramatic resources.[16]

Much like individuals, societies, too, employ memory in the process of accruing a stock of stories through which the collective can appeal to as a shared identity. Stuart Hall refers to this process as "selective canonisation."[17] In his address on the conceptualization of British Heritage, Hall articulates the role stories have in instituting social memory:

> We should think of The Heritage as a discursive practice. It is one of the ways in which the nation slowly constructs for itself a sort of collective social memory. Just as individuals and families construct their identities in part by 'storying' the various random incidents and contingent turning points of their lives into a single, coherent, narrative, so nations construct identities by selectively binding their chosen high points and memorable achievements into an unfolding 'national story'. This story is what is called 'Tradition.' . . . Like personal memory, social memory is also highly selective, it highlights and foregrounds, imposes beginnings, middles and ends on the random and contingent. Equally, it foreshortens, silences, disavows, forgets and elides many episodes which—from another perspective—could be the start of a different narrative. This process of selective 'canonisation' confers authority and a material and institutional facticity on the selective tradition, making it extremely difficult to shift or revise.[18]

For Hall, a social memory is selectively storied and slow to change. This is particularly the case once a story takes root at the level of tradition. These narratives are reinforced at the institutional level and are very effective in informing the beliefs and behaviors of large collectivities.

The use of public narratives as a means in which to draw collectives together is not a new concept. Societies have always used narratives as a means of communicating the boundaries of belonging. Of course, in order for some to belong, it is a necessary implication that others are excluded. In other words, collectivity is often rooted in the paradigms of sameness and difference. Such a framework creates difficulties for societies with multiple collectives to thrive because otherness is seen as a threat

16. MacIntyre, *After Virtue*, 216.
17. Hall, "Whose Heritage," 5.
18. Hall, "Whose Heritage," 5.

to identity. In that case, difference may be viewed through the lens of division rather than diversity. This is becoming particularly problematic as mass migration movements and refugee resettlement challenge views of an imagined homogeneity.

In Western contexts, a person's non-whiteness or European-ness automatically assumes the need for a label of classification or identity that is the "other." These labels are most often socially constructed categories of identification, such as race, nationality, ethnicity, religion, etc. that are reified into individual or collective identity.[19] These classifications are often overly reductive and simplistic representations of complex individuals who may not even identify with the group they are externally classified to belong. More troubling is the potential for these differences to be framed in such a way to view "the other" as an enemy in order to justify hatred and violence. This is often done through public narratives or propaganda. However, this process is not unique to the West. The fear of otherness and viewing others as a threat can be found in every region of the world.[20]

In considering the role of public narratives in the life of our research participants, we must briefly explore media representations of Muslims and more specifically the Pashtun. In addition to sociocultural narratives that are relatively localized, there are global narratives we must consider as well. These narratives tend to transcend boundaries of time and space. As the previous chapter demonstrates, the Internet and computer mediated communication have significant implications for immigrant identity formation. One such implication is the availability of a narrative storehouse that is immense both in size and diversity. This has a significant impact on global narratives such as Islam. One can find a variety of expressions and communities in virtual settings.

The ummah or Muslim community is no longer bound geographically. This means that previous regional boundaries, such as schools of interpretation, are no longer a certainty. The Muslim community in the twenty-first century is transnational and incredibly diverse in its beliefs and practices. This diversity and non-localized expression requires one's sense of belonging to be increasingly imagined rather than experienced. This collectivity is imagined because one could never actually meet the entirety of their collective group. What they have is an imagined belief that there is a community that shares a particular narrative that gives them a collective sense of being.

The increasing number of available narratives in the Muslim world coupled with the number of Muslims makes it incredibly difficult for

19. Brubaker, *Ethnicity Without Groups*.
20. Zizioulas, *Being as Communion*.

non-Muslims to conceptualize what Muslims believe. This is further complicated by the recent shift from print-based epistemology towards media.[21] Given the role of media in informing epistemological assumptions about Islam and Muslims, it is imperative to explore these ideological discourses in American media.

The Medium of Digital Media Discourse

Expressing public narratives of Islam and the Pashtun community through the medium of electronic media has significant implications in identity formation. Neil Postman argued nearly forty years ago that the decline of print-based epistemology and rise of television-based epistemology would lead to complex ideas being reduced to talking points in the form of entertainment thereby "transforming our culture into one vast arena for show business."[22] He considered this to be a dangerous shift in society because of the limitation of electronic media as a medium for communicating complex ideas. This is particularly true concerning television news media where topics or events are discussed in brief segments. According to the Pew Research Center's Journalism Project, the median length of a local television news story with video footage is forty-one seconds.[23] If there is no video footage of the event, the median length drops to twenty-two seconds. The average time allotted for a story on national news networks is higher at two minutes and twenty-three seconds; however, this is still an insufficient length of time to present topics with much depth or nuance. Postman argued that the medium of news media not only shapes the topics but the way in which they are discussed as well. This is certainly the case regarding Islam and Muslims. The insufficient amount of time often results in the adoption of an essentialist paradigm in order to make sense of events involving Muslims.

Essentialists and Nominalists Frameworks

Muslims are often portrayed as either monolithic in belief or a diverse community of interpretation. These two approaches are similar to the cultural essentialist and constructivist paradigms discussed in the previous chapter.

21. Postman, *Amusing ourselves to Death*.

22. Postman, *Amusing ourselves to Death*, 80.

23. The Pew Research Center's Journalism Project, formerly known as the Project for Excellence in Journalism (PEJ) uses a News Coverage Index to analyze nightly news broadcast from American networks NBC, ABC, and CBS. The PEJ data for local news stories includes 33,911 local news stories from 49 stations in fifteen American cities.

Matthew Stone explains these different approaches to Muslims using the philosophical distinction between essentialism and nominalism:

> Roughly, the difference between these views is whether one tends to see abstractions as really real and assign a lesser place to individual or particular existing things (a view called essentialism), or whether one views individual existing things as the primary reality and sees abstractions as ideas or words whose use is helpful for communicating but are not as fully real as individual things (a view called nominalism).[24]

The essentialist, according to Stone, tends to see Islam as the "really real" which may lead to generalizations about what Muslims believe.

The essentialist paradigm often leads to the polarizing dichotomy of Islam as either inherently peaceful or violent. In other words, many Americans become fixated on uncovering the "true nature" of Islam. This, in turn, produces a polarizing discussion of Muslim immigration that often centers on whether or not Muslims can be good American citizens. Those who argue Islam is a violent religion suggest that Muslims come to America under the guise of peace so that they can subvert Western civilization.[25] On the other end of the essentialist spectrum are those who proclaim that Islam is a peaceful religion that has been hijacked by a radical fringe and that Islam is compatible with modernity and democracy.[26] Neither of these positions are particularly helpful in that they do not take into consideration the legitimacy of both peaceful and violent expressions within Islam historically as well as presently. Each of these groups tends to read and interpret the Qur'an and history of Islam selectively rather than understand the diverse representations in the vast corpus of quranic exegetical literature. The same is true for the life of Muhammad. In listening to their competing descriptions of Islam's Prophet one might conclude that essentialists on each end of the spectrum are discussing two different people named Muhammad.

The nominalist tends to focus on individual Muslim experiences, interpretations, cultures and the broader socio-historical development of various Muslim communities. This approach avoids generalizations by recognizing the complexity and diversity within Islam and the variety of factors that are at play within a particular community or individual's interpretation and practice. However, the emphasis on the fluidity and complexity may result in the

24. Stone, *Reaching the Heart and Mind of Muslims*, 8.

25. Emerson, *American Jihad*; Geller, *Stop the Islamization*; McCarthy, *Grand Jihad*; Spencer, *Stealth Jihad*.

26. Abdul-Rauf, *What's Right with Islam*; Esposito and Mogahed, *Who Speaks for Islam*; Lean, *Islamophobia Industry*.

deconstruction of categories making it difficult to make any claims regarding Islam or events involving Muslims.

The essentialist rather than the nominalist position fits the limitations brought on by the medium of electronic news media. Some scholars such as Reza Aslan have attempted to give more complexity to the discussion in television news interviews. However, a brief look at his interview on CNN shows that the journalists were either incapable or unwilling to consider another position other than the essentialist paradigm.[27] It may be, as Postman suggests, the medium of television is insufficient to have complex discussions. Or, perhaps Aslan's approach complicates the connection between religion and violence which may dispel some irrational fears that are a high value in American media production. Regardless, perspectives like Aslan's do not get much news airtime comparable to others. The media analysis research institute Media Tenor analyzed 722 news reports concerning Muslims from 2007–2013. Their analysis revealed that only one percent of the material was discussed by Muslims or experts on Islam. Christian Kolmer, director of policy at Media Tenor, suggests that "voices that refuse to equate Islam and violence are taken up more and more rarely in the media."[28] Thus, nuance is often exchanged for generalizations that are then paired with shocking imagery and a few talking points that often reinforces public fears.

Epistemology of Fear

These stories are often overly simplistic characterizations in a format that is fit for entertainment but not epistemology. Postman suggests that fragmented and incoherent newscasts are driven by an entertainment industry that sells time and therefore cannot afford to discuss any one issue in much depth ([1985] 2005). As a result, he refers to Americans as the "best entertained and quite likely, least well-informed people in the Western world" (106). He cleverly suggests that Americans have a "Now . . . this" worldview:

> "Now . . . this" is commonly used on radio and television newscasts to indicate that what one has just heard or seen has no relevance to what one is about to hear or see, or possibly to anything one is likely to hear or see. The phrase is a means of acknowledging the fact that the world as mapped by the speeded-up electronic media is no order or meaning and is not to be

27. https://www.cnn.com/videos/bestoftv/2014/09/30/cnn-tonight-reza-aslan-bill-maher.cnn.

28. Kolmer, "Terror and Fear Shape the Image of Islam."

taken seriously. There is no murder so brutal, no earthquake so devastating, no political blunder so costly—for that matter, no ball score so tantalizing or weather report so threatening—that it cannot be erased from our minds by a newscaster saying, "Now . . . this."[29]

What Postman observed in 1985 continues to be relevant today. Television news is a multibillion dollar industry that is driven by a bottom line. One of the industry's main commodities is fear. In addition to the "Now . . . this" phrase of news media we have "tune in at eleven to find out . . . " Local news channels in hopes of attracting people to their late-night broadcasts developed a marketing strategy that plays on the fears of their viewers. The thing you need to "find out" about at eleven is often alluded to as a potential threat to the viewer's well-being. This tactic is so commonly used in local news that comedian Ellen DeGeneres developed it into one of her stand-up routines:

> The local news, they want you to watch every broadcast they've got don't they. It's not good enough you are watching the one you're watching, they do these teases to get you to watch later on that are so incredibly cruel. [switches to a newscaster's voice] 'It could be the most-deadly thing in the world and you may be having it for dinner. We'll tell you what it is tonight at eleven!'[30]

The use of fear to generate viewers is common practice in news media. David Altheide recognized the role of news media in generating a public discourse of fear two decades ago saying:

> News perspectives and practices, including the organizational context and use of entertainment formats, promote the problem frame that in turn produces narratives of fear. The perception of many is that life is very problematic, dangerous, and demanding of extreme measures to protect us. Indeed, one of the few things Americans seem to share is the popular culture that celebrates danger and fear as entertainment organized with canned formats delivered through an expansive and invasive information technology.[31]

These news media narratives can shape public perceptions of both who and what to fear. Our televisions and newspapers provide us with "ideal type

29. Postman, *Amusing ourselves to Death*, 99.

30. "Ellen DeGenerous Here and Now." https://www.youtube.com/watch?v=1Pm 9ERE1FhA.

31. Altheide, "News Media," 664.

villains and threats."[32] Before exploring American media's use of fear in representing Muslims, it is worth noting that Muslim majority countries' media representations of the West are equally disingenuous and equally effective in recruiting the imagination of many Muslims to see America as the great Satan or modern day crusaders.

Fear of Muslims in American Media

Some scholars suggest that Muslims have always been constructed as villains in the Western imagination. Sophia Arjana, for example suggests that while the cultural construction of the Muslim identity in the Western imagination is varied, the common thread tends to be the Muslim depicted as a problem:

> Terrorist attacks, wars in Iraq and Afghanistan, the increased movement of Muslim immigrants into northern and western Europe, and the visibility of Islam in general have contributed to a voicing of "the Muslim problem." However, these concerns represent old anxieties that lie within a multiplicity of times and spaces on the pages of manuscripts and canvases of paintings, and works of great drama, poetry, and fiction, within travel diaries and government documents, and on the screens of movie theaters . . . we must look at the numerous fields of cultural production; there, we find a vision of Islam that is both familiar and unsettling. Within it, we must seek what is common. What is common is the Muslim monster.[33]

Arjana suggests that rather than ask "Why do they hate us?," Americans should be asking "Why do we fear them?"[34] She argues that 9/11 reified in the Western imagination 1,300 years of haunting Western constructions of the so called Muslim monster.

Not all media representation of Muslims in media are negative. For example, Evelyn Alsultany argues that following 9/11 there was almost an immediate conflation between Arabs and Muslims in media. She also suggests that in recent years there was a significant shift in media discourse away from the historical stereotypes documented by Arjana. She demonstrates in her research a variety of strategies used by writers and producers to show the complexity of the Muslim world in American media:

Strategy #1: Inserting Patriotic Arab or Muslim Americans

32. Altheide, "News Media," 665.
33. Arjana, *Muslims in the Western Imagination*, 1.
34. Arjana, *Muslims in the Western Imagination*, 7.

Strategy #2: Sympathizing with the Plight of Arab and
Muslim Americans after 9/11

Strategy #3: Challenging the Arab/Muslim Conflation
with Diverse Muslim Identities

Strategy #4: Flipping the Enemy

Strategy #5: Humanizing the Terrorist

Strategy #6: Projecting a Multicultural U.S. Society

Strategy #7: Fictionalizing the Middle Eastern
or Muslim Country[35]

Alsultany suggests these strategies only appear to challenge stereotypes but
fail to do so because Muslims and Arabs , despite being more complex, often remain within a narrative context of terrorism. In other words, while the
Muslim may no longer be the monster, they have yet to escape the horror
film industry. In addition, Alsultany suggests that these "simplified complex
representations" gives the illusion of a "so-called post-race era."[36]

Despite some attempts to offer a more complex view of Muslims in
film and television, many Americans continue to be fearful of Muslims. According to Barry Glassner, the rise in American public fear of Islam and
Muslims was solidified through the use of media narrative techniques following 9/11.[37] He suggests that many Americans, despite living in one of the
safest times in human history, are convinced that the world is falling apart
due to the constant fear mongering of mainstream news media. Glassner
describes the post 9/11 media narrative as follows: "The American way of
life is portrayed as the envy of the world and the storyline is about a great
nation pulling together to fight a common enemy. The villains are from foreign lands, and the heroes of the tale are soldiers."[38] Deepa Kumar agrees
with Glassner's assessment concerning the public narrative of American
exceptionalism in the wake of 9/11: "From then on, US policy was geared
toward 'keeping Americans safe' from Muslim 'evildoers.'"[39]

Much of the news media concerning Islam and Muslims is associated
with violence and terrorism. In a recent study, researchers conducted a
meta-analysis of 345 published media studies concerning Muslim representations from 2000 to 2015 to determine the types of public narratives

35. Alsultany, *Arabs and Muslims in the Media*, 21–26.
36. Alsultany, *Arabs and Muslims in the Media*, 21.
37. Glassner, "Narrative Techniques of Fear Mongering," 819–26.
38. Glassner, "Narrative Techniques of Fear Mongering," 824.
39. Kumar, *Islamophobia and the Politics of Empire*, 113.

shaping Muslim identities.[40] While this study was not specific to American media, their findings revealed that the U.S. media representations of Muslims were more researched than any other country with ninety-nine published studies. In addition, American anti-Muslim sentiments were found to be much higher in the United States compared to other Western nations. The meta-analysis revealed that there was a shift in media representations of Muslims post 9/11. Following the attacks on the World Trade Center, media coverage of Islam was mostly negative and primarily discussed in the context of extremism and violence. This was particularly the case in U.S. media representations:

> Several studies have focused on media representations of wars within and between Muslim countries, with special emphasis on the wars in Afghanistan (2001–present) and Iraq (2003–2011). Researchers comparing the USA and the foreign media observed that the US media used pro-war and anti-Muslim/Arab frames, while the media outside of the USA were anti-war and more humanistic in their portrayals.[41]

Considering the consistent themes of negative news media since 9/11, it should come as no surprise that Americans are increasingly fearful and suspicious of Muslims and Islam. A recent survey of American fears by Chapman University revealed 41 percent of Americans were afraid of a terrorist attack making it the second greatest fear behind government corruption.[42] Moreover, a 2016 survey by Pew Research Center revealed that 80 percent of Americans believe ISIS is America's greatest global threat.[43]

American fears of domestic terrorism made Islam and Muslim immigration a significant talking point in the political campaigns for the 2016 presidential election. While many of the Republican candidates did not support Donald Trump's calls for a Muslim ban, the majority of American registered voters did. After winning the election, Trump issued an executive order temporarily banning entry into the U.S. from seven majority Muslim countries. According to a 2017 Politico survey, 55 percent of American registered voters either strongly agreed (35 percent) or somewhat agreed (20 percent) with Trump's order.[44] Some are suggesting that there is a correlation with the increase of negative media attention during the two-year election campaign and an upsurge in hate crimes against Muslims. According

40. Ahmed and Matthes, "Media Representation of Muslims," 219–44.
41. Ahmed and Matthes, "Media Representation of Muslims," 15.
42. Chapman University, "America's Top Fears 2016."
43. Drake and Doherty, "How Americans view the U.S. in the World."
44. Shepard, "Majority of Voters Back Trump Travel Ban."

to the CAIR 2017 Civil Rights Report, hate crimes against Muslims have increased by 584 percent (440 incidents) from 2014 to 2016.[45] One of the cited reasons for the significant increase was a "toxic political environment," including anti-Muslim rhetoric by elected officials and presidential candidates.[46] The problem may not be the anti-Muslim political rhetoric or the government policies that target Muslims, but rather the increased news media attention of the rhetoric and policies that have made anti-Muslim sentiments so pervasive. Governmental policies targeting Muslims and the use of Islam as the enemy of America is not unique to Donald Trump or the current Republican Party.

"Us" versus "Them" in National News Media

Edward Said suggests that Islam filled the vacuum of America's enemy that would justify the continued expansion of the military industrial complex following the end of the Cold War. The news media was the means through which Islam came to symbolize "America's major foreign devil."[47] He suggests that the media reinforced an "us" versus "them" narrative where both the Muslim and Western world are depicted as opposing forces of good and evil:

> The conflict between "Islam" and "the West" is very real. One tends to forget that all wars have two sets of trenches, two sets of barricades, two military machines. And just as the war with Islam seems to have unified the west around opposition to Islam's power, so too has the war with the West unified many sectors of the Islamic world.[48]

While Said wholeheartedly rejects these media characterizations and the clash of civilizations narrative, he recognizes that these stories have taken root in the imagination of both Westerner and Muslim general populations alike. How one determines which side is good or evil will depend on the side they are on.

The 1979 siege of the Grand Friday Mosque in Mecca is a clear example of the "us" versus "them" public propaganda narratives on both sides. On November 20, 1979, Juhayman al-Oteibi and his followers, barricaded themselves inside the Mosque with estimates of 50,000–100,000 hostages. Immediately, the Carter administration accused Ayatollah Khomeini in

45. CAIR, "CAIR Civil Rights Report 2017," 2.
46. CAIR, "CAIR Civil Rights Report 2017," 14.
47. Said, *Orientalism*, 7.
48. Said, *Orientalism*, 65.

Iran for taking over Islam's holiest site in hopes of spreading Shia Islam. Khomeini, in turn, accused the United States, in cooperation with the Jews, of orchestrating the siege in response to the ongoing American embassy hostage crises in Iran. Despite the fact that Juhayman was working for neither the Americans nor the Iranians, the accusations of each government captured the imaginations of their respective sides. Following the Ayatollah's proclamation, Muslim protests and riots took place outside American embassies, consulates, and even some American expatriate homes. These riots were not confined to Iran but stretched across the globe.

Media Double Standard

The violent Muslim characterization, according to Said, is perpetuated through a media double standard whereby when violence is committed by a Muslim there is an assumed religious motivation while non-Muslim violence has no such religious presumption:

> "Islam" seems to engulf all aspects of the diverse Muslim world, reducing them all to a special malevolent and unthinking essence. Instead of analysis and understanding as a result there can be for the most part only the crudest form of us–versus–them. . . . Of course no one has equated the Jonestown massacre or the destructive horror of the Oklahoma bombing or the devastation of Indochina with Christianity, or with Western or American culture at large; that sort of equation has been reserved for "Islam."[49]

This double standard is present in American news media where violence committed by Muslims is often attributed to theological motivation with little to no exploration of other contributing factors while religious motivation is rarely considered for the same crimes committed by non-Muslims.

For example, a recent study that analyzed news archives from local television news (CBS, ABC, and NBC Nightly News) and cable news (FOX News, MSNBC, and CNN) from 2008 to 2012 found that Muslims were disproportionately associated with terrorism.[50] The study revealed that while Muslims only represented 6 percent of domestic terrorism, 81 percent of the news media reporting on domestic terrorism was directly associated with being Muslim. The other 94 percent of domestic terrorist activity conducted by non-Muslims received only 19 percent of the news coverage. When

49. Said, *Orientalism*, 9.
50. Dixon and Williams, "Changing Misrepresentation of Race and Crime."

comparing this study to similar ones conducted before 9/11, the researchers found a significant shift in media overrepresentation and misrepresentation from African Americans to Muslims and Latinos.

The study argues that the national news media platform is the space where political discourse takes place. Prior to 9/11, the war on drugs and crime, particularly in the black community, were the political talking points of the day. The current shift demonstrates that the political discourse has shifted away from America's war on drugs towards America's war on terror and immigration policies. Another suggested cause for the media and journalistic bias was that "news stories get greater attention if they identify a phenomenon as an intruder or threat (e.g., Muslim extremists threaten national security)."[51] This phenomenon is known as the ethnic blame discourse. The blame discourse has less to do with ethnicity and more to do with identifying a group or "them" as the problem or potential threat to the majority or "us." Identifying Muslims as the problem/threat is unique in that it is not a race or ethnicity but rather a religious community (or theological ideology when speaking of Islam) that becomes the unifying factor put forth in media discourse.

This theological generalization and determinism is further perpetuated in the media by attributing religious motivation to young Muslims who join radical movements such as ISIS. Muslims who join radical movements are often portrayed as being motivated by an apocalyptic vision of ushering in a new Islamic caliphate. This too is an oversimplification as to the variety of motivating factors for some Muslims who are joining the ranks of radical groups. There are indeed some who are driven by a theology of an eschatological apocalypse, but even they may have other contributing factors as well. It is imperative to take into consideration the various reasons that some Muslims join radical movements rather than appeal to an overarching narrative of a civilization clash driven by theology. Nabeel Jabbour, for example, suggests at least ten reasons that Muslims are joining the Islamic State.[52] Only one of Jabbour's reasons is theologically related. The other nine relate to sociocultural, historical, economic, and political factors. We must not forget that groups like ISIS pay competitive monthly salaries to their fighters. On that same note, we must bear in mind that some, like the senior leadership of Al-Qaeda, left considerable wealth to live in the caves of Afghanistan to achieve their eschatological vision.

The reasons for joining groups like ISIS are multidimensional and fluid. One particular reason, according to Lydia Wilson, is the desire to belong.

51. Dixon and Williams, "Changing Misrepresentation of Race and Crime," 35.
52. Jabbour, "10 Reasons Muslims are Eager to Join ISIS."

Wilson suggests that a popular ISIS propaganda narrative is the creation of a utopian society where young Muslims can find belonging.[53] This narrative has a dual function in that it is used to recruit new fighters and reinforce the commitment of those who belong when they have doubts:

> This narrative not only attracts idealistic young Muslims but it helps encourage people already in the Islamic State who are discouraged by the hardships they encounter: the lack of electricity, Western luxuries, and sometimes food and basic medical supplies and, in some areas, the constant bombardment. Of course it is hard, the narrative tells them, because this is the beginning; everything new must be built with sacrifice and effort. The brutality of the ISIS interpretation of sharia, when witnessed in person, can be a shock, but this too can be overcome, ISIS argues, using the narrative of a new state: once people are used to the law, there will be less crime and thus, inevitably, less need to punish people. In other words, these are just birthing pains. Use of the utopian ideal as a motivator to fight and struggle has many precedents. The most obvious parallel in the twentieth century is communism, which called on people to make huge sacrifices to support what they believed was a socially just system on earth, as represented in George Orwell's 1984 by the character Boxer, a strong but easily persuaded workhorse who regularly tells himself, "I will work harder" to overcome any problems that the new system produces. . . . A comparison can also be made with the Hitler Youth movement, which captured large numbers of German youth in pursuit of a better world. It was based on an ideology of racial purity that invoked nostalgic images of the German Volk to build an idealized version of what the German race was when it was strong, and what therefore should be recreated. This method of reading history to build a vision for the future strong enough to motivate people to fight and die is seen in the propaganda of ISIS, which uses the Qur'an and the hadith, the sayings and doings of the Prophet, to define and illustrate the ideology.[54]

Wilson uses the aforementioned comparisons to demonstrate that the utopian narrative is not unique to ISIS or Islam. This desire to belong is a more significant draw for joining ISIS than radical ideology according to Wilson:

> Our initial research into the motivations of those who have traveled to and fought for the Islamic State show they are not so

53. Wilson, "Understanding the Appeal of ISIS," 5.
54. Wilson, "Understanding the Appeal of ISIS," 6.

interested in the ideology—for a start, many expressed confusion over the concepts of caliphate, jihad, and sharia—but were attracted to the sense of brotherhood. One major reason defectors give for leaving the Islamic State is disillusionment over finding the same racism, inequality, and corruption that exists in their own countries, and perhaps even worse.[55]

The draw of belonging is particularly strong for Muslim youth living in the West especially if they are feeling marginalized or rejected because of their faith traditions. These youths are particularly vulnerable to a narrative of belonging that is derived from the Qur'an and hadith, even if they do not understand the religious ideology. The perception of shared religious identity may deepen and reinforce a sense of brotherhood and belonging despite the theological confusion. This narrative provides people with an opportunity to live and potentially die for something bigger than themselves.

One factor not mentioned by Wilson is the fluidity of the process of joining and remaining in a radicalized group like ISIS. While the initial draw may be brotherhood or belonging, it does not necessarily mean this draw will endure. For example, it may be the case that a fighter joins a radical movement for a sense of belonging but is quickly disenchanted by disunity and re-narrates their commitment to the ideological or vice versa. In other words, what draws a person to join a movement may not necessarily be the thing that keeps them in the movement. Motivations for joining and remaining in radicalized groups like ISIS are fluid and varied. The complexity of this process goes beyond what can be effectively discussed in the format of news media. Perhaps the insufficiency of the medium to debate these multiple factors associated with the radicalization of individual Muslims or the rise of radical Islam perpetuates the "us" versus "them" narrative. As Postman reminds us, "forms of media favor particular kinds of content."[56]

According to historian Thomas Kidd, the contentious relationship between Islam and political elites of the United States is not new. He suggests that the negative characterization of Islam and Muhammad through public narratives can be traced back to the founding fathers:

> In the last public act before his death, Benjamin Franklin parodied a proslavery speech in Congress by comparing it to a fictitious proslavery address by a North African Muslim pirate named Sidi Mehemet Ibrahim. Like proslavery southerners, the Algerian argued that he could not accept the end of Christian slavery because it would hurt the interest of the Algerian state,

---

55. Wilson, "Understanding the Appeal of ISIS," 9.

56. Postman, *Amusing ourselves to Death*, 9.

unfairly deprive Muslim slave masters of property, and release dangerous slaves into a vulnerable society.[57]

Benjamin Franklin's parody was published in the major northern newspapers according to Kidd. He further suggests that Franklin's use of polemical Islam was not unique. In fact, he argues that descriptions of Muhammad as demon possessed and Islam as inherently violent were common practice throughout American history, particularly from conservative Protestants.

Evangelical "Us" Versus "Them"

In light of the ethnographic emphasis on reflexivity, this section explores the role of American evangelical Christians in generating negative stereotypes of Muslims and perpetuating the "us" versus "them" narrative in public discourse. A recent study by Lifeway Research revealed that nearly half of the Christian pastors in the U.S. believe ISIS represents the true nature of Islam.[58] However, it is important to acknowledge that the evangelical Church in America is no more monolithic than Islam. There are American evangelicals actively promoting a more nuanced and balanced approach to understanding Islam and Muslims.[59] However, these Christians seem to get far less publicity in mainstream media and their message has yet to take root within the American evangelical community. A 2015 survey conducted by the Public Religion Research Institute found that 73 percent of white evangelicals believed the values of Islam were not compatible with the values of America.[60] Similarly, a recent Pew Research study concluded that 72 percent of white evangelicals believed that there was a "natural conflict between Islam and democracy."[61] This makes sense considering so much of evangelical leadership believes ISIS members are the real Muslims. The debate over whether or not Islam is compatible with democracy or the imagined values of America is an important discussion. The problem is not in the debate but rather the lack of balance and complexity in public discourse on this issue, particularly among some evangelicals.

57. Kidd, *American Christians and Islam*, 1.

58. Smietana, "Research: 1 in 3 Americans Worry About Sharia Law."

59. Adeney, *Daughters of Islam*; George, *Father of Jesus the God of Muhammad*; Greenlee, *Longing for Community*; Kraft, *Searching for Heaven*; Loewen, *Woman to Woman*; Medearis, *Muslims Christians and Jesus*; Parshall, *Cross and the Crescent*; Reisacher; *Joyful Witness* Shenk, *Journeys of the Muslim Nation*; Stone, *Heart and Mind of Muslims*.

60. Jones et al., "Anxiety Nostalgia and Mistrust."

61. Mohamed et al., "U.S. Muslims Concerned About Their Place in Society."

Some conservative evangelical leaders use the stereotype of the violent Muslim to perpetuate the "us" versus "them" narrative. Franklin Graham regularly takes this position in public forums. His most recent comments come from a 2016 Facebook post following the Pope's comments that the current wars were not religious. Graham disagreed:

> Pope Francis said Wednesday that "the world is at war," but he said it was not a war of religion. I agree that the world is at war—but I disagree that it's not a war of religion. It is most certainly a war of religion. Religion is behind the violence and jihad we're seeing in Europe, the Middle East, Asia, and here in this country. It's a religion that calls for the extermination of "infidels" outside their faith, specifically Jews and Christians. It's a religion that calls on its soldiers to shout "Allahu Akbar" ("God is Great" in Arabic) as they behead, rape, and murder in the name of Islam. Radical Islamists are following the teachings of the Qur'an.[62]

The reverend Graham is also an outspoken critic of Muslim immigration. It was Graham who first publicly suggested a temporary ban on Muslims entering the U.S. following the shootings in Chattanooga, TN where Muslim immigrant, Muhammad Youssef Abdulazeez, shot and killed four U.S. Marines. Graham posted the following on his Facebook wall:

> Four innocent Marines (United States Marine Corps) killed and three others wounded in #Chattanooga yesterday including a policeman and another Marine—all by a radical Muslim whose family was allowed to immigrate to this country from Kuwait. We are under attack by Muslims at home and abroad. We should stop all immigration of Muslims to the U.S. until this threat with Islam has been settled. Every Muslim that comes into this country has the potential to be radicalized—and they do their killing to honor their religion and Muhammad. During World War 2, we didn't allow Japanese to immigrate to America, nor did we allow Germans. Why are we allowing Muslims now? Do you agree? Let your Congressman know that we've got to put a stop to this and close the flood gates. Pray for the men and women who serve this nation in uniform, that God would protect them.[63]

---

62. Facebook post Franklin Graham July 31, 2016: https://www.facebook.com/FranklinGraham/posts/1211701438886035.

63. Facebook post Franklin Graham July 17, 2015: https://www.facebook.com/FranklinGraham/posts/967305353325646.

Graham's social media post reinforces the "us" versus "them" narrative by evoking the memories of the Second World War by comparing the Muslim world with the nation of Japan and Germany. Graham has also been an outspoken supporter of President Trump's travel ban as well. According to a recent survey by Pew Research, 76 percent of white evangelicals agree with Trump and Franklin's call for a moratorium on Muslim immigration.[64] One group of pastors in North Carolina purchased billboard space along I-40 to show their support for a Muslim immigration ban with the following message:

> Why Support President Trump's Immigration Ban??? [sic] 19 Muslim Immigrants Killed 2977 Americans September 11, 2001

The North Carolina Pastors Network offered the following explanation for the billboard:

> As a lone voice of truth in a desert wasteland of political correctness, we have chosen to prominently place this billboard for maximum impact on the westbound lane of I-40 in western North Carolina. We understand that the challenge we face today is not primarily political, but rather spiritual. If the 19 Muslim immigrants that attacked America on September 11th had become born again believers in Jesus Christ prior to that dreadful day, there would have been no "September 11th". The dilemma we face with Islamic terrorism is one of the religion itself. Plain and simple, Islamic ideology/theology is the problem.

Another publicly outspoken Pastor against Islam is Robert Jeffress of First Baptist Dallas. The church's YouTube channel features a Sunday sermon in which Jeffress publicly proclaimed that "Islam is a false religion based on a false book written by a false prophet."[65] The YouTube channel also displays a question and answer session in which Jeffress describes Islam as evil and Muhammad as a child rapist. In addition to the YouTube channel, Jeffress regularly appears on national news outlets publicly denouncing Islam as violent and oppressive. In one particular interview with Fox host Sean Hannity, Pastor Jeffress was a panel guest with Imam Mohammad Ali Elahi of the Islamic House of Wisdom in Dearborn, Michigan. Jeffress's comments about Islam and Muhammad are as follows:

> Muhammad was nothing but a blood thirsty warlord who beheaded 600 Jews who would not follow him into battle. And I know that not everyone likes what Donald Trump says, but

64. Smith, "Most White Evangelicals Approve of Trump Travel Prohibition."

65. "Dr. Jeffress Responds to Dallas News Columnist." https://www.youtube.com/watch?v=lzpJHIhH6Hc.

> Donald Trump was right when he said 'There is something within Islam itself that causes its followers to hate us.' Not all Islamics [sic] are certainly terrorists, only 5 percent are. But 5 percent of 1.5 billion people is 75 million radical Muslims in the world. How did so many people get their religion wrong? . . . They are following Muhammad is what they are doing. They are following his example.[66]

Following the Orlando night club shooting carried out by Omar Mateen, Jeffress released a video through the church YouTube channel suggesting that the massacre was "another demonstration of the difference between Christianity and Islam."[67] While Jeffress admits that most Muslims are not violent, he suggests that it is only because they do not understand their religion or else they would be. In other words, true Muslims are violent and the peaceful Muslims are simply nominal or cultural believers. It is worth noting that Jeffress served as an evangelical advisor to Trump during his presidential campaign. After Trump won the election, Jeffress gained further media attention when he preached at the morning service for incoming President Trump on inauguration day and continues to serve as an evangelical advisor to the administration.

Evangelical's Use of the Essentialist Framework

Much like the media discourse, the evangelicals who promote the "us" versus "them" narrative utilize an essentialist framework to discuss Islam and Muslims. This framework is argued by some evangelical scholars as the only way to understand Islam. For example, a recent publication by the evangelical journal *Global Missiology* featured three articles by anonymous authors arguing for the essentialist position regarding Islam. The first anonymous author suggests,

> Today Islam is claimed by about 1.5 billion. But this entire population is not all involved with militant activities. Roughly speaking, only 20% of Muslims seriously practice Islam, and about 10% support militant activities themselves. This means that our real enemy, militant Islam, is resident among only about 150 million people.[68]

---

66. "Dr. Jeffress on Hannity." https://www.youtube.com/watch?v=M3rKBgC3MIA.

67. "Dr. Jeffress Addresses Orlando Massacre and Radical Islam." https://www.youtube.com/watch?v=o-utAWzEb3Y.

68. One Anonymous, "9/11: Did We Learn Anything," 3.

The *Global Missiology* website describes itself as a "professional and academic electronic journal serving researchers, practitioners and scholars internationally," yet, Anonymous Author One offers no citation for the claim that only 20 percent of the Muslim world is serious about their faith or that 10 percent of the Muslim world supports militant activity. In my own research, the only source suggesting that there are 10 percent or 150 million Muslims who support militant Islam comes from a December 6, 2010 radio broadcast by Glenn Beck.

In the most recent study by the Pew Research Center concerning the favorability of ISIS, only three countries had more than 10 percent favorability: Senegal (11 percent), Malaysia (11 percent), and Nigeria (14 percent). Indonesia, the country with the largest Muslim population had only 4 percent of the participants favorable to ISIS.[69] There is no reliable research to suggest how many Muslims are the "real enemy". What we can be certain of is that more American evangelical pastors believe ISIS represents the true nature of Islam than Muslims themselves. There is also concern with the assertion that only Muslims "seriously practicing Islam" are militant. This gives the impression that the core of the religion is essentially violent and that those who engage in militant activity are all theologically motivated.

The essentialist narrative often argues that "real Islam" is located in the life or Sunnah of the Prophet Muhammad and the Qur'an. Anonymous Author Two explains this position as follows:

> Islam is in the midst of the greatest religious revival in world history. It is an 'essentialist' revival clearly defined by a return to primeval Islam, a return to 'essential' Islam. What is, then, the essence of Islam? Clearly Islam as a religion focuses on two things. First, the Qur'an as the dictated Word of Allah is 'essential' to Islam. You simply cannot make sense of the Muslim world apart from that. Second, Islam is 'based' on the 'Sunna' or behavior of the Prophet. Muslims believe in a Holy Book and in the Holy example of a perfect person, Muhammad. You simply cannot be a Muslim without accepting both of these foundations without reservation. Even slight variations from this theme puts you outside of Islam.[70]

What Anonymous Author Two fails to acknowledge is the various interpretations of the Qur'an and hadith. Rather, he suggests that there is only one true Islam and that the arguments for diversity of faith or so called many

---

69. Poushter, "Muslim Populations, Much Disdain for ISIS."

70. Two Anonymous, "Essentialism and Islam," 3.

Islams are "a false notion."[71] His argument is that Muslim theological diversity will eventually lose out to the true or orthodox Islam. The author goes on to suggest that the repulsive actions of ISIS, including rape and sex slavery, are within the teachings of Islamic orthodoxy and the Prophet Muhammad and therefore "no Sunni Islamic council on earth has condemned ISIS for its systematic rape of Yazidi women."[72] He concludes his paper by suggesting that it is impossible to understand Islam from any other perspective than the essentialist paradigm and that "The Western world, and Evangelical Christians must understand Islam "as it is", not as they imagine it to be."[73]

Allowing Muslims to speak for themselves may be a better strategy for understanding the teachings of Islam, particularly when it comes to the actions of ISIS. Muslim scholars have overwhelmingly condemned the actions of ISIS. One of the most prominent examples is the open letter sent from 126 Muslim scholars to Abu Bakr Baghdadi in 2014:

> During your sermon dated 6th of Ramadan 1435 AH (4th July 2014 CE), you said, paraphrasing Abu Bakr Al-Siddiq 'If you find what I say and do to be true, then assist me, and if you find what I say and do to be false, then advise me and set me straight.' In what follows is a scholarly opinion via the media. The Prophet said: *'Religion is [rectifying] advice.'* Everything said here below relies completely upon the statements and actions of followers of the 'Islamic State' as they themselves have promulgated in social media—or upon Muslim eyewitness accounts—and not upon other media. Every effort has been made to avoid fabrications and misunderstandings. Moreover, everything said here consists of synopses written in a simple style that reflect the opinions of the overwhelming majority of Sunni scholars over the course of Islamic history.[74]

The letter goes on to condemn several of the actions of the Islamic state including, coercion in conversion, torture, declaring apostates, mutilation, and the treatment of women, particularly the slavery and rape of the Yazidis. The open letter concludes with a call to repentance: "Reconsider all your actions; desist from them; repent from them; cease harming others and return to the religion of mercy." It is true that many Muslim scholars are unwilling to consider ISIS members apostates based upon their deplorable actions. That may be because it is not the place of Islamic scholars

---

71. Two Anonymous, "Essentialism and Islam," 7.

72. Two Anonymous, "Essentialism and Islam," 4.

73. Two Anonymous, "Essentialism and Islam," 7.

74. www.lettertobaghdadi.com.

to engage in the behavior they already declared to be un-Islamic, namely declaring Muslims apostates. It could be argued that Anonymous Author Two is arguing for an imagined Islam that harkens back to the seventh century rather than acknowledging the real Islam in the twenty-first century is a diverse community of interpretation that includes both violent extremists as well as pacifistic groups like the Gülen movement as well as everything in between. Each group wholeheartedly believes that their view is the truest representation of Islam. The suggestion that seventh-century Islam is an imagined one is further discussed in chapter six.

Diverse Communities of Interpretation rather than "Us" and "Them"

A community of interpretation framework accepts the influence of the complex theological and historical processes that informs the construction of religious groups.[75] This framework recognizes that no community of faith exists in a vacuum devoid of historical and sociocultural experience. This experience for religious collectivities is similar to the sociocultural collectivities in that it employs a highly selective memory of people and events. This selective memory is reinforced through public religious narratives in order to reinforce the desired religious identity. Therefore, it should not come as a surprise that the evangelical demonized representations of Muhammad are not an accepted representation for many Muslims despite the fact that the stories originate from Muslim sources. While the religious texts are important, they should not be looked at as a determining factor in the beliefs and actions of particular groups. This is not an elevation of personal or collective experience above revealed text but rather a linking of the two together. Finally, this perspective recognizes that diversity of belief in religion is not a recent phenomenon.

Violent movements are not new or unique to Islam. Diverse religious sects are present in Judaism and Christianity as well. First-century Judaism had a variety of religious sects according to Ida Glaser:

> By the time of Jesus, several groups represented different ideas of keeping the covenant, and of dealing with Greek culture and dealing with Roman occupation. That is, they had different answers to the questions 'Who are the true Jews' and 'How should the Jews relate to other peoples?'[76]

---

75. Said, *Orientalism*, 337.
76. Glaser, *Bible and Other Faiths*, 142.

Glaser points out that there was a variety of theological, sociocultural, and political beliefs that separated the Pharisees, Essenes, Zealots, Sadducees, and Herodians. Some of the theological differences were minor but others were considered essential aspects of Judaism such as the law, the covenant, and eschatology. Richard Horsley documents an additional religious sect called the Sicarii. This group is often seen as zealot assassins. However, according to Horsley, this group was not a faction of the Zealots but an entirely separate group with their own theological and political aspirations. The Sicarii regularly used terrorist acts as a means of propagating their theological and political aspirations:

> The terrorist tactics of Sicarii were threefold, according to Jose-phus's reports: selective, symbolic assassinations; more general assassinations along with destruction or plundering of the prop-erty of the wealthy and powerful; and kidnapping. Other com-mon tactics of terrorist groups, such as sniping and sabotage against the military or indiscriminate attacks in public places, are not mentioned by Josephus. In all cases the attacks by the Sicarii appear to be highly discriminate and always directed against fellow Jews, not against Roman soldiers or civilians.[77]

The goal of the Sicarii was to overthrow the yoke of the Romans and free the people from their aristocratic religious elite that were in collusion with the foreign occupiers. Horsley suggests they were driven by an eschatologi-cal discourse that included the ushering in of a messianic ruler. Given the diversity of first-century Judaism, it would be a difficult task to ascribe the Sicarii, or any other of the aforementioned group as the "true Jews". Espe-cially considering that, as Glaser suggests, the majority of first-century Jews did not belong to any one of these groups. Rather, most Jews were simply trying to serve God in a difficult setting.

Diverse Groups in the Protestant Reformation

Christianity has also had a diversity of religious groups throughout his-tory. The irony of some conservative evangelicals using the essentialists paradigm is that they often go to great lengths to clarify the complexity of their particular faith expression within the broader context of Chris-tian history, yet, they do not afford Muslims the same privilege. There is a sense of a double standard in some American evangelical representations of Islam as fixed and monolithic while seeing their own faith as diverse

---

77. Horsley, "Sicarii," 439.

and fluid. For example, Christian acts of violence are often relegated to the pre-reformation Catholic Crusades and Inquisition or the individual acts of people falsely claiming to be Christian. This is because most American evangelicals tend to believe their faith is essentially peaceful. In a 2011 survey conducted by the Public Religion Research Institute, 85 percent of white evangelicals agreed that if a person, who claimed to be Christian, committed an act of violence in the name of Christianity that they were not true Christians. However, when it came to Islam, 45 percent agreed that if an act of violence was committed by a person, who claimed to be Muslim, in the name of Islam then they were true Muslims.[78]

It is worth noting however that some of the most violent years in Christian history are the fifty years before and after Martin Luther nailed his ninety-five theses to the door in Wittenberg in 1517. The Christian violence during the sixteenth century included both Catholics and Protestants. However, Protestants tend to narrate their history through the lens of suffering at the hands of Catholics during the reformation and Catholics do likewise. There are public monuments to reinforce these narratives of suffering as well. During the course of this research I came across one such monument while attending an academic conference on Muslim-Christian Relations in Oxford, England. Near the center of the city stands the Martyrs Memorial commemorating Thomas Cranmer, Hugh Lattimore, and Nicolas Ridley who were burned to death for their Protestant faith in 1555. The inscription on the memorial reads:

> To the Glory of God, and in grateful commemoration of His servants, Thomas Cranmer, Nicholas Ridley, Hugh Latimer, Prelates of the Church of England, who near this spot yielded their bodies to be burned, bearing witness to the sacred truths which they had affirmed and maintained against the errors of the Church of Rome, and rejoicing that to them it was given not only to believe in Christ, but also to suffer for His sake; this monument was erected by public subscription in the year of our Lord God, MDCCCXLI.

Stories of the Oxford Martyrs are included in books and sermon illustrations throughout the Protestant Church to reinforce the narrative of the peaceful Protestants suffering at the hand of the Catholic Church.

While touring the church next to the Martyrs Memorial, a local guide encouraged me to visit a similar memorial only a few blocks away. The monument is a simple plaque that states,

---

78. Cox et al., "What It Means to Be American."

> Near this spot George Nichols Richard Yaxley Thomas Belson
> Humphrey Pritchrey were executed for their Catholic Faith 5
> July 1589 [*sic*]

Both priests, Nichols and Yaxley, were hanged, drawn, and quartered.
Their body parts were displayed throughout the city as a reminder of the
punishment for practicing the former religion of Catholicism. The two
laypersons were also hanged for their association with the priests and par-
taking the sacraments. In a period of less than forty years, both Catholics
and Anglicans are martyred in Oxford by one another for their expression
of Christian faith. Some may argue that these deaths had less to do with
religious belief and more to do with political power. However, the same
arguments could be made by Muslims in the twenty-first century. The
question is whether or not the same lens of interpretation would be used
to evaluate the current situation in many Muslim contexts? The Catholic
and Anglican memorials in the city of Oxford demonstrate the complexity
of seeing religion as a community of interpretation that selectively draws
from its historical experience which is storied and in some cases memori-
alized in monuments and plaques.

Some of the more radical religious movements spawned by the Reformation are reminiscent of the first-century Jewish Sicarii and current
trends within Islam. In 1534, a radical Anabaptist and self-proclaimed
prophet named John Matthys lead an uprising in the city of Münster, Germany. Matthys gave the inhabitants of the city three options: leave the city,
recognize him as God's prophet and be re-baptized, or die by the sword.[79]
The majority of the Lutherans and Catholics left the city. A little more than
a month later, Matthys was killed outside the city walls by those he had
previously driven out.

Fellow Anabaptist and trained tailor John of Leiden gathered the followers and told them that he had received a revelation about the death of
Matthys before it happened. In addition to this prophecy, John of Lieden
explains that God had instructed him to set up a theocracy and make the
city of Münster the New Jerusalem. His eschatological utterances included
a system of governance where the city would be ruled by twelve elders, appointed by him, to represent the twelve tribes of Israel. They would rule by
the divine law of the Old Testament, punishing those who broke the law
with the sword. His revelations included the institution of polygamy and
permission to marry his predecessor's widow.

Eventually John's divine inspirations instructed him to crown himself
King of the New Jerusalem and ruler from the throne of David. He declared

---

79. Horsch, "Rise and Fall of the Anabaptists of Muenster." 129–43.

Matthys's widow to be his new wife and Queen of the New Israel. The New Israel, however did not last more than a year. Eventually the city was taken back by the Catholics but not after many failed attempts. It is said that in prison, John of Leiden repented of his errors and admitted to never having received any divine revelation. He was tortured, killed, and his body was placed on display in a cage as a public example.

We tend to frame our religious identity at the intersection of our personal and collective experience that is informed by our memory and experience. For this reason, the Catholic martyrs of Oxford and the extremism demonstrated in Münster are likely unfamiliar stories to many American evangelical Christians. If a community of interpretation wants to reinforce a narrative of peace, then it will selectively choose peaceful narratives and ignore the ones that would suggest otherwise. The same is true of historical figures that are instrumental to the theological development of a faith tradition. Protestant Christians are well aware of the reformers' theological ideas and have no problem quoting, for example, the words of Luther or Calvin as the definitive proof text in a sermon. However, few Christians are aware of Calvin's support of putting heretics and adulterers to death and encouraging rape victims to marry their assailant in accordance with the Old Testament law.[80]

Few Christians are likely aware of Luther's justification for anti-Semitism in his 1534 publication, *On the Jews and their Lies*. Luther explains his rationale in writing the book as follows:

> I had made up my mind to write no more either about the Jews or against them. But since I learned that these miserable and accursed people do not cease to lure to themselves even us, that is, the Christians, I have published this little book, so that I might be found among those who opposed such poisonous activities of the Jews who warned the Christians to be on their guard against them. I would not have believed that a Christian could be duped by the Jews into taking their exile and wretchedness upon himself. However, the devil is the god of the world, and wherever God's word is absent he has an easy task, not only with the weak but also with the strong. May God help us. Amen.[81]

Luther proposes that Christians use "sharp mercy" with the Jews in order that some might be saved from the fires of hell. His "sincere advice" includes the following seven actions against the Jews:

80. Gordon, *Calvin*.
81. Luther, *On the Jews and their Lies*, 121.

First, to set fire to their synagogues in schools . . . Second, I advise that their houses also be razed and destroyed . . . Third, I advised that their prayer books and Talmudic writings, in which such idolatry, lies, cursing, and blasphemy are taught, be taken from them . . . Fourth, I advise that their rabbis be forbidden to teach henceforth on pain of loss of life and limb . . . Fifth, I advise that safe–conduct on the highways be abolished completely for the Jews . . . Sixth, I advise that usury be prohibited to them, and that all cash and treasure of silver and gold be taken from them and put aside for safekeeping . . . Seventh, I recommend putting a flail, an ax, a hoe, a spade, a distaff, or a spindle into the hands of young, strong Jews and Jewesses and letting them earn their bread in the sweat of their brow.[82]

He concludes his advice by suggesting that this form of sharp mercy will only reform the Jews slightly and therefore it is best to simply expel them from the country. Many evangelical Christians would likely disassociate themselves from Luther's beliefs regarding the Jews. It may be the case that most Christians are unaware of the above quote considering communities of interpretation have a selective memory when it comes to hagiography. It is not that individual Christians have intentionally ignored these writings but rather they are ignored at a collective level in that they are not incorporated as part of religious identity. In other words, the public narrative of the Sunday sermon is likely not quoting from *On the Jews and their Lies*.

Conclusion

Both Muslims and Christians are communities of interpretation. The adherents of these two faiths make up more than half the world's population. Their religious identities are conceptualized in the overlap of the individual experience and the broader sociocultural and historical experience of the collective. These collective identities are rooted in historical, present, and eschatological contexts. Each faith has a variety of expressions regarding the interpretations of their religious texts as well as their religious history. The same is true for key figures within the religious traditions as well.

Evangelical narratives of the inherent violence in Islam and the peacefulness of Christianity almost always come down to a comparison between the person of Christ and Muhammad. The problem with the comparison is that there is an underlying assumption that all Christians and Muslims are in agreement about the life of Christ and the life of Muhammad. This

82. Luther, *On the Jews and their Lies*, 110–14.

is clearly exhibited among evangelicals in the ongoing public debate over whether a believer should arm themselves and if necessary, take the life of another individual. If Jesus is the model and he was indeed a peaceful martyr, why are evangelicals so evenly divided over whether or not Christians can carry weapons?

This debate became a public spectacle when the President of Liberty University, Jerry Falwell Jr., encouraged students to get their concealed weapon permits following the terrorist attacks in San Bernardino saying:

> I always thought that if more good people had concealed-carry permits, then we could end those Muslims before they walk in and kill. I just wanted to take this opportunity to encourage all of you to get your permit. We offer a free course. Let's teach them a lesson if they ever show up here."[83]

Liberty is the largest Christian college in the United States and following his comments there was an eruption of cheers from the audience. Pastor John Piper publicly responded to Jerry Falwell Jr.'s comments through the Desiring God Website, suggesting that it was not biblical to encourage Christian citizens to carry arms for self-protection. The only exception, according to Piper, is if the Christian is serving in the military or as a policeman. Both Piper and Falwell quote Jesus to defend their positions. Falwell Jr. stated the following in the Liberty University News Service:

> It just boggles my mind that anybody would be against what Jesus told his disciples in Luke 22:36. He told them if they had to sell their coat to buy a sword to do it because he knew danger was coming, and he wanted them to defend themselves.[84]

Piper on the other hand quotes John 18:36: "My kingdom is not of this world. If my kingdom were of this world, my servants would have been fighting, that I might not be delivered over to the Jews. But my kingdom is not from the world." He further suggests that Falwell Jr. misunderstands the words of Jesus in Luke 22.

To further complicate matters, the earliest liturgies of the Church disagree with Piper's assessment that Christians can fight in the military. According to the second-century *Apostolic Traditions of Hippolytus*, before baptism there should be an inquiry as to the trade of the one desiring baptism. The following tradition applied to those who served in military service:

---

83. CNN, "University president to students: Arm yourselves." https://www.youtube.com/watch?v=zHmwD2VElyE.

84. Fallwell, "President Thanks Students for Support."

> A soldier of the civil authority must be taught not to kill men and to refuse to do so if he is commanded, and to refuse to take an oath; if he is unwilling to comply, he must be rejected. A military commander or civic magistrate that wears the purple must resign or be rejected. If a catechumen or a believer seeks to become a soldier, they must be rejected, for they have despised God.[85]

This did not remain the position of the church following the just war theory of Augustine, but the example brings up an interesting discussion regarding the interaction of religious text alongside religious tradition. There is wide debate among Christians as to the life of Christ and what it means to follow him. Concerning Muhammad, the debate among Muslims may be even larger considering there is far more written about Muhammad than Jesus and the vast majority of Muslims either do not have access to these writings or cannot understand the languages in which these books are printed. It should come as no surprise then that various Muslims have a variety of views about the life and deeds of Muhammad. However, it should be noted that these sources are becoming increasingly available in multiple languages on the internet and in print.

The current trend by some evangelical conservative groups is to reinforce an "us" versus "them" narrative where devout Muslims are essentially violent while cultural or nominal (in name only) Muslims are peaceful. If evangelical Christians wanted to take a position of understanding Muslims, it would be more appropriate to view them in light of the context of a religious reformation that is similar to that of the Protestant Reformation. In saying this, I am not advocating the position that has been espoused by Nabeel Qureshi who states:

> This might sound shocking, but consider: Just as the Protestant Reformation was an attempt to raze centuries of Catholic tradition and return to the canonical texts, so radical Islam is an attempt to raze centuries of traditions of various schools of Islamic thought and return to the canonical texts of the Quran and Muhammad's life.[86]

Qureshi argues that there are only three options for Muslims today: apostasy, apathy, or radicalization.[87] In a 2015 seminar at Christ Community Chapel, Qureshi stated that if he were still a Muslim, he would "have a hard

---

85. Hippolytus, *Apostolic Traditions of Hippolytus*, 42.

86. Qureshi, *Answering Jihad*, 75.

87. Qureshi, *Answering Jihad*.

time not going to Syria right now to fight for ISIS, it seems like they are doing what Islam commands."[88]

It may be more appropriate to suggests that Islam is in the middle of a reformation and much like the Protestant Reformation, the vast majority of people in both contexts are caught in the middle of shifting religious, social, economic, and political power structures as well as splinter groups such ISIS or the Münster rebellion. This view may afford more understanding and care for Muslims than the fear that may result from a narrative suggesting that the faithful Muslim is a violent Muslim.

The public narratives of the violent Muslim are prevalent in American media and particularly among many American evangelicals. This may cause a great deal of stress on Muslim immigrant identity formation considering the inner and outer role of these narratives in this process. The Pashtun ethnicity has an equally troubling sociocultural perception in America that is explored in the next chapter.

88. Christ Community Chapel, April 29, 2015. "Q&A Does Islam Really Teach Peace?" https://www.youtube.com/watch?v=XNseMjQkxvI.

5

Transnational Pashtun Narratives

THIS CHAPTER DISCUSSES THE complex relationship between the Pashtun and the United States. Consecutive presidential administrations have propagated competing narratives about the Pashtun over the last fifty years. In the 1980s, the Pashtun were celebrated by the Carter and Reagan administrations as U.S. allies against the Soviet Union's spread of communism. Then, following the attacks on 9/11, the Pashtun were presented as enemies of the U.S. and at least partially responsible for the attacks on the World Trade Center. In other words, the Pashtun have been presented as both "us" and "them" in recent American history. The irony of these competing ascribed identities is that the common denominator that served to make the Pashtun both allies and enemies is jihad. [1]

Propaganda Narratives

We must consider the role of war propaganda when exploring the recent public narratives of the Pashtun generated by the U.S. government. The "us"

---

1. President Reagan declared March 21, 1982 Afghanistan Day and dedicated the launch of the Columbia Space Shuttle to the people of Afghanistan. Following a meeting in the Whitehouse with the Pashtun chairman of the Afghan resistance fighters November 12, 1987, Reagan addressed the nation saying: "Well, we've just held a very useful and, I might say, brief but also, I'll add, a very moving discussion with Chairman Yunis Khalis of the Islamic Union of Mujahidin of Afghanistan and other members of his distinguished delegation. I expressed our nation's continued strong support for the resistance and our satisfaction with the large step the Afghan resistance took toward unity in choosing a chairman for the first time. This new political milestone demonstrates that the people of Afghanistan speak with one voice in their opposition to the Soviet invasion and occupation of their homeland. . . . On behalf of the American people, I salute Chairman Khalis, his delegation, and the people of Afghanistan themselves. You are a nation of heroes. God bless you" (Ronald Reagan Presidential Library, https://www.reaganlibrary.gov/archives/speech/remarks-following -meeting-afghan-resistance-leaders-and-members-congress).

versus "them" narrative serves an important role in generating public support for the United States' ongoing Global War on Terrorism (GWOT). Edward Bernays, considered to be the father of public relations, defined propaganda as "A consistent, enduring effort to create or shape events to influence the relations of the public to an enterprise, idea or group."[2]

While the word today has negative connotations, this was not always the case. According to the OED, the term propaganda has its origins in the post reformation Catholic Church. In 1622, Pope Gregory XV commissioned a College of Cardinals for the *Propaganda Fide* or propagation of faith through missionary priests. In 1627, under Pope Urban VIII, this became the College of Propaganda. Bernays suggests that the word "took on a decidedly sinister complexion" following WWI when it was used to garner public support for the war.[3] He argues that most people who view propaganda negatively are unaware of their own propaganda statements that are merely opinions stated as facts. It is not until a differing opinion is presented as a fact that the label of propaganda becomes applicable. Bernays argues that everyone is under the influence of propaganda, though they are likely unaware. He suggests that "virtually no important undertaking is now carried on without it."[4] He posited that propaganda is all around us all the time, shaping and influencing how we perceive the world:

> The conscious and intelligent manipulation of the organized habits and opinions of the masses is an important element in democratic society. Those who manipulate this unseen mechanism of society constitute an invisible government which is the true ruling power of our country. We are governed, our minds molded, our tastes formed, our ideas suggested, largely by men we have never heard of. This is a logical result of the way in which our democratic society is organized. Vast numbers of human beings must cooperate in this manner if they are to live together as a smoothly functioning society.[5]

Bernays recognized the power of using propaganda narratives to garner public support. Whether through pictures, audio, or written stories, the goal of propaganda is to create a cohesive narrative through manipulating circumstances in the collective imagination.

Propaganda is not limited by rationality. In fact, it tends to appeal more to emotions than logic. Whether or not a propaganda narrative is

---

2. Bernays, *Propaganda*, 52.
3. Bernays, *Propaganda*, 49.
4. Bernays, *Propaganda*, 52.
5. Bernays, *Propaganda*, 37.

true is irrelevant. The goal is to recruit the imagination rather than the intellect. This can be achieved by re-narrating an old story within the collective memory or by inventing an entirely new one. The goal of the propaganda narrative is "to swing a whole mass of group emotions."[6] In the twenty-first century, digital media is the primary medium by which a small number of people who understand the psychosocial processes of the masses organize what would otherwise be chaos for the average American. Bernays argues that this small number of people are often politicians, teachers, ministers, or novelists. These people narrow the broad field of competing ideas into a smaller and more manageable size for the general public. What is left after this process are a few socially acceptable narratives from which the general public can choose.

Pre-9/11 U.S. Pashtun Propaganda of "Us"

The Pashtun have been allies and, more recently, enemies of the United States. Following the Soviet invasion of Afghanistan in 1979, U.S. influence in the region was under significant threat. The invasion of Afghanistan was particularly troublesome for the U.S. considering it had lost its influence in Iran earlier that year with the overthrow of the Shah during the Islamic Revolution. In order to stop the impending spread of communism through Central Asia, and prevent Iranian influence in the region, the U.S. in cooperation with Pakistan and Saudi Arabia, armed the mainly Pashtun mujahideen to fight the Soviet invaders. Over the next decade, the U.S. supplied arms to these Pashtun fighters in hopes of dismantling the Soviet Union through a proxy war.

The U.S. support of the mujahideen included a propaganda war in which the "us" versus "them" narrative aligned the U.S. and Muslim jihadists against the Soviets. One means of achieving this was through affirming the Pashtun faith in God as a means to overthrow atheistic Soviet invaders. The Cold War documentary *Soldiers of God* displays video footage of the National Security Advisor Zbigniew Brzezinski personally exhorting the mujahideen in their jihad. He speaks to them through a translator:

> We know of their deep belief in God, and we are confident that their struggle will succeed. That land over there is yours. You will go back to it one day, because your fight will prevail and

6. Bernays, *Propaganda*, 74.

you'll have your homes and your mosques back again, because your cause is right and God is on your side.[7]

The narrative of God being on the side of the mujahideen reinforced the belief that the war they were fighting against Soviet atheists was in fact a holy war or jihad.

The U.S. partnered with the Kingdom of Saudi Arabia to propagate this violent version of Islam. Brzezinski convinced the Saudi government to match the U.S. financial contributions in the region which are estimated to be a total of $3 billion.[8] The Saudi interest in the region was to support the Sunni majority of Afghanistan and to limit the Iranian influence among the minority Shia population. The Pakistani government also supported the import of Saudi Wahhabism as a counter narrative to the rise of Pashtun nationalism in Afghanistan. The two competing public narratives for the Pashtun became national and religious identity. The U.S. government opted to promote the religious identity narrative.

One reason for promoting the religious identity over Pashtun identity was the increasing presence of foreign fighters from all over the Arab world. These fighters were recruited by Saudi Arabia to join in the jihad in Afghanistan. Andrew Coulson suggests that prior to the U.S. involvement, the Afghan resistance was driven by tribal allegiances rather than radical Islamist ideology.[9] The Pashtun have a long history of blood feuds and tribalism (see chapter 2). In order to overcome the internal strife among the Pashtun tribes and unify them with incoming foreign fighters, the U.S., with the help of Saudi Arabia and Pakistan, made Islam the rallying cry against the Russians. Ahmed Rashid explains,

> With the active encouragement of the CIA and Pakistan's ISI, who wanted to turn the Afghan jihad into a global war waged by all Muslim states against the Soviet Union, some 35,000 Muslim radicals from 40 Islamic countries joined Afghanistan's fight from 1982 to 1992. Tens of thousands more came to study in Pakistani *madrasahs*. Eventually more than 100,000 foreign Muslim radicals were directly influenced by the Afghan jihad. The camps in Pakistan and Afghanistan where they trained became virtual universities for promoting pan-Islamic radicalism in Algeria, Egypt, Yemen, Sudan, Jordan, the Philippines, and Bangladesh.[10]

---

7. Coombs et al., *Soldiers of God.*
8. Coulson, "Education and Indoctrination in the Muslim World," 1–36.
9. Coulson, "Education and Indoctrination in the Muslim World," 1–36.
10. Rashid, "Taliban," 7.

In addition to providing arms and training to the jihadists, the U.S. provided the educational curriculum for madrassas that promoted the violent version of Islam.

Propaganda through Textbooks

In order to further reify the religious identity of the Pashtun, the U.S. funded and produced educational textbooks that propagated the narrative of holy war against the Soviet infidels. Coulson explains:

> Between 1986 and 1992, USAID underwrote the printing of explicitly violent Islamist textbooks for elementary school children. The University of Nebraska, Omaha (UNO), oversaw this $50 million contract with the Education Center for Afghanistan (ECA), a group jointly appointed by the seven mujaheddin [sic] organizations that the ISI and CIA had taken under their wing.[11]

In order to provide oversight and management of the USAID grant money, the Education Sector Support Project (ESSP) was created in 1986. The ESSP's final project assessment documents how the textbook project had to choose between writing new texts or updating existing ones. Because of time constraints they chose to update and revise. The primary revisions, according to the report, included strengthening the religious theme of jihad:

> Revisions consisted mainly of bringing the text up to date regarding the political reality of present day Afghanistan, adding topics relevant to the Jehad [sic], and strengthening certain religious themes. These were all appropriate revisions, and they were accomplished with admirable speed.[12]

According to the report, Afghans were responsible for the decisions regarding the content in the textbooks but the U.S. UNO team was working to "tactfully exert some influence over some content decisions by means of indirect persuasion."[13] The report does not specify which content was a direct result of the UNO team's persuasion. That said, the objectives of dismantling the Soviet Union and partnering with Saudi Arabia has led some scholars to speculate that the U.S. influence included the propagation of the violent version of Islam found in the textbooks.[14]

11. Coulson, "Education and Indoctrination in the Muslim World," 17.
12. USAID, "Mission to Pakistan and Afghanistan," 10.
13. USAID, "Mission to Pakistan and Afghanistan," 11.
14. Burde, Schools for Conflict or Peace.

The textbooks produced were in Dari and Pashto (the two primary languages of Afghanistan) and distributed in both Afghanistan and Pakistan. In addition to children's textbooks, the U.S. developed a two-volume adult literacy set called "Alphabet of Jihad Literacy". According to another USAID report, the mujahideen were offered literacy courses from 1987 to 1992. The report documents providing 43,694 mujahideen with literacy training from the "Alphabet of Jihad Literacy" curriculum.[15] The reach of the primary school educational textbooks was significantly larger:

> The project printed and distributed approximately 15 million textbooks to primary schools in all 29 provinces of Afghanistan and in limited numbers to schools in the refugee camps in Pakistan. Over 1,600 primary schools and 446,000 students received ESSP textbooks in Afghanistan, and 1,031 primary schools and 167,022 students received ESSP textbooks in the refugee camps in Pakistan.[16]

Craig Davis provides translated samples of the primary educational textbooks in his research. One particular text mentioned by Davis is an elementary literacy alphabet book that promotes jihad as well as violent imagery against the Russians:

> *Alif* [is for] Allah. Allah is one.
>
> *Bi* [is for] Father (*baba*). Father goes to the mosque. . .
>
> *Pi* [is for] Five (*panj*). Islam has five pillars. . .
>
> *Ti* [is for] Rifle (*tufang*). Javad obtains rifles for the Mujahidin. . .
>
> *Jim* [is for] Jihad. Jihad is an obligation. My mom went to the jihad. Our brother gave water to the Mujahidin. . .
>
> *Dal* [is for] Religion (*din*). Our religion is Islam. The Russians are the enemies of the religion of Islam. . .
>
> *Zhi* [is for] Good news *(muzhdih)*. The Mujahidin missiles rain down like dew on the Russians.
>
> *Shin* [is for] Shakir. Shakir conducts jihad with the sword. God becomes happy with the defeat of the Russians. . .
>
> *Zal* [is for] Oppression (*zulm*). Oppression is forbidden. The Russians are oppressors. We perform jihad against the oppressors. . .

15. USAID, "Mission to Pakistan and Afghanistan," 8.
16. USAID, "Mission to Pakistan and Afghanistan," 7.

> *Vav* [is for] Nation (*vatn*). Our nation is Afghanistan. . . . The
> Mujahidin made our country famous. . . . Our Muslim people
> are defeating the communists. The Mujahidin are making our
> dear country free.[17]

The above is one example of the educational texts funded and produced
by the U.S. that had the effect of indoctrinating children in the region towards a militant version of Islam. In addition to militancy, the texts were
designed to reinforce animosity towards the Soviets. According to Davis,
even the math textbooks, both at the elementary and secondary levels,
used militant imagery to teach:

> One group of mujahidin attack 50 Russian soldiers. In that at-
> tack 20 Russians were killed. How many Russians fled? . . . The
> speed of a Kalashnikov bullet is 800 meters per second. If the
> Russian is at a distance of 3200 meters from a mujahid, and that
> mujahid aims at the Russian's head, calculate how many seconds
> it will take for the bullet to strike the Russian in the forehead.[18]

Dana Burde also surveyed the literature produced with the USAID grant.
In her review of a book designed to teach fifth grade Pashto speakers basic
Dari language, she notes the following definitions given for jihad and the
mujahideen:

> *Jihad*—It is obligatory for Muslims to fight in the way of God.
> The Prophet said wage jihad against kafirs [infidels] with your
> wealth, with your life, and with your speech. The Muslims of
> Afghanistan by the order of God and His Prophet, started jihad
> against the Russian Communists and their slaves. In this cause,
> they lost their wealth and their lives, and achieved manifold suc-
> cess. We read about that in the newspapers and magazines of
> Islamic revolution every day.
>
> *Mujahideen*—We Muslims wage jihad in the way of God. With
> the power of belief and faith in God, we began jihad against
> the Russian unbelievers, empty handed. The brave mujahideen
> attack the communist Russian unbelievers from every side and
> capture/seize their weapons with the help of God, the great
> and the exalted. Also, they inflict defeat/destruction on the
> enemies of our faith and our homeland. Hence, we can say that
> whatever successes that are the destiny of mujahideen are a re-
> sult of believing in God and are in accordance with the law of

17. Davis, "'A' Is for Allah, 'J' Is for Jihad," 90.
18. Davis, "'A' Is for Allah, 'J' Is for Jihad," 93.

God and a result of acting upon the sharia of the Holy Prophet (Peace Be Upon Him).[19]

The U.S. did not create the content of these texts but did choose to underwrite the production, despite the violent indoctrination that would ensue. According to Davis, these violent images were officially to be removed from the textbooks in 1992. However, in his field research Davis found the unedited versions still being printed in both Afghanistan and Pakistan as late as 2000.[20]

It is an oversimplification to suggest that the U.S. created the mujahideen or the ideology of Islamic radicalism. The Islamic resistance in Afghanistan and the ideology of jihad was present before U.S. involvement as was Saudi Arabia's export of violent extremist ideology. The influence of scholars such as Abdul A'la Maududi (1903–1979) and Sayyid Qutb (1906–1966) were already beginning to take root in the region. Nevertheless, the U.S. did use the resurgence of violent Islam as a means to achieve their political goals, ultimately, the collapse of the Soviet Union. While the U.S. did not create jihad, according to Coulson, they "helped militarize modern Islam."[21] It may be more appropriate to suggest that the U.S. reified an already present violent Islamic identity as a call to transcend national, political, ethnic, and tribal divisions in the region. This is particularly troubling considering that many of the foreign fighters that were armed by the U.S. to fight the Russians would eventually form the group Al-Qaeda and use their relationships with the Pashtun in Afghanistan to set up their operations.

Post-Cold War, "Us" becomes "Them"

After the collapse of the Soviet Union, some of the fighters who were previously "us" quickly shifted to "them" with the formation of Al-Qaeda. The same is true of the Pashtun who, following 9/11, were largely represented in American media as the Taliban. Media scholars documented a significant shift in the use of media for wartime propaganda by the U.S. government following 9/11.[22] One significant shift was the creation of the Office of Strategic Influence (OSI) in order to facilitate propaganda both at home and abroad. After information regarding the "tactical deception" of the OSI was leaked to

19. Burde, *Schools for Conflict or Peace*, 78.

20. Davis, "'A' Is for Allah, 'J' Is for Jihad," 90.

21. Coulson, "Education and Indoctrination in the Muslim World," 15.

22. Campbell, "Cultural Governance and Pictorial Resistance," 57–73; Snow and Taylor, "Revival of the Propaganda," 389–407.

the press, Secretary of Defense Donald Rumsfeld announced that the office would be officially shut down.[23] However, Campbell suggests that the closing of the OSI simply meant that the activities will be carried out by other offices within the Pentagon. The use of propaganda has been employed by radical groups such as Al-Qaeda and ISIS as well. While the issues of propaganda are complex, the narratives put forth by the U.S. and radical Muslim groups are rather simple. Following 9/11, the pervasive narrative reinforced by both the U.S. and Al-Qaeda was one of good versus evil. Who was good and who was evil was dependent upon the narrator.

Following 9/11 the "us" versus "them" narrative dominated the media discourse. Both the U.S. and Al-Qaeda leadership offered competing narratives as to the reasons for war. The U.S. declared Al-Qaeda as evil and an enemy of freedom. Their hatred of freedom and democracy was given as the reason for their horrendous acts of terrorism. On the evening of the 9/11 attacks President Bush's brief speech explained:

> Today, our fellow citizens, our way of life, our very freedom came under attack in a series of deliberate and deadly terrorist attacks. The victims were in airplanes, or in their offices; secretaries, businessmen and women, military and federal workers; moms and dads, friends and neighbors. Thousands of lives were suddenly ended by evil, despicable acts of terror. . . . America was targeted for attack because we're the brightest beacon for freedom and opportunity in the world. And no one will keep that light from shining.[24]

Nine days later on September 20, 2001, President Bush reinforced this narrative when he addressed the American people and a joint session of Congress:

> Tonight we are a country awakened to danger and called to defend freedom. Our grief has turned to anger, and anger to resolution. Whether we bring our enemies to justice, or bring justice to our enemies, justice will be done. . . . On September the 11th, enemies of freedom committed an act of war against our country. . . . Americans are asking, why do they hate us? They hate what we see right here in this chamber: a democratically elected government. Their leaders are self-appointed. They hate our

23. Campbell, "Cultural Governance and Pictorial Resistance," 60.

24. https://georgewbush-whitehouse.archives.gov/news/releases/2001/09/200 10911-16.html.

freedoms: our freedom of religion, our freedom of speech, our freedom to vote and assemble and disagree with each other.[25]

President Bush went on to describe Al-Qaeda as a radical fringe group that hates freedom and democracy and "perverts the peaceful teachings of Islam." He outlined their plan to destroy Western civilization and force everyone to adhere to their radical teachings that "hijack Islam." The President further explained that America was at war with an ideology of evil but that good would prevail.

Al-Qaeda tells a counternarrative that has less to do with freedom and democracy and more to do with American foreign policy in majority Muslim regions. The U.S. is likened to medieval crusaders who desire to dominate Muslim lands under the false pretenses of spreading freedom and democracy. For Osama Bin Laden, the greatest offense was the presence of U.S. troops in the Arab peninsula:

> It is not concealed from you that the people of Islam had suffered from aggression, iniquity and injustice imposed on them by the Jewish-Christian alliance and their collaborators to the extent that the Muslims' blood became the cheapest and their wealth and assets looted by the hands of the enemies. Their blood was spilled in Palestine and Iraq. The horrifying pictures of the massacre of Qana, in Lebanon are still fresh in our memory. Massacres took place in Tajikistan, Burma, Kashmir, Assam, Philippine, Fattani, Ugadin, Somalia, Eritrea, Chechnya and in Bosnia Herzegovina. Massacring Muslims that sent shivers in the body and shook the conscience. All of that happened and the world watched and heard, and not only did not respond to these atrocities, but also with a clear conspiracy between America and its allies prevented the weaklings from acquiring arms to defend themselves by using the United Nations as a cover. Muslims became aware that they were the main targets of the Jewish-Crusader alliance of aggression. The false propaganda regarding human rights have vanished under the tribulations and massacres that were committed against Muslims everywhere. This last aggression was the worst catastrophe that was inflicted upon the Moslems since the death of the Prophet. That is, the occupation of the land of the two holiest sites, Islam's own grounds, the cradle of Islam, source

---

25. https://georgewbush-whitehouse.archives.gov/news/releases/2001/09/200 10920-8.html.

of the Prophet's mission, site of the Ka'bah was launched by the Christian army of the Americans and their allies.[26]

Al-Qaeda's war against the U.S. is far more complex and historically based than the disliking of American democracy and freedom. Osama Bin Laden remains rather consistent as to why he declared war against the U.S. and its allies. The same is true of the current leader of Al-Qaeda Ayman Zawahiri. Zawahiri released an audio statement on February 24, 2004 through Al-Jazeera concerning Al-Qaeda's war with the West. While it was the head scarf ban in France that prompted Zawahiri's message, he ends his recording specifically condemning what he considers to be oppressive foreign policies implemented by the United States:

> The Zionist-Crusader West considers freedom sacred as long as it is its freedom to steal the wealth of others and plunder their resources. But when freedom becomes a means of resisting the West or choosing Islam as a way of life, jihad, and resistance, it becomes terrorism, narrow-mindedness, and fanaticism that should be dealt with by tank shells and aircraft missiles. . . . Banning the hijab in France is consistent with the burning of villages along with their people in Afghanistan, demolishing houses over their sleeping residents in Palestine, and killing the children of Iraq and stealing its oil under false pretexts. . . . It is consistent with tormenting prisoners in the cages of Guanta- namo and torturing Muslims in the prisons of our leaders, the friends of the United States. It is consistent with the right that the United States granted itself to kill any human being or ar- rest anyone anywhere and deport and detain him anywhere for any duration of time, without anyone daring to ask why, how, where, or even when this person was arrested. It is consistent above all with the banning of nuclear weapons everywhere, except Israel. The banning of the hijab is consistent with all these crimes. It shows the scope of the Zionist-Crusade's moral and doctrinal hypocrisy and the extent of its savagery in its war against Islam and Muslims.[27]

Both the U.S. and radical Islamist groups have worked hard to garner sup- port for their cause through propaganda narratives. Both have produced media material that position themselves as being motivated by justice while their opponents are motivated by evil. While these public narratives are oversimplifications of the complex history of the relationship between the

26. Combating Terrorism Center, "Declaration of Jihad against the Americans."

27. Zawahiri audio transcript from Al-Jazeera.

U.S. and the rise of Islamic extremism, they remain very effective in recruiting people to join sides in the battle of "us" versus "them."

Recent Pashtun Public Narratives

In some sense, the Pashtun are caught between the U.S. and the radical Muslims that continued on in their jihad after expelling the Soviets from Afghanistan. The Taliban, a group made up of mostly ethnic Pashtun, filled the vacuum of power following the end of the Soviet occupation. Most of the Taliban came from the Pashtun refugee camps where the textbooks promoting a violent version of Islam were distributed during the Cold War. The brutality of the Taliban included public stonings and beheadings in the national soccer stadium of Kabul. Following the attack on 9/11, the Pashtun Taliban was considered guilty by association. In the speech delivered to the joint session of congress, President George Bush had this to say to the former allies of the U.S.:

> By aiding and abetting murder, the Taliban regime is committing murder. And tonight the United States of America makes the following demands on the Taliban. Deliver to United States authorities all of the leaders of Al Qaeda who hide in your land. Release all foreign nationals, including American citizens you have unjustly imprisoned. Protect foreign journalists, diplomats and aid workers in your country. Close immediately and permanently every terrorist training camp in Afghanistan. And hand over every terrorist and every person and their support structure to appropriate authorities. Give the United States full access to terrorist training camps, so we can make sure they are no longer operating. These demands are not open to negotiation or discussion. The Taliban must act and act immediately. They will hand over the terrorists or they will share in their fate.[28]

The Taliban refused to give up Osama Bin Laden to the U.S. and recommended that he be tried in an Islamic court to determine whether or not he was guilty of any crimes. On October 7, 2001, the U.S. in cooperation with the United Nations, began bombing Afghanistan in order to remove the Taliban from power.

The actions of the U.S. in the Pashtun regions of Afghanistan and Pakistan during the Cold War continue to be problematic. On April 24, 2009, Secretary of State Hillary Clinton discussed how the U.S. involvement in the

28. https://georgewbush-whitehouse.archives.gov/news/releases/2001/09/200 10920-8.html.

region during the Soviet occupation continues to bring challenges in the region, particularly in Pakistan:

> We have a history of moving in and out of Pakistan. Let's remember here, the people we are fighting today we funded twenty years ago. And, we did it because we were locked in the struggle with the Soviet Union. They invaded Afghanistan and we did not want to see them control Central Asia. And we went to work. And it was President Reagan in partnership with the Congress led by Democrats who said, "You know what? Sounds like a pretty good idea. Let's deal with the ISI and the Pakistani Military, and let's go recruit these mujahideen. That's great let's get some to come from Saudi Arabia and other places importing their Wahhabi brand of Islam so that we can go beat the Soviet Union!" And guess what? They retreated, they lost billions of dollars and it led to the collapse of the Soviet Union. So there is a very strong argument which is, "It wasn't a bad investment to end the Soviet Union." But let's be careful what we sow because we will harvest. So, we then left Pakistan. We said, "Ok fine. You deal with the stingers that we've left all over your country. You deal with the mines that are along the border. And by the way, we don't want to have anything to do with you. In fact we're sanctioning you." So we stopped dealing with the Pakistani military and with ISI and we now are making up for a lot of lost time.[29]

Secretary Clinton's words are reminiscent of Jimmy Carter's National Security Advisor Zbigniew Brzezinski's comments concerning the justification of arming Muslim jihadists: "What is more important in world history? The Taliban or the collapse of the Soviet empire? Some agitated Moslems or the liberation of Central Europe and the end of the Cold War?"[30]

Pashtun in the News Media

Many Pashtun immigrants suffer from a complex global media dilemma because of their Muslim faith and ethnic heritage. The events of 9/11 and the Taliban were likely the first introduction to the Pashtun for many Americans. Unfortunately, much of the media coverage of the Pashtun since 9/11 continues to be in the context of ethnic connections to terrorism.[31] Some

---

29. CNN, April 24, 2009. http://edition.cnn.com/TRANSCRIPTS/0904/24/ltm.01.html.

30. Gibbs, "Afghanistan," 242.

31. Rashid, "Pashtuns want an Image Change."

American media reports have suggested that the Pashtun are prone to radicalization due to ethnic and religious identity.[32] While research on transnationalism has shown that political events in the country of origin can have an impact on the political ideology of the immigrant community abroad, there is no empirical evidence indicating Pashtun immigrants are predisposed to radicalization. Nevertheless, media outlets continue to connect Pashtun heritage and Islam as determining factors in recent radicalization of some Pashtun immigrants.

For example, Faisal Shahzad, a Pashtun and a naturalized American citizen, is serving six life sentences in a federal prison for attempting to detonate a car bomb in New York City's Times Square. According to an ABC World News report, Shahzad showed no remorse in the courtroom and, after hearing his sentence, said "Allahu Akbar" and that he would "sacrifice a thousand lives for Allah." Shahzad also stated, "the war with Muslims has just begun" and "the defeat of the U.S. is imminent, God willing."[33] Shahzad, a former financial analyst with a Master's Degree in Business Administration traveled to Waziristan in the Northwest frontier of Pakistan, to train and plot his attempted terrorist attack.

Waziristan is part of Northwest Pakistan's Federally Administered Tribal Areas (FATA) and is predominantly inhabited by Pashtun. It has become a breeding ground for radicalized Islamist groups such as the Taliban, the Haqqani Network, and Al-Qaeda.[34] Consequently, Waziristan is the most targeted area of the FATA in American drone strikes.[35] Shahzad's Pashtun heritage is suspected for his transnational connections in Waziristan and a possible motive for his attempted terrorist attack.[36] Shahzad's story is one of many accounts that have made Americans poignantly aware of the Pashtun people. Although Shahzad's Times Square bomb failed to detonate, news regarding the incident was still widespread.[37]

Pashtuns have drawn further media attention because of the Pashtun involvement with insider attacks—Afghan soldiers who turn their weapons on allied coalition soldiers. According to the Department of Defense, insider attacks are predominately carried out by Pashtun.[38] The ongoing conflict

32. Elliott et al., "For Times Sq. Suspect"; Kaylan, "Immigration, Terror and Assimilation"; News Week, "Pashtuns May Bring The Afghan War Home To America."

33. Katersky, "Faisal Shahzad."

34. Lunn and Smith, "AfPak Policy and the Pashtuns."

35. Cavallaro et al., "Living Under Drones."

36. Elliott et al., "For Times Sq. Suspect."

37. Ackerman, "Time Square Bomber Suspect"; Baum, "Failed Times Square Bomber"; Hays, "Times Square Car Bomb Suspect"; Wilson, "Shahzad Gets Life Term."

38. Tilghman, "DoD."

in Afghanistan and Pakistan brings considerable negative media attention for the Pashtun.[39]

The case could be made that Shahzad's radicalization had little to do with his Pashtun heritage and that he is an anomaly. It is worth noting, however, that Shahzad is not the only naturalized American Pashtun immigrant to engage in terrorist activity. Mohammad Junaid Barbar is also an American naturalized Pashtun who traveled to Northwest Pakistan and trained with Al-Qaeda. Barbar assisted in planning the 7/7 attacks on the London Underground railway system. Also, Najibullah Zazi, much like Shahzad and Barbar, is a Pashtun who spent a good part of his life in the U.S. until returning to Northwest Pakistan to train and plot with Al-Qaeda for a terrorist attack. He was arrested for planning to carry out the attack on the New York City subway system. Pashtun immigrants also have been arrested in Spain, Denmark, and Great Britain for suspected terrorist activity.[40]

The two most recent terrorist attacks in the United States were also carried out by Pashtun immigrants. On June 29, 2016, Omar Mateen killed forty-nine people at an LGBTQ Pulse nightclub in Orlando, Florida. This was the deadliest mass shooting by a single person in the United States. Omar's father Seddique Mir Mateen attracted media attention for being the host of a Pashtun nationalist's television show from which he publicly praised the Taliban. Omar Mateen swore allegiance to the Islamic State before his act of terror. Similarly, Sayeed Rizwan Farook and his wife Tashfeen Malik pledged allegiance to the Islamic State before killing fourteen people in San Bernardino. The couple's Pashtun ethnicity has not been emphasized by media outlets.

Though similarities surrounding the aforementioned cases are uncanny, the question remains as to whether these incidents are coincidental or if the Pashtun are predisposed to radicalization as some have claimed. Whether or not their Pashtun heritage played a role in their radicalization and terrorist activities is debatable. What we know with certainty is the potential power of a narrative that claims their Pashtun heritage is responsible. While the narrative of the violent Muslim Pashtun is not new (see early ethnographic representations in Ch.2), we are seeing a revival of the cultural and religious determinism of the early twentieth century in some current media representations of the Pashtun.

39. Filkins, "Nation Challenged"; Greenway, "War with the Wrong Enemy"; Karon, "Taliban and Afghanistan"; McGirk, "Pashtun."

40. Newsweek, "Pashtuns May Bring The Afghan War Home To America."

This negative stereotyping of the Pashtun is not unique to Western media. Farooq Yousaf suggests that there has been a recent campaign in Pakistan to profile those who are ethnically Pashtun as potential terrorists.[41] Official notices have been circulated encouraging the report of anyone who looks Pashtun or is wearing Pashtun attire. Yousaf says that the implication is that if a person is Pashtun then they are a potential terrorist. This negative stereotyping of the Pashtun in Pakistan is not a recent phenomenon. According to Yousaf the Pashtun have always been perceived and characterized as barbaric. Many Pashtun believe they are misrepresented and "caught in the middle of warmongers, extremists and militants."[42] Pashtun politician Mehmood Khan Achakzai stated, "The world is asking 'who are you Pashtuns' . . . around the world we are accused of being terrorists, but tolerance is in our blood—it is taught by our mothers."[43]

Conclusion

The violent public narratives for Pashtun immigrants are concerning. The checkered history of the United States with the Pashtun may create a deep sense of mistrust for American Pashtun immigrants. The ongoing negative media associating the Pashtun with violence and terrorism leave many feeling misunderstood and misrepresented by their societies of origin and resettlement. For example, in March of 2009, Pashtun immigrants (approximately 200) took to the streets of New York "to let the world know that Pashtuns are not terrorists, they are not the Taliban."[44] Pashtun immigrants in America may also experience discrimination from their countries of origin for being too American. They are often ostracized by their extended families back home where anti-American sentiments are prevalent. Many Pashtun immigrants feel they have one foot in their home country and another in America but are welcome in neither.[45]

This ongoing tension between the nation-states of origin and resettlement is a potential strain on the identity formation of Pashtun immigrants. Prevalent negative views toward Muslim immigrants have potentially negative effects for both Muslims and America. There is a direct correlation between immigrant attitudes and the perceived attitude of the host society.[46]

41. Yousaf, "Pakistan's Pashtun Profiling."
42. Rashid, "Pashtuns want an Image Change."
43. Rashid, "Pashtuns want an Image Change."
44. Babar and Semple, "In Brooklyn, Pashtuns March Against the Taliban."
45. Zaheer, "'I Am a Khan, I Am Not a Terrorist' Say Pashtuns in New York."
46. Phinney et al., "Ethnic Identity, Immigration, and Well-Being," 493–510.

Immigrants who believe that the host society is hostile or unwelcoming may abandon their ethnic identity or more deeply identify with the ethnicity that is perceived as marginalized or threatened. The pressures of abandoning an ethnic identity or deeply identifying with a group that has a perception of marginalization may have adverse effects on an individual's emotional well-being.[47] This is understandable considering the relationship between sociocultural narratives and identity.

The next chapter illustrates how narrative identity can go beyond the binary framework of essentialism and constructivism by assessing the life history of Sayyid Qutb. Qutb is a well-known historical figure in the Muslim world whose life illustrates the complexity and tension of an individual's attempt to reconcile competing narrative identities in a transnational context.

47. Phinney et al., "Ethnic Identity, Immigration, and Well-Being," 493–510.

6

Narrative Identity of Sayyid Qutb (1906–1966)

THIS CHAPTER EXPLORES THE life history of Sayyid Qutb in order to illustrate the process of narrative identity formation. Using well-known and
documented historical figures to demonstrate theories of identity is well
documented in social science.[1]

Sayyid Qutb is considered by many to be one of the most influential
people in developing the ideological framework for those who carried out
the attacks of 9/11. His 1964 work, *Milestones*, is often cited as a seminal
text that informs the violent versions of Islam employed by groups such
as Al-Qaeda and ISIS. The discussion of Qutb's ideas are often reduced to
an identity crisis he experienced during his two-year visit to the United
States as a foreign exchange student.[2] However, a brief look at Qutb's life
history demonstrates a far more complex process of competing narrative
identities that started long before he visited America. I argue in this chapter
that *Milestones* is Qutb's attempt to re-narrate his previous experiences and
beliefs to coincide with his imprisonment and suffering at the hands of fellow Muslims. Being a powerful story teller, Qutb re-invents the so called
"unique quranic generation" as a historical collectivity that embodies his
new beliefs and gives meaning to his suffering. In other words, *Milestones* is
Qutb's articulation of a narrative identity that is rooted in the re-imagined
collectivity where he and others can find a sense of belonging.

Competing Global Narratives in Childhood

Qutb was born in the upper Egyptian village of Musha in 1906. At this
time, the overarching competing global narratives concerned British colonialism and the rule of the Ottoman Empire. The 'clash of civilizations'

1. Erikson, *Gandhi's Truth*; *Young Man Luther*.
2. D'Souza, *Enemy at Home*.

narrative was prevalent in the life of Qutb long before Samuel Huntington popularized the phrase in 1993. He recalls in his childhood memoirs, *A Child from a Village*, how his father's home was the secret meeting place for those in the village that supported the Egyptian Nationalist Party.[3] The political party was adamantly opposed to the British occupation of Egypt and desired to maintain strong ties to the Ottoman Empire. The party was pushed underground following the British invasion in 1882. As a boy, Qutb was allowed to attend some of these secret meetings and was given the role of reading the newspaper to those who gathered in his father's home. When the meetings were only adults, he recalls having to strain to hear the discussions from another room. The transnational connection with the Ottoman Empire and the disdain for the British occupiers during WWI provided a clear "us" versus "them" narrative for Qutb as a child:

> The feelings of the entire village were on the side of Turkey, the State of the Islamic Caliphate, and against the Allies, who represented the "unbelievers" and were fighting Islam. It seemed that certain feelings were beginning to ferment. He [in his memoir, Qutb refers to himself in third person] remembers that now and realizes that even though he was a child he, like the men, had the feeling that some as yet ill-defined thing was going to happen. He did not know what it was or how it would occur, but that it would definitely happen. Secret meetings took place at his house. Doors were shut and voices were reduced to whispers. These meetings impressed in his mind this ill-defined thing that he did not know.[4]

Qutb was not completely aware of what was happening though he recalls feeling like he was a part of something bigger than himself. His shared experiences of patriotism, and an imagined connection to the Caliphate gave a sense of invigoration to his young soul.

Qutb was given two books that further stoked the fires of his new-found affections for the Islamic Caliphate and Egyptian nationalism: the poetry of Thabit al-Jurjawi and the Islamic historical work of Muhammad Khudari. Qutb says of Thabit al-Jurjawi that "He found in this poetry words that nourished in his soul the spirit of patriotism, a spirit that had been awakened by the family atmosphere in which he lived and the general atmosphere that was as if charged with electric currents ready to explode."[5] He became interested even further after learning that al-Jurjawi had become a political

3. Qutb, *Child from a Village*.
4. Qutb, *Child from a Village*, 92.
5. Qutb, *Child from a Village*, 94.

prisoner and his book was officially banned by the government. The author's sacrifice gave the book an increased value for Qutb and reified in him a sense of collective identity that was marginalized by the West.

As for Khudari's historical text, Qutb was thrilled to read that the author had feared sections of his book praising the Ottoman viceroy of Egypt would likely be removed due to government censorship. Qutb recalls thinking "He had in his hands two valuable and rare books containing patriotic material of the kind that his soul thirsted for."[6] Qutb, being convinced of their rarity, began memorizing and, in some cases, transcribing copies of these works. These authors were also the sources for Qutb's patriotic speeches during the Egyptian Revolution. According to Qutb, his speeches were weak; nevertheless, he persisted in delivering them in meeting halls and mosques at the age of ten.

One can only imagine the disappointment of Qutb following the dismantling of the Ottoman Empire and the abolishment of the Islamic Caliphate in 1924. The competing global narrative of the West against Islam is further reified into the mind of Qutb with the subsequent British colonialism he experienced as a young adult. In addition to the competing global narratives, Qutb documents in his childhood memoir a continual struggle between the folk practices and beliefs of his village upbringing and the modernism he experienced in his primary education.

Competing Sociocultural Narratives in Childhood

Qutb begins his childhood memoir by introducing the prevalence of traditional or folk religious practices that were enmeshed in the Muslim beliefs and practices of his family and village. The opening lines of his book detail a man in Qutb's local village who was endowed with supernatural power known as Shaykh Naqib:

> More than a quarter century has passed since these events, but even today he cannot recall them without feeling in his body a shudder that silently penetrates his bones, as if his blood had turned to ice water. It was this man with disheveled hair and torn clothing, sometimes naked with nothing to cover his body, wandering about the streets and alleys of the village with a stick in his hand that struck at everything and everybody . . . The man used to tear his clothes to shreds and then roll in the mud or pour dust over his head and naked body, until the dust and mud coating his skin formed a new set of clothes, replacing the

6. Qutb, *Child from a Village*, 94.

torn and discarded ones. He used to run through the streets of
the village screaming in a shrill, terrifying voice, "Allah! Allah!
Allah!"[7]

Qutb recalls the adults in the village revered the man as a saint saying, "He is
no longer an ordinary person; he is no longer subject to the rules of society.
He has been endowed with sainthood and no longer belongs to the earthly
realm in which we live."[8]

Despite the elders' claims of sainthood, Qutb was never quite comfortable with the man's behaviors. He was terrified of him, as were most of the
children in the village. It was said that the man's walking stick came from a
tree in Paradise and had been dipped seven times in the well of Zamzam.[9]
The villagers believed that the stick had healing power. However, Qutb and
his friends had their own version of why the man carried the stick. The boys
believed the stick could lengthen upon command and be used to "burn their
backs or break their ribs."[10] He describes the feelings he and his companions
experienced when they would encounter the man on the road:

> There had been times when he was walking alone or with his
> companions and *Shaykh Naqib* suddenly appeared, they knew
> not from where. What he knew was that their mouths went dry
> and their feet froze to the ground when he appeared at the end
> of the road, even if he were dozens of meters away from them.
> Their legs became paralyzed, their eyes stared at him without
> blinking, their hearts beat violently but they could not move
> a muscle.[11]

Qutb and his friends knew they could not outrun the man for they had
been told that he attended the Friday prayers in Mecca each week by taking only one step.

Qutb did what he could to avoid Shaykh Naqib until the day he injured his neck playing a game with his friends. When he did not seem to be
recovering, Qutb overheard a village woman suggest that his mother take
him to Shaykh Naqib to be healed. She was instructed to follow the Shaykh
until he laid down to sleep for the night. Once he was sleeping, she needed
to lay the young boy next to him and he would be cured by sunrise. Qutb
recalls being utterly terrified at the proposal:

7. Qutb, *Child from a Village*, 1.
8. Qutb, *Child from a Village*, 5.
9. The well believed to be provided for Hagar in the desert and located in Mecca.
10. Qutb, *Child from a Village*, 3.
11. Qutb, *Child from a Village*, 3.

Why not then send him to the snake pit or the lion's den? Indeed, why not put him face-to-face with the devil? Or was it he who was crazy? Although he did not believe for one instant that the woman seriously meant what she said, he cannot remember any terror that so penetrated his whole being throughout the rest of his life as this one did when he heard that sick joke.[12]

Qutb's mother refused the woman's advice and instead chose to leave Qutb's fate to "the knowledge and power of God."[13]

Qutb's opening story sets the stage for much of his memoir. The competing narratives of the spiritual powers associated with the traditional village beliefs are consistently contrasted with the knowledge and power of God which often takes the form of modern science and medicine. That said, there are times in which Qutb lends credence to the work of spiritual powers in conjunction with the knowledge of modern medicine. For example, he recounts how his own brother was strangled to death as a child by his *qarina* (spirit double) because his aunt was unable to get him to the local healer in time. Interestingly, Qutb suggests that the *qarina* was able to accomplish this through a tetanus infection resulting from a lack of modern medical techniques:

The baby frothed and foamed at the mouth and turned dark or even black. Just as the suffering appeared to be unbearable, the fit would subside and the baby would settle down, until it seized him again. There was no doubt about it: It was the *qarina*. The beauty and health of the child had vexed her, filling her with envy of the family, so that she began to strangle the baby . . . On the seventh day, during one of the acute attacks, the newborn gasped his last breath. Tetanus had overcome him as a result of the nonsterile knife used by the midwife to cut the umbilical cord. The tetanus microbe clung to it, causing the wound to be infected. There it remained for the duration of its incubation period, which ranges between four to six days. With that, the *qarina* had accomplished her mission, venting her fury at the beautiful baby boy.[14]

That same day, Qutb was given an amulet to wear with the picture of Solomon to protect him from evil. He wore the amulet until his mother had another child. Qutb's brother was given the amulet to protect it from the fate of their previous sibling.

12. Qutb, *Child from a Village*, 6.
13. Qutb, *Child from a Village*, 1.
14. Qutb, *Child from a Village*, 63–66.

Aside from this incident, Qutb tends to represent the village traditions as "superstitions and quackery" when compared to the "enlightened
ones of the village" who believed in modern medicine.[15] This is most evi-
dent in his recollection of a particular Ramadan *iftar* [the meal for breaking the fast] when his entire family came down with a sickness that caused
everyone profuse vomiting. The initial thought of the villagers was that
the food was poisoned from reptile saliva. Another possibility was that
the food was cursed by envy of the Qutb family's prosperity. Qutb, looking
back, suggests a different hypothesis to the traditional beliefs in unclean
animal poisons and curses. "The real cause was either eating food that had
spoiled after being left for two or three days or, alternatively, the copper
oxide that had accumulated in the copper pots and pans, but it was always
ascribed to the 'smelling of snakes.'"[16] Qutb recalls his father being an enlightened man who was uninterested in folk remedies. Rather than call
upon a local healer, Qutb's father asked the local physician to come and
treat his family. Qutb's description of the doctor amidst the large crowd
gathered in his home that day provides some insight as to his early affec-
tion for modern science over folk practices:

> Among these relentlessly moving and numerous crowds there was
> one man who stood out. He was tall, slender, and of light com-
> plexion. He was dressed in a clean, white *jallabiyya* [traditional
> garmet], tailor-made in the urban style, not the village style, with
> a clean, white scarf over it, and wore elegant leather slippers on
> his feet. This elegant man who stood out from the whole crowd
> was issuing orders but in a friendly, gentle, and graceful manner,
> and his orders had to do with quantities of milk being brought,
> into which he personally dissolved a special substance and then
> had them taken to the sick people in glasses. He was the one in
> charge of treating this vast number of sick people.[17]

The medicine provided by the doctor worked, and according to Qutb, "this
increased his fame and raised his prestige, so that many more came to him,
even those who were not believers in modern medicine."[18]

One particular story of Qutb's childhood reveals a possible turning
point from the traditional beliefs of the village toward modern science. He
tells the story how one of his childhood friends was possessed by a demon
after seeing a black tomcat on a moonless night. Qutb recalls everyone

15. Qutb, *Child from a Village*, 51.
16. Qutb, *Child from a Village*, 48.
17. Qutb, *Child from a Village*, 49.
18. Qutb, *Child from a Village*, 51.

screaming and running when they saw the apparition except for his friend Gomaa. When the boys realized that Gomaa was not with them, they returned only to find him lifeless but still breathing:

> To no avail they attempted to arouse him. They stood for a long time at that terrifying spot before banding together to carry him to a safe place. His house was not far. They knocked at the door and his grandmother opened it to be confronted with the body of her grandson. She was troubled and alarmed, especially after she heard the story, and became convinced that the boy was possessed by an *'ifrit* [demon or evil spirit].[19]

The grandmother proceeded to employ traditional healers to deliver the boy. Qutb says that she spent all of her savings on various rites and exorcisms. After three months, the boy died. Qutb says that the whole event is "etched in his mind and its memory cannot be erased."[20] He was only seven years old at the time and in the second grade. The event with Gomaa had a profound effect on Qutb. He did not believe Gomaa was possessed but simply fainted and likely hit his head during the fall:

> Gomaa turned clumsy and his feet would not obey him, so he stammered and became agitated. The children's sudden movement had scared the tomcat so that it began to run to and fro. The poor boy reckoned that the *'ifrit* was talking to him, and with that he finally lost his balance and fell down in a dead faint. Our friend observed his dear companion fall but in this situation he could not help him.[21]

It seems this event was a turning point for Qutb because he specifically mentions being unwilling to return to the place where Gomaa died until he changed his beliefs about the *'afarit* [demons or evil spirits], something he would eventually do with the help of his state school headmaster.

Synthesizing Islam and Modernism through Education

The setting of Qutb's exploration of modern science over the spirit world of his village upbringing is in the state primary school. Qutb remembers tension between the state primary school and the local quranic school. He recalls the day a qualified teacher arrived from the city and replaced the

19. Qutb, *Child from a Village*, 61.
20. Qutb, *Child from a Village*, 61.
21. Qutb, *Child from a Village*, 60.

local village Shaykh who had no credentials other than having memorized
the Qur'an. Immediately rumors were circulated that the government
school was trying to end quranic instruction and memorization for children. The disenfranchised Shaykh notified Qutb's father personally of the
situation and the boy was immediately transferred from the state school
to the village *kuttab* (quranic school). The following quote is Qutb's recollection of his feelings on the first day of Qur'an school. It is necessary to
quote him at length in order to clearly demonstrate how his early experiences led him to believe that the religious school was significantly inferior
compared to the state school.

> He does not remember his small heart ever feeling as much
> anxiety as it did on that day, or his breast being so constricted
> and narrowed. Our Master, Shaykh Ahmad, received him
> kindly with smiles and promptly sat him down beside him-
> self, whereas the other youths of the *kuttab* sat on a mat in the
> middle of the room or on a bench running around the wall
> of the room. But none of this decreased his resistance. He was
> accustomed to being greeted each morning by that neat clean
> building, with its rooms whitewashed and its courtyard spread
> with sand. He was used to sitting in the school chairs with their
> receptacles for books, implements, notepads, and his fine writ-
> ing slate. In the *kuttab*, by contrast, there were no seats with
> book receptacles, nor bells, classrooms, books, inkwells, chairs.
> Instead there was a tin sheet upon which the students would
> write with ink made from indigo or lamp soot or a similar sub-
> stance. The students carried their inkwells and pens in their
> hands wherever they went. If they recited what was on their
> slates to Our Master and he found that they had memorized it,
> then they would clean them and write other verses of the Qur'an
> on them. Their manner of erasing them was filthy, because they
> would spit on them, rub them with their hands, and then wipe
> them off with the edge of their garments. Consequently their
> clothes were always stained with ink. He was appalled by the
> fact that Our Master, when he was correcting the slates with red
> ink and noticed an error in what was written, would promptly
> lick off the incorrect words with his tongue and then wipe the
> slate clean with the edge of his palm. The student would then
> write the correct words. If a student needed to go out to attend
> a call of nature he did not raise his finger, as did the students
> in the school; rather he snapped his fingers and called out:
> "Our Master! Our Master!" If Our Master acknowledged the
> request he would touch together the fingers of his two hands

and say: "Permission granted!" Then the student would leave and might possibly not return for the rest of the day. In any case, our child's soul was filled with repugnance at everything that surrounded him. He felt bitter, abject loneliness. When he returned to his house he was determined that he would never go back to that filthy place, no matter how much he might be threatened or reproached. He confided this urgent desire to his mother, and her eyes filled with tears.[22]

The next morning, without his father's permission, Qutb skipped Qur'an school and returned to the state school. Upon hearing the boy's story, the headmaster convinced his father that Qutb's intellect would not be recognized in the quranic school. Despite the Shaykh's disappointment, Qutb was allowed to return to the state school for his primary education.

Upon returning to the state school, Qutb had a new found Islamic missionary zeal. He described the state school as "a holy place like a *mihrab* for prayer."[23] He wanted to demonstrate to the quranic school and any villagers who thought he was compromising the Islamic faith that they were mistaken. He fully believed that the Qur'an could be studied alongside a broader secular curriculum. In order to prove his point, he gathered a group of students together in the state school to begin memorizing the Qur'an. In his fourth year at the age of ten, Qutb had memorized the Qur'an in its entirety. He also formed a team that would compete against village Qur'an schools in recitation competitions. Qutb's team won on more than one occasion, effectively silencing any opposition to his attending a state school.

While he had effectively shown the compatibility of the Qur'an and modern education, his traditional village beliefs were not so easily reconciled. Over a period of three years, with the help of his school headmaster, Qutb and his friends were able to renegotiate their belief systems regarding the spirit world. The non-material world went from an all-encompassing aspect of daily life to the sidelines of folklore and superstition for Qutb. However, this was not an easy transition. He recalls how the headmaster strived to free the boys from the fear of the spirit world that was deeply embedded into their lives:

> Because dozens of these images, myths, and accounts were constantly being impressed on his young mind, how could he ever have been able to change his beliefs about the *'afarit*? Yet this happened when a young headmaster came to the school. He was deeply concerned about the moral and spiritual education

22. Qutb, *Child from a Village*, 19–20.
23. Qutb, *Child from a Village*, 21.

of the students and did not simply limit himself to dry scholas-
tic subjects. When he saw how the myth of the 'afarit occupied
a solid place in the perceptions and feelings of the students,
he tried as much as he could to purify their minds of it. He
said to them, 'All talk about these 'afarit is superstition based
on ignorance, and all the tales about those who unexpectedly
encountered 'afarit are fabricated for some ulterior purpose,
or else are simply imagined. The cats, dogs, and other animals
that many people think are 'afarit are in fact real animals. Fear
and dread create these thoughts in people, especially since they
meet them in the dark, where they cannot see forms clearly.'
He made this subject the focus of conversation in many of his
classes, until some of the students were almost at the point of
believing what he said.[24]

The problem, according to Qutb, was that he and his classmates had both
experienced the supernatural and had been told several stories about the
spirit world. Therefore, the intellectual arguments of the headmaster were
insufficient on their own in changing the student's beliefs. Qutb describes
the spirit world as having a grip on his young imagination.

Qutb found it necessary to have new experiences to "demolish these
beliefs and to establish new ones in their place."[25] The headmaster provided
such experiences for Qutb and his classmates. For example, after hearing the
students explain that there was a particular alleyway in the village where the
rabbits were inhabited by spirits after midnight, the headmaster scheduled a
fieldtrip. He encouraged the boys to join him in visiting the haunted alleyway
at the appointed time of spirit possession in order to catch a rabbit for closer
examination. Qutb and five of his classmates participated. The headmaster
caught one of the rabbits and took it back to the classroom in order to show
the boys that their fears were irrational. The headmaster designed other similar experiments to free the boys of their fear of spirits.

Before long, Qutb found himself intentionally walking by the places
where people believed the spirits dwelled. However, he often carried matches
with him as a cautionary protection since the 'afarit were supposedly afraid
of light. Eventually Qutb overcame his fears of the 'afarit and they became
nothing but folklore for him. Nevertheless, he admits they continue to haunt
him in his dreams, saying "the myth of the 'afarit is more deeply embedded
in his soul than education, and that the 'afarit that inhabited his mind in
childhood and youth will inhabit his imagination forever."[26]

24. Qutb, *Child from a Village*, 70.
25. Qutb, *Child from a Village*, 71.
26. Qutb, *Child from a Village*, 77.

Competing Narratives of Tribalism and Nationalism

There were some traditional village traditions rooted in tribalism that Qutb found repulsive. For example, the tribal blood feuds in the villages terrified Qutb as a child. He recalls vendetta killings being gruesome and frequent. As a result, many of the villagers lived in a perpetual state of fear and suspicion. He saw family honor as the root of the revenge killings which led to an endless cycle of violence:

> These incidents occurred all the time, and their fire kept burning generation after generation. Perhaps a man was killed who had one young child. The child's mother, along with the rest of the people in the village, would keep telling him the story of his father's murder until he was ready to take vengeance simply because he had the strength to do so. Only then was the funeral of the father performed and only then did his family accept condolences; otherwise, the family would continue to be shamed before the village. None of them could raise their heads before he took vengeance.[27]

Qutb recalls two particular revenge incidents that were "inscribed in the boy's memory and imagination." The first incident was when someone killed all but one of his aunt's livestock. He remembers the cattle being "either stabbed in the stomach, their guts ripped apart, or poisoned by a caustic substance." He saw the cows writhing on the ground in pain and remembers thinking it was "particularly horrible and cruel" because the cows suffered but they had committed no offense.[28]

The second incident was not witnessed personally by Qutb, but it was the "talk of the whole village." He had heard the story told more than a dozen times and despite the fact that the story "made his body tremble," Qutb frequently recalled scenes in his imagination.[29] The story is about the murder of three young men by their uncle. One of the young men married his cousin against his uncle's will. The uncle demanded that his nephew divorce his daughter. When the young man refused, the uncle proceeded to file a lawsuit in the local Shari'ah Court. The young man was poor and had no animal to ride to the court. So, in order to make it to the court when it opened at sunrise, he and his two brothers set out on foot while it was still dark. When the uncle learned that the boys would be walking, he hired two armed men to assist him in ambushing them along their way.

27. Qutb, *Child from a Village*, 102.
28. Qutb, *Child from a Village*, 103.
29. Qutb, *Child from a Village*, 103.

The three boys were brutally murdered by their uncle. Qutb recounts how one of the boys pleaded for mercy,

> He pleaded with his monstrous uncle in a way that would have softened iron, saying to him: 'Why do you want to kill me, uncle? What wrong have I done to you? Do not my brothers suffice? You have already killed your opponent so let me go. My mother is alone and I am her only support now that my brothers are gone and the only support of the small child that your brother left behind. Free me for God's sake and I will remain silent about all that has happened. I swear to you!' But the pitiless uncle did not listen to any of that. He was afraid that if he freed him, the third brother would testify against him and his two accomplices. It is said that the third brother kept pleading for half an hour, but his uncle never softened up. In the end, the two thugs finished off the poor man.[30]

According to Qutb, there was a fourth brother that was only a small child when this incident occurred. Though he was too small to enact revenge, Qutb used to imagine such an ending in which the "fourth boy had drawn his knife and slashed open the belly of the savage uncle. Even though he knew that had not happened and never would, his imagination always completed the story with that desired end."[31] For Qutb, the story lacked a sense of justice, a problem that he found endemic to the tribalism of his youth.

The Need for Social Justice

The theme of social justice is prevalent in Qutb's memoir, particularly in his interactions with the annual migrant workers that assisted on his family farm. Each year, the same migrant workers would come to help work the fields in the village. It was through the lives of these foreign workers that Qutb came to realize the amount of wealth that his village and family possessed by comparison. While many of the villagers looked down upon these foreign workers because they were poor, Qutb viewed them as friends. He says that they "had entered into something like a family relationship" despite the fact that the only thing they shared in common was Islam.[32] He remembers his father feeding the workers better than what was expected. Qutb also made sure that his friends had plenty to eat, even waking up early to bring them extra portions of food while they were in the fields. Then,

30. Qutb, *Child from a Village*, 104.
31. Qutb, *Child from a Village*, 121.
32. Qutb, *Child from a Village*, 116.

according to Qutb, there was an event that took place with these migrant workers that he "will never forget as long as he lives."

The workers asked if they could exchange their daily food for a raise in their daily wage. Qutb's father reluctantly agreed after making it known that he was offended at the rejection of his hospitality. Qutb's father assumed that the workers were able to save money by rationing food they prepared themselves. However, when Qutb saw what the workers were eating, something equivalent to cabbage soup, he told his father and asked him to come and see for himself. Qutb's father was amazed at how little each one was willing to eat in order to gain a small increment in pay. He agreed to give the pay increase and continue feeding the migrant workers as a result. The workers praised Allah for his provision through Qutb's father. That night, Qutb learned how privileged he was. The simple foods that he had taken for granted were foods that these migrant workers only tasted on special occasions. Qutb's interaction with these foreign workers started an internal struggle that he would continually reflect upon into adulthood:

> He learned many things, whose profound effects on his soul and whose harsh impact on his feelings have only become evident as he now reflects on them from time to time, and feels shame in the depth of his soul and contempt for himself and his people. He is a robber. He has robbed these "foreigners" and many millions like them who create the wealth of the Nile Valley yet go hungry. He is a robber! If there were a just law in the valley, it would send him to prison before those multitudes whom the law counts as robbers and criminals. This was the feeling that always kept coming over him whenever he sat down to eat rich food or sweet fruit or luxurious sweets or whenever he enjoyed the simple pleasures of life amidst the millions of deprived.[33]

Qutb's inner conflict over his privilege and the needs of others is something that haunted him throughout his life. In some sense, the reflexivity in Qutb's writing gives the impression that he may have been struggling to reconcile his adult social status as an intellectual elite with the village boy who befriended the foreigner. He goes to great lengths in explaining that his reasons for leaving the village had more to do with others than his own personal ambition.

33. Qutb, *Child from a Village*, 124.

A Vision to become an Intellectual

Qutb's vision of leaving Musha and becoming an intellectual started the day he realized that his mother was counting on him to provide for the family in ways his father had not. The day he saw his mother crying because his father had sold some of the family farm to pay off debt had a profound effect on ten-year old Qutb. He felt the weight of the responsibility of his mother's words, "Listen, sir, you must get back what your father has lost!"[34] His mother told him exactly how he should go about getting back the land. He was to leave the village to further his education in Cairo and then earn enough money to purchase back the land. It was at this moment that Qutb's past experiences and present circumstances gave him a sense of vision and hope for the future:

> Thus the first seed of real responsibility was sown in his soul. He knew now why his mother was pushing his education so fast and why she had been so eager for him to go to the primary school rather than the *kuttab*. He had to repair the building before it collapsed. . . . There was a task that awaited him, and he was like a soldier prepared for the struggle, drafted for this task, which his mother had both prepared him for and hidden from him from the first day he was taken to school. Then she had revealed it to him the day he came in and saw her crying! He had to restore to the family the prestige and money it had lost![35]

Qutb believed that it was his fault that his family wealth was depleted. He knew that his father had made financial sacrifices for his education. This gave him a sense of purpose in pursuing further education in Cairo. He found a sense of identity in achieving the plan that his mother set out for him.

Qutb studied at the teacher training college of Dar al-'Ulum in Cairo. The school had a broad curriculum which included quranic exegesis alongside the more modernist subjects such as science and math. Qutb biographer John Calvert describes it as a conservative transitional college that bridged the gap between the narrow Islamic curriculum of Al-Azhar and the new modern education that was imported from the West.[36] Qutb graduated in 1933 with a degree in Arabic and Literature. His father died the same year he completed his education. Rather than returning home to care for his family, Qutb took various elementary teaching positions in and around Cairo. He

34. Qutb, *Child from a Village*, 129.
35. Qutb, *Child from a Village*, 130, 134.
36. Calvert, *Sayyid Qutb and the Origins of Radical Islamism*.

eventually settled in Hulwan, a suburb of Cairo, where he would bring his mother, brother, and three sisters to live with him.

Conflicting Narratives for Egypt

The inner turmoil concerning the conflicting narratives of westernization and traditional conservatives can be seen throughout Qutb's literary work while living in Cairo.[37] Qutb joined a group of young literary intellectuals who had a vested interest in developing a new identity for an independent Egypt that was characterized by secular modernism and cultural revivalism.[38] In his personal life, Qutb began having second thoughts about the value of modernism. He struggled to adjust to the modernization that he had idealized as a child. Qutb collaborated with his brother and two sisters to publish a 1945 work titled the *Four Phantoms* in which they document their struggles to belong in Hulwan. The death of their mother in 1940 may have further exasperated the feelings of isolation and loss of historical continuity with their village pasts. Qutb writes "We are exiles; we are the small branches whose roots have withered after their estrangement from their native soil. And how far are the branches from establishing themselves in the foreign soil."[39]

Much of Qutb's literary work during his time in Hulwan seems to reflect his inner discontent with intellectualism and modernism. He mourns the loss of a simpler life now that he was experiencing the realities of the city life that left him feeling disillusioned. He also begins to mourn the loss of the spiritual mysticism of his youth in exchange for rationalism. According to Calvert, "He comes across very much as the outsider, a young man at odds with the banality of existence, who reaches for and sometimes catches a glimpse of a higher spiritual truth. He is of a type well represented in European Romantic and Existentialist literature."[40] Like the European Romantics, Qutb's writings take on the notion of a misunderstood spiritual mystic who was disenchanted with the intellectualism and modernism produced by the enlightenment. Qutb began to idealize a Sufi asceticism that was not so different from the Shaykh Naqib that he so feared in his childhood.

The shift towards spiritual mysticism may have been a reaction to Qutb's distaste for Western materialism and individualism. He feared that Western influence might ruin the moral fabric of Egyptian society. Qutb

37. Calvert, *Sayyid Qutb and the Origins of Radical Islamism.*
38. Calvert, *Sayyid Qutb and the Origins of Radical Islamism.*
39. Calvert, *Sayyid Qutb and the Origins of Radical Islamism,* 66.
40. Calvert, *Sayyid Qutb and the Origins of Radical Islamism,* 69.

was beginning to question whether the benefits of modernity were worth
the encroaching liberalism he was witnessing in Cairo. He spent a good
portion of the 1940s working in the Education Ministry Office of General
Culture hoping to see a modernized Egypt that retained its cultural con-
servativism come to fruition.

The establishment of Israel and the Palestinian refugee crises may
have been the breaking point for Qutb. Calvert documents a decisive shift
concerning the relationship between Islam and modernity in three books
published by Qutb after 1948:

> The books represent a sea change in Qutb's ideological orienta-
> tion. Up to this point, he had expressed his hope for Egypt's fu-
> ture in terms of secular nationalism, believing that the Egyptian
> people had a spiritual disposition that set them apart from the
> materialism and aggressiveness of the Western nations. Islam,
> in his previous understanding, stood with the Arabic language
> and Egyptian history as a marker of Egypt's collective identity,
> but was not sufficient itself. As Qutb had written in 1946, 'The
> question for me is my honour, my language, and my culture.'
> However, writing in 1948, he began explicitly to base his call for
> a just political, economic and social order on the teachings of
> the Qur'an and the example of the Prophet. Drawing on these
> sources, he began to fashion a theological argument that ad-
> dressed the contemporary Egyptian contexts of political and
> social strain, especially the extreme social-class inequality that
> existed at the national level. At the heart of his discussion was
> an explicit moral and ethical concern for disenfranchised and
> downtrodden Muslims in Egypt and the wider *Umma*.[41]

Calvert goes on to document how Qutb expected the British support
of Israel but was surprised by the United States' role. It was at this point
that Qutb began to lump all Western countries together in a unified attack
against the East and more specifically the Muslim world. This was another
turning point for Qutb. He no longer seems interested in conceptualizing
an Egyptian national identity. The plight of the Palestinians forced Qutb to
consider a broader collective identity that transcended the borders of Egypt
and included the global Muslim community.

At this point, Qutb began showing interest in the ideology promoted by
Hasan al-Banna and the organization he founded, the Muslim Brotherhood.
He was becoming increasingly skeptical of his previous belief that the tech-
nological and scientific advances of Westernization could be separated from

41. Calvert, *Sayyid Qutb and the Origins of Radical Islamism*, 127.

the materialism and moral corruption of traditional culture. This was further confirmed when the Egyptian Ministry of Education sent Qutb to the United States to learn how to replicate the Western model of education.

Qutb's Visit to America

Qutb's visit to America confirmed his suspicions that his life-long dream of integrating Islam and modernity through Western education was an impossibility. While Qutb was thoroughly impressed with American technological advances, they were overshadowed by the culture which he considered to be devoid of morality and spirituality. He documents his experience in a published 1951 essay titled *The America I have Seen*. Qutb argues that the success of material production through technological advances led Americans to go backwards toward a primitive state where animalistic behaviors were normalized. He associates this primitive state of being with pre-Islamic Arabia by using the term *Jahiliyya*. For example, he documents the American obsession with football as follows:

> It seems the American is primitive in his appreciation of muscular strength and the strength of matter in general. To the extent that he overlooks principles, values, and manners in his personal life, in his family life, and in his social life, except in the realm of work, and economic and monetary relationships. This primitiveness can be seen in the spectacle of the fans as they follow a game of football, played in the rough American style, which has nothing to do with its name (football), for the foot does not take part in the game. Instead, each player attempts to catch the ball with his hands and run with it toward the goal, while the players of the opposing team attempt to tackle him by any means necessary, whether this be a blow to his stomach, or crushing his arms and legs with great violence and ferocity. The sight of the fans as they follow this game, or watch boxing matches or bloody, monstrous wrestling matches . . . is one of animal excitement born of their love for hardcore violence. Their lack of attention to the rules and sportsmanship to the extent that they are enthralled with the flowing blood and crushed limbs, crying loudly, everyone cheering for his team. Destroy his head. Crush his ribs. Beat him to a pulp. This spectacle leaves no room for doubt as to the primitiveness of the feelings of those who are enamored with muscular strength and desire it.[42]

42. Qutb, "America I have Seen," 6.

It could be argued that there is some cultural misunderstanding that plays into Qutb's assessment of American culture and that his perspective on American football is a misrepresentation of the game. However, recent studies showing the potential long-term effects of playing football and the potential for traumatic brain injuries (TBI) lends some credence to his observations.

Qutb was particularly disturbed by the religious beliefs and practices he encountered in America. He found it difficult to comprehend why there were so many churches in each town especially considering his observation that most people did not attend except for special holidays. This led Qutb to conclude that "there is no one further than the American from appreciating the spirituality of religion and respect for its sacraments, and there is nothing farther from religion than the American's thinking and his feelings and manners."[43] In describing the church service he says:

> You will find it difficult to differentiate between it and any other place. They go to church for carousal and enjoyment, or, as they call it in their language "fun." Most who go there do so out of necessary social tradition, and it is a place for meeting and friendship, and to spend a nice time . . . In most churches there are clubs that join the two sexes, and every minister attempts to attract to his church as many people as possible, especially since there is a tremendous competition between churches of different denominations. And for this reason, each church races to advertise itself with lit, colored signs on the doors and walls to attract attention, and by presenting delightful programs to attract the people much in the same way as merchants or showmen or actors. And there is no compunction about using the most beautiful and graceful girls of the town, and engaging them in song and dance, and advertising . . . The minister does not feel that his job is any different from that of a theater manager, or that of a merchant. Success comes first and before everything, and the means are not important, and this success will reflect on him with fine results: money and stature. The more people that join his church, the greater is his income. Likewise, his respect and recognition is elevated in the community, because the American by his nature is taken with grandeur in size and numbers. It is his first measure of the way he feels and evaluates.[44]

He writes about a church dance he attended where the minister dimmed the lights and played "Baby, it's Cold Outside" on the gramophone before leaving the youth to privately enjoy one another's company. He says that "arms

43. Qutb, "America I have Seen," 9.
44. Qutb, "America I have Seen," 10.

wrapped around waists, lips pressed to lips, and chests pressed to chests. The atmosphere was full of desire."[45]

He was convinced that Christian ministers were using attractive young women as a means to draw young men to their churches. This led Qutb to conclude that American ministers were more concerned about the size of their congregations than the morality and spiritual maturity of those attending. Much like in Egypt, Qutb was especially bothered by the free mixing of genders in America. He titles one section of his essay *The Appearance of the American Temptress*:

> The American girl is well acquainted with her body's seductive capacity. She knows it lies in the face, and in expressive eyes, and thirsty lips. She knows seductiveness lies in the round breasts, the full buttocks, and in the shapely thighs, sleek legs and she shows all this and does not hide it. She knows it lies in clothes: in bright colors that awaken primal sensations, and in designs that reveal the temptations of the body— and in American girls these are sometimes live, screaming temptations! Then she adds to all this the fetching laugh, the naked looks, and the bold moves, and she does not ignore this for one moment or forget it![46]

Qutb found American culture to be hypersexualized. He describes conversations with both males and females who had reduced sexual activity to mere biology and therefore devoid of any moral obligation. While the Americans saw their freedom to explore sexuality as a symbol of intellectual progression, it reminded Qutb of the primitiveness of "the days when man lived in jungles and caves."[47]

Qutb's Return to Egypt

When Qutb returned to Egypt, he was granted the opportunity to effect change following a military coup in 1952. Qutb served as a cultural advisor to the new regime of the Revolutionary Command Council (RCC). He was tasked with reforming the educational curriculum that would shape a new identity of Egyptian nationalism. However, Qutb was no longer interested in developing propaganda inspiring a national identity. His imagined Egypt had Islam as the unifying fabric of society rather than the secular nationalism he had once anticipated. Once Qutb realized his Islamized vision for

45. Qutb, "America I have Seen," 14.
46. Qutb, "America I have Seen," 13.
47. Qutb, "America I have Seen," 5.

Egypt was not shared by the RCC leadership, he left his position of influence to join the Muslim Brotherhood.

Qutb officially joined the Muslim Brotherhood in 1953, and he was quickly promoted to a leadership position within the organization as the head of Islamic Da'wa. Qutb's role was to develop propaganda literature that would recruit the masses towards the Brotherhood's Islamist ideology. Much of what Qutb produced was censored by the Egyptian government. However, outside of Egypt, his calls for an Islamic revival as a means to resist the crusading West was growing in popularity. Qutb's religious propaganda was viewed as a political threat to the nationalist identity put forth by the RCC. In 1954, Qutb and 450 other Brotherhood members were arrested and put in jail.[48] They were eventually released and allowed to meet under the condition that they disengage from all political activity.

Qutb and the Brotherhood were not deterred by the regime's threat of imprisonment. The Brotherhood continued their political activity underground. Qutb began writing and circulating secret tracts exposing the RCC regime's capitulation to Western imperialism.[49] It was not long, however, before the Brotherhood members were rounded up and arrested. This time, the Brotherhood was being charged with conspiring in the attempted assassination of Egyptian President Gamal Abdel Nasser. Qutb denied the Brotherhood's involvement claiming that they were being framed by a "Zionist Crusader."[50] Qutb was tortured in prison while awaiting trial. At one point during his hearing, he lifted his shirt to show the proof of his mistreatment to the prosecutor.[51] Qutb was found guilty and sentenced to fifteen years in prison for his anti-government political activity.

The Impact of Imprisonment on Qutb's Identity

There was a significant shift that took place in Qutb while in prison. Calvert documents some of the torture tactics that were employed against Qutb and the Brotherhood in order to break their Islamist identity:

> Guards suspended prisoners with their arms tied behind their heads, beat them with clubs, or subjected them to the viciousness of attack dogs. As the guards marched arrivals down the

48. Calvert, *Sayyid Qutb and the Origins of Radical Islamism*.

49. Calvert, *Sayyid Qutb and the Origins of Radical Islamism*.

50. Calvert, *Sayyid Qutb and the Origins of Radical Islamism*, 192.

51. Calvert, *Sayyid Qutb and the Origins of Radical Islamism*.

gloomy passageways in chains, they could hear the cries and desperate shouts of fellow Muslim Brothers.[52]

Another event in prison may have had an even deeper psychological effect on Qutb. A rumor was circulated that members of the Brotherhood were going to be executed during their hard labor in the rock quarries. When the men refused to come out of their cells, the guards opened fire, killing twenty-one of Qutb's companions and wounding many more. Qutb was in the infirmary that day because of his failing health. He only learned of the situation when he saw his friends being brought in for treatment, covered in blood. Calvert suggests this was the breaking point for Qutb:

> The massacre elicited terrible emotions in Qutb. He was convinced that 'Abd al-Nasser's agents had encouraged the Brothers to strike in order to justify their murder. Qutb carried within him intense anger and bitterness at the Free Officers. Because of them, he and other Muslim Brothers had endured arrest and torture. He had come to believe that the regime was atheistic and in the grip of Zionists and Western "Crusaders", most especially the United States. All of this rankled. However, the 1957 massacre was the last straw. In his mind, it revealed the true, naked character of the Nasserist revolution. Qutb was full of indignation and outrage.[53]

Qutb's prison experience led him to conclude that the disease resulting in the primitive behaviors he observed in America had already infected Egypt and were spreading. The charitable views of Western intellectualism were abandoned by Qutb, as was his empathy for those who differed from him. In the book, *Milestones*, Qutb outlines a plan to combat Western influence in the Muslim world by restoring Islam to its original glory.

Milestones: A Re-imagined Islamic Identity

Qutb uses his mastery of Romantic literary technique to re-imagine the "unique quranic generation" of the *Rashidun* (the first four Caliphs in Islam) as the embodiment of Islam's original glory. His theoretical framework is an attempt to shift the public discourse towards the revival of a previous imagined community that arranged all areas of life solely on the Qur'an. He argues that this early Muslim community was not unified by

---

52. Calvert, *Sayyid Qutb and the Origins of Radical Islamism*, 197.
53. Calvert, *Sayyid Qutb and the Origins of Radical Islamism*, 202.

national or tribal ties but rather a collective belief; they were united under the banner of Islam.

> In this great Islamic society Arabs, Persians, Syrians, Egyptians, Moroccans, Turks, Chinese, Indians, Romans, Greeks, Indonesians and Africans were gathered together—in short, peoples of all nations and all races. Their various characteristics were united, and with mutual cooperation, harmony and unity, they took part in the construction of the Islamic community and Islamic culture. This marvelous civilization was not an 'Arabic civilization', even for a single day; it was purely an 'Islamic civilization'. It was never a 'nationality' but always a 'community of belief.'[54]

What made the Islamic civilization pure was the source from which the Islamic community derived its sense of being and way of life. According to Qutb, this early Muslim community drank from the single spring of the Holy Qur'an. "The Holy Qur'an was the only source from which they quenched their thirst, and this was the only mould in which they formed their lives."[55] Qutb includes the teachings of Muhammad and his Sunnah as well. He argues that Muhammad embodied the character of the revelations he received and therefore his life and teachings were an offspring of the quranic fountainhead.

The purity of the quranic spring is what sets this generation apart for Qutb. They are distinct from all other Muslim communities in that they never allowed additional sources to direct their daily life. In other words, there was no acculturation in the life of this early Muslim community. There was no syncretism in their religious beliefs and practices because they refused to allow their fountainhead to be diluted with other religions, philosophies, cultures, or civilizations.

For Qutb, the progressive nature of Muhammad's revelations demonstrates that the early Muslim community's daily lives were directed solely by the Qur'an and centered around the worship of God. He argues that verses were given through the Prophet only as situations arose giving the Qur'an a deterministic and transformative power in the life of the Muslim community:

> When a person embraced Islam during the time of the Prophet—peace be on him— he would immediately cut himself off from *Jahiliyyah* (pre-Islamic ignorance). When he stepped into the circle of Islam, he would start a new life, separating himself completely from his past life under ignorance of the Divine

54. Qutb, *Milestones*, 49–50.
55. Qutb, *Milestones*, 16.

Law. He would look upon the deeds during his life of ignorance with mistrust and fear, with a feeling that these were impure and could not be tolerated in Islam! With this feeling, he would turn toward Islam for new guidance; and if at any time temptations overpowered him, or the old habits attracted him, or if he became lax in carrying out the injunctions of Islam, he would become restless with a sense of guilt and would feel the need to purify himself of what had happened, and would turn to the Qur'an to mould himself according to its guidance.[56]

Qutb argues that these Muslims would renounce their former *Jahiliyyah* beliefs, traditions, culture, and even relationships. There was a clear shift in identity that was demonstrated cutting off all influences from their *Jahili* society in favor of a life derived from the revelations given through Muhammad.

Competing Narratives of *Jahiliyyah* and Islamic Identity

Qutb uses the competing narrative identities of *Jahiliyyah* and the unique quranic generation as a metaphorical framework to validate his bifurcated categories of identity:

> We are also surrounded by *Jahiliyyah* today, which is of the same nature as it was during the first period of Islam, perhaps a little deeper. Our whole environment, people's beliefs and ideas, habits and art, rules and laws is *Jahiliyyah*, even to the extent that what we consider to be Islamic culture, Islamic sources, Islamic philosophy and Islamic thought are also constructs of *Jahiliyyah*.[57] ([1964] 2003:20)

Qutb believed that Muslims were deceived into thinking that their societies were Islamic when they were in fact *Jahili*. In his view, there are only two collective identities or societies in the world, the Islamic and the *Jahili*.

> The Islamic society is that which follows Islam in belief and ways of worship, in law and organization, in morals and manners. The *Jahili* society is that which does not follow Islam and in which neither the Islamic belief and concepts, nor Islamic values or standards, Islamic laws and regulations, or Islamic morals and manners are cared for. The Islamic society is not one in which people call themselves 'Muslims' but in which the Islamic law

56. Qutb, *Milestones*, 19.
57. Qutb, *Milestones*, 20.

has no status, even though prayer, fasting and Hajj are regularly observed; and the Islamic society is not one in which people invent their own version of Islam, other than what Allah and His Messenger—peace be on him—have prescribed and explained, and call it, for example, 'progressive Islam.'[58]

Qutb accused the so called "Muslim" societies of practicing *shirk* [a grave sin of adding partners to God]. The charge was not due to their association of a partner with God but for instituting another way of life besides the Divine Shari'ah.

> Although they still believe in the Unity of God, still, they relegated the legislative attribute of Allah Almighty to others and submit to this authority, and from this authority they derive their systems, their traditions and customs, their laws, their values and standards, and almost every practice of life.[59]

In other words, by forcing Muslims to submit to man-made laws, governments were effectively suspending God's sovereignty and dominion on the earth and making all Muslims guilty of idolatry. Qutb argued that only the Divine law of God was to be obeyed by Muslims rather than the man made laws of secular governments.

Qutb applies his binary framework to individuals as well. There are only two individual identities of people in the world: Muslims who have submitted themselves to God and his Messenger and those who follow the way of *Jahiliyyah*. Individuals are either in the "party of God" or of "Satan and rebellion."[60] Qutb believed that many so called "Islamic" societies and individual so called "Muslims" were truly in a state of *Jahiliyyah* because they were drinking from a polluted spring. The corruption of the source meant that Muslims no longer understood the meaning of their faith. He maintained that it is the confession of the creed alone that makes a person a Muslim, but insists that it must penetrate deep into the heart of the individual and be manifested in their behaviors. Qutb argues that the unique quranic generation had such an understanding of the creed:

> They knew very well that the proclamation, 'There is no deity worthy of worship except Allah' was a challenge to that worldly authority which had usurped the greatest attribute of Allah, namely, sovereignty. It was a rebellion against all modes of behaviour which have been devised under this usurpation and was a

58. Qutb, *Milestones*, 93.
59. Qutb, *Milestones*, 82.
60. Qutb, *Milestones*, 117.

declaration of war against that authority which legislates laws not permitted by Allah Almighty. It was no secret to the Arabs—who knew their language very well and knew the real meaning of the message, 'La ilaha illa Allah', what its significance was in relation to their traditions, their rule and their power. Hence they greeted this call, this revolutionary message, with anger, and fought against it with that vigour which is known to everyone.[61]

For Qutb, the very nature of the creed made it politically subversive in that it made God the sole ruler of mankind and no other. He desired that contemporary Muslims would heed this call to overthrow the influences of *Jahiliyyah* that were tainting the pure message of Islam.

Qutb was particularly concerned with Western *Jahili* societies. While they appeared to be civilized because of their scientific and technological advances, Qutb argues that their lack of family values and morality clearly demonstrated their backwardness:

If the family is the basis of the society, the basis of the family is the division of labour between husband and wife, and the upbringing of children is the most important function of the family, then such a society is indeed civilized. In the Islamic system of life, this kind of a family provides the environment under which human values and morals develop and grow in the new generation; these values and morals cannot exist apart from the family unit. If, on the other hand, free sexual relationships and illegitimate children become the basis of a society, and if the relationship between man and woman is based on lust, passion and impulse, and the division of work is not based on family responsibility and natural gifts; if woman's role is merely to be attractive, sexy and flirtatious, and if the woman is freed from her basic responsibility of bringing up children; and if, on her own or under social demand, she prefers to become a hostess or a stewardess in a hotel or ship or air company, thus spending her ability for material productivity rather than in the training of human beings, because material production is considered to be more important, more valuable and more honourable than the development of human character, then such a civilization is 'backward' from the human point of view, or 'Jahili' in the Islamic terminology.[62]

Qutb believed that the gender roles and the intermixing of sexes had a particular deterministic effect on a society. He calls the West's "emancipation of

61. Qutb, *Milestones*, 25.
62. Qutb, *Milestones*, 97–98.

women" a "vulgarity," and insists that the "free mixing of the sexes" is "animal like behavior."[63] The only solution according to Qutb was the Islamic safeguards provided through the institution of a Divine law.

Divine Shari'ah and Jihad

Only when the Divine Shari'ah is instituted can a society be considered truly Islamic according to Qutb. He believed that Shari'ah Law had all the answers necessary for day to day life as well as instruction on how to govern the people, "everything legislated by God for ordering man's life; it includes the principles of belief, principles of administration and justice, principles of morality and human relationships, and principles of knowledge."[64] For Qutb, it is only through obedience to the Divine law that man is able to live in harmony with the created order. This Divine system was to be universally applied throughout the earth in order to provide mankind a sense of peace. It is only through submission to the Divine system that a person can be considered truly Muslim. The Islamic society he envisioned would have the distinction among all other systems of being "based on worship of God alone."[65]

Qutb called upon true Muslims to institute such an Islamic society. Once this Islamic society was established, it would have the responsibility to free other peoples from the *Jahili* societies so that they too could submit themselves to God alone. Qutb believed it was the responsibility of the Islamic society to "annihilate all those political and material powers which stand between people and Islam."[66] They have a "God given right to take control so that it may establish the Divine system on earth."[67] This was to be achieved through waging jihad (holy war). Qutb conceptualized jihad as having both an internal and external component. The believer must first "fight a great battle within himself against Satan, against his own desires and ambitions, his personal interests and inclinations, the interest of his family and of his nation."[68] Qutb believed that once a Muslim society is revived through internal jihad, and Shari'ah Law was the ruling factor in the lives of the people, then the world would see that Islam had something

63. Qutb, *Milestones*, 139.

64. Qutb, *Milestones*, 107.

65. Qutb, *Milestones*, 78.

66. Qutb, *Milestones*, 57.

67. Qutb, *Milestones*, 78.

68. Qutb, *Milestones*, 71.

to offer that all other religions and world systems did not, namely morals, ethics, and values.

In order for the come and see approach to work, an external jihad would need to be waged as well. Only when Muslims were free from the oppressive secular governments that were in place would they be free to devote themselves to God alone. Following the jihad against the secular Muslim governments, the rest of the *Jahili* societies would become the target of jihad. Qutb believed that Islam must be proclaimed to all peoples, and servitude of man-made government institutions must be stopped on a global scale.

> Islam is not a heritage of any particular race or country; this is Allah's religion and it is for the whole world. It has the right to destroy all obstacles in the form of institutions and traditions which limit man's freedom of choice. It does not attack individuals nor does it force them to accept its beliefs; it attacks institutions and traditions to release human beings from their poisonous influences, which distort human nature and which curtail human freedom. It is the right of Islam to release mankind from servitude to human beings so that they may serve Allah alone, to give practical meaning to its declaration that Allah is the true Lord of all and that all men are free under Him.[69]

He argued that God alone is to be the ruler of men; and that when governments stand in the way of men being ruled by God alone, Muslims are to "strike hard at all those political powers which force people to bow before them and which rule over them."[70] This was not a call to forced conversion as Qutb upheld the belief that there should be "no compulsion in religion."[71] However, he did advocate the forceful removal of the obstacles that did not allow people to "accept or reject it [Islam] with an open mind."[72]

Qutb's views of an Islamic society that would reflect the unique quranic generation of the *Rashidun* may be a romanticized re-narration of Islamic history. We must keep in mind that two of the four Caliphs were murdered by fellow Muslims. Granted, the murder of Ali was carried out by those labeled as *Kharijites* (defectors of the Muslim community) because of their refusal to recognize the Caliphate. Ironically, the label of *Kharijite* is often applied to those who uphold Qutb's vision for an Islamic society. The label was also applied to Qutb himself by the Egyptian government for his unwillingness

69. Qutb, *Milestones*, 75.

70. Qutb, *Milestones*, 61.

71. Qutb, *Milestones*, 63.

72. Qutb, *Milestones*, 63.

to recant his writings and support Egyptian nationalism.[73] Qutb refused to accept the label arguing that he would never accuse a Muslim of being a *kafir* (unbeliever) who had made the confession.

Conclusion

A brief look at the life history of Sayyid Qutb demonstrates the effectiveness of conceptualizing identity as relationally constituted at the intersection of personal, global, and sociocultural narratives. Qutb, throughout his life, struggled to reconcile the competing narratives of Western secular modernism and Eastern quranic traditionalism. As a young boy, he seemingly abandons the folk traditions of his village upbringing for the secular model posited in Western secular education. In his early adult life, Qutb recognizes the shortcomings of tribalism that divides his homeland and limits social justice and begins working towards the creation of a national identity. However, Qutb becomes disenchanted with the rise of nationalism when he sees there is no room in the national imagination for his Muslim brothers across the national boundary in Palestine. Qutb, similar to his childhood experiences with the migrant workers, internalized the suffering of others and in turn could not reconcile a personal or collective identity that ignored their plight. Qutb's beliefs were further challenged when he was sent to prison by the government that he spent his life helping to develop and tortured by people who were supposed to be in the same community of faith. It seems fair to suggest that Qutb had an identity crisis during the last decade of his life in prison where he penned *Milestones*.

Given the context, it seems appropriate to read *Milestones* as Qutb's attempt to reconcile his past experiences and imprisonment into a cohesive story that gives meaning to his suffering as well as hope that others may join him in his cause. In other words, *Milestones* is the embodiment of Sayyid Qutb's narrative identity where he is attempting to regain a sense of self that is only dependent upon Islam and the Muslim community as he imagines it. Since Qutb was not able to find a suitable narrative identity within the Egyptian sociocultural stock of stories, he resurrected one from the seventh century. Qutb finds his sense of belonging by transcending time and space and rooting himself in shared beliefs with the seventh century unique quranic generation. He considers himself in relationship to this true Muslim community through faith and "a sacred and eternal bond of love" that surpasses the relationships of even blood relatives.[74] This imagined community transcends

73. Calvert, *Sayyid Qutb and the Origins of Radical Islamism*.
74. Qutb, *Milestones*, 120.

all the identities that had become fractured in Qutb's life. Not only was there no longer a need for national, ethnic, tribal, or familial identity for Qutb, he now believed these groupings contained elements of *shirk* because the groupings were not based upon shared belief.

In addition to reconstructing his beliefs concerning collective identity, Qutb re-narrates the purpose behind his lifelong pursuit of Western education. In doing so he is able to regain a sense of historical continuity that suggests his forty years of Western influenced academia was not wasted:

> The person who is writing these lines has spent forty years of his life in reading books and in research in almost all aspects of human knowledge. He specialized in some branches of knowledge and he studied others due to personal interest. Then he turned to the fountainhead of his faith. He came to feel that whatever he had read so far was as nothing in comparison to what he found here. He does not regret spending forty years of his life in the pursuit of these sciences, because he came to know the nature of *Jahiliyyah*, its deviations, its errors and its ignorance, as well as its pomp and noise, its arrogant and boastful claims. Finally, he was convinced that a Muslim cannot combine these two sources, the source of Divine guidance and the source of *Jahiliyyah*, for his education.[75]

Qutb reframes his educational pursuits as preparation to warn other Muslims to avoid the allures of the West. While Qutb believed that his Islamic consciousness had been purified from the Western influences of his youth, it should be noted that Qutb seems unaware that much of *Milestones* is rooted in Western philosophy. His emphasis on personal identity, personhood, and freedom of choice are influenced more by enlightenment thinkers than the Qur'an.

Qutb was found guilty of sedition and sentenced to death by hanging. It is said that upon receiving his sentencing Qutb said "Praise be to God, I performed jihad for fifteen years until I earned this martyrdom."[76] The death of Sayyid Qutb has only increased the popularity of his writings in the Muslim world. His resurrection of the *Rashidun*, contrasted with *Jahiliyyah*, continues be an effective public narrative of "us" versus "them" around the globe.

---

75. Qutb, *Milestones*, 113.

76. Calvert, *Sayyid Qutb and the Origins of Radical Islamism*, 251.

7

Three Young Men from Kabul

THIS CHAPTER IS A case study of three young men who recently immigrated to the United States from Kabul, Afghanistan. Each of these
research participants received Afghan Special Immigrant Visas (SIV).
The program was initiated to provide a path to American citizenship for
Afghan nationals who assisted the United States Armed Forces during
Operation Enduring Freedom. SIV applicants are required to demonstrate
that they were employed by or on behalf of the United States government
in Afghanistan for a minimum of one year, and that, because of their employment, they face an ongoing and serious threat to their lives in their
countries of origin. Names and specific details of their stories have been
changed in order to protect their identity.

Ibrahim had been living in the United States for less than a year when
we first met. When I told Ibrahim of my research, he immediately recruited
his roommates, Ahmed and Yusuf. My hope was to document the process
of these young men negotiating their Pashtun identity. However, I quickly
realized that I was far more interested in conceptualizing identity through
an ethnic framework than my research participants.

Five minutes into my first visit, Ahmed turns on the TV and begins
streaming YouTube videos from Afghanistan. He quickly filters through
clips until he finds a video of a wedding party dancing the *Attan* (a traditional Pashtun dance). Yusuf begins dancing the *Attan* while his roommates cheer him on. The song ends and a winded Yusuf sits down with us
at the table. As the laughing and joking wane, I expect the young men to
explain the significance of the *Attan* but there is little discussion concerning the meaning of the dance. Rather, these young men simply reminisce
about how they miss going to weddings back in Kabul where dancing the
Attan is a popular pastime with friends. I inquire further, "Does this dance
remind you of your culture back home?" Ahmed's response was telling.
"This isn't really our culture . . . this is a dance they do in the villages."
I reply, "This is a traditional Pashtun dance, isn't it?" They look at me
puzzled. It was as if I had asked a trick question. Yusuf replies, "Anyone

can dance the *Attan*." All three laugh, and Yusuf returns to another *Attan* demonstration.

Yusuf, more than his roommates, loves to dance. There were times I would come by the apartment and the music would be so loud that I would have to wait for the break between songs to knock. He would greet me at the door, sometimes winded and drenched in sweat. For Yusuf, dancing was a way to return home in his imagination. The *Attan* has a special place in his heart, but not because of its ethnic origin. The dance is a reminder of wedding parties and, more specifically, friendships he has back home. He does not associate the *Attan* with Pashtun culture any more than Americans associate the Chicken Dance with Swiss-German culture.[1]

While these young men are using computer mediated communication, particularly social media, to renegotiate and reinforce a sense of transnational identity, it is not rooted in ethnicity but rather the geographical space of Kabul. In fact, these three young men lived together for nearly six months without knowing or discussing each other's ethnic backgrounds. Only Ibrahim's parents are both ethnically Pashtun. Yusuf and Ahmed both have ethnically mixed homes. Yusuf's father is Pashtun, but his mother is Tajik. Ahmed's parents are Uzbek and Tajik. There is a sense of hesitancy with these young men in discussing their ethnic backgrounds. Not only are these young men uninterested in ethnic identity, they are noticeably opposed to categorizing themselves ethnically. This makes sense considering the two who are ethnically mixed, but it is true for Ibrahim as well. All three agree that the ethnic divisions of Afghanistan are problematic, and therefore defining oneself ethnically is uncommon in their experience. They have similar feelings about religious identity. Each of them are highly critical of any ethnic or religious exclusivity. For, Ibrahim, religious exclusivity is a big problem in the world that could be solved if people understood that there is no difference between Islam, Christianity, and Judaism. He explains,

> The Qur'an or the Bible are for our instruction and guidance. There is no difference in any of the four books: Tauraut, Zabur, Injeel or Qur'an. People use these religions as a tool so that they gain power and make money. They use it to convince people to fight for them or motivate them to kill other people for them. The people who are doing this to make money, they know that there is no difference. If you went to my village and I say you are a Christian, they won't like it. They will say, "If he is a Christian then he is an infidel." These people don't know that Christians are following Isa al-salaam, that's Jesus's name in Arabic. The

1. The chicken dance is a popular American wedding party dance that has little to no connection with its Swiss-German roots.

same thing will happen if you are a Jew. If you say, "I am Jewish" they might kill you. But why? They are following the Prophet Musa or Moses. If they knew they were following Musa they would not want to kill them. It is really about money. Here if I say I am a Muslim, they will think to themselves, "You must be a terrorist and you probably beat women." I think it would be better if we didn't look at what people did but what do the books say? Groups like ISIS, what they do is not in the Qur'an, but the people don't know. The books are 99.9 percent the same.

Ibrahim calls himself a Muslim but quickly clarifies that he is not a religious person. He does not want to be associated with the Mullahs in Afghanistan. He believes that the religious elite in Afghanistan are a major part of the problems in the country.

Competing Narratives of Rural Afghanistan and Kabul

When I inquire further about the importance of ethnicity and cultural differences, they tell me that these things only matter in the rural villages of Afghanistan, not in Kabul. Ibrahim explains, "In the city, people are very diverse and educated. In the rural areas people keep separate from each other because of culture." He says this is particularly the case among the Pashtun areas of Afghanistan. Ibrahim is rather critical of the traditional village life, describing it as archaic and unwilling to change. He is particularly critical of the cultural practices concerning gender roles.

> This is quite embarrassing, but in the villages the men eat before the women and the women can only eat after the men are full. The people in Kabul do not like to give their daughters to the village family members because they are afraid of how they would be treated. If you go to my village you cannot even wear pants. You have to wear traditional clothes. The women wear the hijab and you can only see one eye. The husband is the only one allowed to see the whole body. You also have to grow a beard or else you are not considered a man.

Kabul, on the other hand, Ibrahim describes as comparable to New York City. He explains that there is no single nationality or ethnicity in Kabul, rather there are all sorts of peoples from all over the world. Almost inevitably, descriptions of Kabul are in contrast to rural villages. Kabul is depicted as a progressive city very much under the influence of the West, while the villages are associated with being traditional and conservative.

The words traditional and conservative seem to have little connection with morality. For example, Ibrahim shares about a traditional practice in the city of Kandahar that he and the others find morally repulsive. "Some areas of rural Afghanistan, like Kandahar, are famous for really big guys going after beautiful teenage boys." He further explains by telling a popular joke told in Kabul, "If you find money on the street don't bend over to pick it up because maybe someone from Kandahar set a trap for you." Yusuf adds, "It is called *Bacha Bazi*. It means like gay or something." Ibrahim attributes the practices of Kandahar as "traditional." *Bacha Bazi* literally translates "boy play." The practice has outraged many in Kabul but continues without repercussion in parts of rural Afghanistan.

For these young men, the traditional culture and conservative beliefs of rural Afghanistan are not of much value, and in most cases, traditional behaviors are described as backwards. In their opinions, it is the traditional beliefs and culture that keep the rural people separated, and it is often the cause of violence in Afghanistan. Yusuf, Ibrahim, and Ahmed believe that if rural people were educated they may see the value and beauty of diversity and tolerance that is enjoyed in Kabul. In Ibrahim's opinion, many of the historic and present problems of Afghanistan have to do with a lack of education which results in a sort of tribalism that needs to be replaced by the value of diversity, a value he attributes to the West.

The others agree with Ibrahim; on several occasions they describe the rural people as backwards in much of their thinking and practices. Yusuf, like Ibrahim, has strong opinions about the mistreatment of women in rural Afghanistan, "In the village, the women work at home, and only the men go outside. Daughters are not even allowed to go to school or university." He further discusses how women are treated like property. Ibrahim agrees, saying that in rural villages, wealth is demonstrated by how many wives you can support. He recalls hearing how his grandfather took an additional wife to gain a particular place of power within his village. According to Ibrahim, success in the villages is associated with power. In his experience, an individual's power is dependent upon how many males are in the family to protect family interest. He contrasts this with Kabul where he asserts that the success of an individual is measured by the quality of their education and employment as well as material possessions. When I ask if any of them would consider marrying a girl from their family villages, they answer emphatically, "no." Marriage with someone in the village would mean a stronger connection with their village relatives. Neither they nor their families in Kabul are interested in strengthening that bond.

Each of the guys agree that visiting villages was not something Kabul residents desire to do very often. Their reasoning was largely because of the disparity in cultural expressions and the potential danger they could encounter while visiting. These three young men have little positive to say about rural Afghanistan or the cultural traditions that are preserved in the villages. Each of them have extended families in villages, but their interactions with them were intentionally limited. As far as they could tell, the primary relationship between those who lived in Kabul and their rural extended family members was limited to financial support or providing housing when someone came to Kabul for a short visit. Even the practice of hospitality in the villages was something that Ibrahim saw as impractical for those living in Kabul:

> If you come to my house in Kabul, I can provide you food, and I can keep you one or two days because everyone is busy. But, if you go to the village you can stay with them for years and they won't even ask when you are going to leave their house. They are very connected to their traditional culture.

Neither Ibrahim, Yusuf, nor Ahmed believe relationships with extended family members in villages are important to their daily lives. The dangerous travel conditions outside of Kabul provided legitimate excuses for not visiting their village relatives. Yusuf describes how his Uncle had been kidnapped while returning from Kabul to the village:

> He was driving back to the village from Kabul and a car stopped him and took him. They called my family and said to give them $100,000 or they would kill him. After one week, the government caught the people who did it. The main guy was our own relative. Now he is spending his life in jail.

The others agree with Yusuf and explain that this is a common practice in rural Afghanistan. The assumption is that if you live in Kabul, then you are rich, and, therefore, at risk of being kidnapped. Whether or not safe travel routes would increase their interaction with their village relatives is debatable considering their negative beliefs regarding traditional culture. While multiple examples are given to explain the superiority of Kabul over the rural villages, one that continually rises to the surface is a disdain for village homogeneity when compared to the diversity of Kabul.

Competing Narratives of America and Kabul

Interestingly, these young men associate the diversity of Kabul with Western influence. However, during their first six months in America, their belief that ethnic plurality is a Western value is challenged. Upon entering the United

States, these young men were resettled into a low-income apartment complex. According to them, their neighbors were primarily African American, Latino, and other refugees. They were disappointed that the social gatherings, at least in their perception, were centered around racial or ethnic boundaries. They had hoped to make a variety of friends, like they had back in Kabul, but instead, they found themselves only welcomed by fellow Afghans. They were thankful for the small Afghan community, but they felt isolated from the broader American community. Yusuf tells me how some of his Afghan friends who came to America for college warned him not to come. "They said 'don't go there because you will feel homeless.' I have been trying to adjust, but I miss my home." In six months, none of the three have made any significant friendships with Americans. At first, they wondered whether it was because they were Muslim immigrants. However, they eventually conclude that it is more likely that American culture is not friendly. Ibrahim explains:

> Here it is really quiet and very slow. We grew up in the middle of Kabul city—it is like New York, busy all the time, very crowded with people. Here you don't see people on the street, neighbors do not talk to each other. We have a neighbor and a couple of times we said hi and she just ignored us. I don't think it is because we are Afghani. I think neighbors here just don't talk to each other. In our culture, you have to have respect for your neighbor. If your neighbor is sick or has a need, you have to try to help them. Even if you are not in a position to help them, still you have to try your best. That's the culture. I think it comes from the religion. It does not matter in Kabul what the ethnic background of your neighbor is; you care for them because they are your neighbor.

I was able to experience some of this during my visits. Almost nightly one of the married Afghan neighbors brings them food. One particular neighbor, a Pashtun named Amman, shares with me that the Afghan families are concerned that if they do not send food, the young guys may not eat. He jokes that he was not sure whether or not they know how to cook. He further explains that his wife regularly makes food for a single Afghan mother as well. Amman was unaware of the ethnic backgrounds of his Afghan neighbors.

Public Narratives of Christianity and Islam and the Impact of Acculturation

In addition to the lack of diversity, Ibrahim, Yusuf, and Ahmed discuss the difficulties of adjusting to the overt displays of Western immorality they regularly encounter. Ibrahim's most shocking experience since moving to America happened at Gold's Gym: "I had never seen a woman naked dancing her body in front of me. She only had on two small pieces of cloth to cover her special parts. The rest of her was naked!" Yusuf had not been to the gym but he too was overwhelmed with the culture of sexual promiscuity. He was shocked to see the number of women who have children but no husbands. He recalls one interaction with a neighbor in his apartment complex:

> She told me she was not married but she had two kids. I asked her, "How can you have two kids and still be single?" She replied, "One night stands." I didn't know what that meant when she said it. But it really shocked me to find out that people are having sex before marriage. My friend told me that finding a girl who is eighteen years old and is still a virgin is very rare. This really shocked me.

Their initial perception of American culture is that it is chaotic and dangerous. Life in the United States was not what they anticipated, and they are experiencing a great deal of culture shock.

Someone told them that America used to be more traditional when people upheld Christian values. That same person invited them to a church service, but they found themselves disillusioned there as well. They had hoped to meet people who shared their conservative values, particularly when it came to gender roles. However, as they entered the sanctuary, they were immediately consumed with the way women dressed. Yusuf was surprised that none of the women were wearing head coverings. He shares that he had studied the Bible while he was living in Afghanistan, and that he did not understand why none of the women were wearing the *hijab* (head covering) like the Bible commanded. Yusuf is referring to 1 Corinthians 11:1–16 where the Apostle Paul commends the church in Corinth for upholding the tradition of women wearing head coverings.

By and large, American evangelicals do not wear head coverings. The Council of Biblical Manhood and Womanhood (CBMW), a conservative evangelical proponent for complementarianism, suggests that a head covering is not a timeless symbol of feminine submission and therefore unnecessary. Instead, the CBMW encourages Christians to look for "culturally appropriate expressions of masculinity and femininity" in order to demonstrate the created order of submission and headship.[2] Ironically, one could argue that the CBMW is ignoring the broader global and historical understanding of the head covering in favor of the influence of American feminism. This of course begs the question as to who should

2. Piper and Grudem, *Central Concerns about Manhood and Womanhood,* 50.

determine whether or not something is culturally relevant. While the majority of American Christians may agree that the head covering is not an American cultural symbol of submission, the lack of head coverings was a stumbling block for Yusuf, Ibrahim, and Ahmed. These young men represent a microcosm of an increasing global phenomenon of acculturation due to mass migration. This increasing integration of cultures may require a fresh look at contextual theology to determine what practices are culturally appropriate expressions of faith.

It was not only the lack of head coverings that were a distraction for these young men. "Church was like a party," according to Yusuf. "Lots of ladies were wearing necklaces and short shorts to show off their style." Ibrahim agrees, "The ladies' clothes grab your attention." He goes on to explain that in his view, women are very attractive to men and they dress in a way that the devil can use to distract the men from reading the Bible or worshiping.

Yusuf shares how, after the service, one person asked him to explain the Qur'an to him. He replied, "That is not something we can discuss in one hour. We need at least one year to discuss the Qur'an." The person then proceeded to explain the Bible to him, and, according to Yusuf, he was trying to convert him by convincing him that Christianity was better for him than Islam. Yusuf was not convinced. On the contrary, they left the church more convinced of Islam's superiority. In addition to what they considered inappropriate clothing, the guys were surprised by how Christians handled their Bibles. Ibrahim feels that they had no respect for the Bible. He explains:

> When we carry the Qur'an, we carry it with respect. We use a cover and we put it on the top [points to the table]. But in the church, I saw that the Bible was here [points to ground]. I even picked up a couple of the Bibles and put it on top because this was disrespectful. We believe in all four books, and it is disrespectful when you see a Bible lying in front of you on the floor. These are words from God. You can't leave them on the floor. You even have to clean your body, your hands and mouth before you read the Qur'an. I don't know how it works in church but I was really surprised when I saw Bibles lying everywhere.

The experience at church was further confirmation for these young men that America was not the place they imagined. In some respects, their church experience challenged their views of religious plurality. While they had no intention of visiting any more churches, they did express gratitude for one church member, a former missionary, who stops by their apartment for an occasional visit.

I visited the church three times on my own to observe what they experienced. It is a conservative, non-denominational church with a mix of traditional and contemporary worship. Ironically, this particular church has a reputation for having a *significant* emphasis on cross-cultural missions. According to the missions' pastor, more than half the congregation has been on an international mission trip. Regardless, the religious expressions in this particular church were not conservative enough for the young men to feel comfortable.

Neither Yusuf, Ibrahim, nor Ahmed seem aware of their own ethnocentrism as they described their experiences in America. Initially, their mutual condemnation of the rural villagers for being too conservative and the Americans for not being conservative enough may seem hypocritical. However, it may be that the dissonance between these spaces is an attempt to develop a new narrative to help cope with their present struggle to belong. Polarizing rural Afghanistan and America seems to help reinforce their imagined, and arguably idealized, city of Kabul at the center of this tension. The best parts of America were interlaced with the best parts of rural Afghanistan in their descriptions of Kabul despite the fact that the best parts of America were being consistently disconfirmed in their actual experiences. One way of alleviating this mental conflict was for Yusuf, Ibrahim, and Ahmed to imagine that their current problems would be alleviated if they moved to larger city in the United States.

Lack of Meaningful Work

As previously mentioned, Ibrahim, Yusuf, and Ahmed worked for or on behalf of the United States government in Afghanistan. Each of them believe that their jobs in Afghanistan were a significant contribution to their homeland. All three had fled the city of Kabul in their youth when the Taliban took over, and all three returned as young adults when the Taliban were removed. Each of them recall watching the news reports of the U.S. invasion and, upon returning to Kabul, all three secured jobs hoping to assist in rebuilding the Afghan government.

Each of them had what they considered to be prestigious high paying jobs in Afghanistan. Both Ibrahim and Yusuf worked for defense contractors in Kabul and Ahmed worked directly with the military as a translator. Both Ibrahim and Yusuf have professional degrees, and they self-describe as being some of the highest paid Afghan civilian contractors in Kabul. Neither Ibrahim nor Yusuf are able to find work in their field of study. Ibrahim is currently working as a grocery bagger while he continues sending out resumes. Both Yusuf and Ahmed are working in fast-food restaurants. While they are all grateful to have jobs, none of them are finding much meaning in their current employment.

Transnationalism through Computer Mediated Communication

Computer mediated communication back home may be a barrier to Ibrahim, Yusuf, and Ahmed integrating into American society. They spend a significant amount of time on social media with family and friends back in Kabul. It is rare to see Ahmed not wearing his Bluetooth ear piece. Sometimes he has friends or family connect with him through Skype just so he can listen to their conversations as if he were sitting with them in the room. The ability to maintain significant relationships back in Kabul through social media may be hindering them from pursuing meaningful relationships in their new sociocultural context. What they miss most about home is not necessarily the culture but the city of Kabul, more specifically, the relationships they left in Kabul.

All three are homesick and are struggling to cope with their sadness. They do not feel like they belong in America, but they know that they cannot return to Afghanistan. The disconfirmation of the America that they imagined has resulted in them believing they are trapped. In one of my visits, I ask, "besides dancing the *Attan*, what makes you feel better?" Almost without hesitation, they reply "music!" They share three songs that are repeatedly playing on YouTube in their apartment. All three songs have one thing in common. The common denominator is surprisingly not culture or language. The songs are in Dari, Pashto, and English. The common theme in all three songs is the city of Kabul. Here are some of the lyrics translated by Ibrahim: "Kabul is heaven on earth. No other city in the world can compete with my beautiful Kabul, including Paris and London." Ibrahim further explains the allure of Kabul:

> It's not because Kabul is very modern, but there is a deep connection for a lot of Afghans. Friends in Kabul are different. If you have a friend there, they are friends forever. Even after my dad died, his friends would still come to my house to check on us and take care of us.

The band that the guys were most excited about is Kabul Dreams, the first rock band in Afghanistan. Kabul Dreams is a three-man band with whom Ibrahim, Yusuf, and Ahmed have a lot in common, maybe more

than they realize. Not only is the band named after the dream to some-
day return to Kabul, but each band member is also from a different ethnic
background. They all speak different mother tongues of Uzbek, Pashto, and
Dari. Each of the three band members were forced to flee Kabul in their
youth because of the Taliban, and all three returned to Kabul after the U.S.
occupation. The band's Facebook page says, "You destroyed, we will build
back up." Similarly, they are also now living abroad after receiving regular
death threats from the Taliban. The band members, much like Ibrahim,
Yusuf, and Ahmed, imagine a day when Kabul will be restored to peace.
In order for that to take place, the ethnic and tribal identities need to be
replaced by a new sociocultural narrative of national identity.

The competing narratives of ethnic, tribal, and national identities in
Afghanistan are prevalent in Kabul. The country of Afghanistan, and more
specifically the residents of Kabul, have endured national, ethnic, tribal, and
religious violence for almost half a century. The complexity of the ethnic
and tribal diversity is summarized well in the fiction novel *A Thousand
Splendid Suns* by Afghan-American Khaled Hosseini:

> Though Tariq and his parents were ethnic Pashtuns, they spoke
> Farsi when Laila was around for her benefit, even though Laila
> more or less understood their native Pashto, having learned it in
> school. Babi said that there were tensions between their people
> the Tajiks, who were a minority, and Tariq's people, the Pash-
> tuns, who were the largest ethnic group in Afghanistan. Tajiks
> have always felt slighted, Babi had said. *Pashtun kings ruled this
> country for almost two hundred and fifty years, Laila, and Tajiks
> for all of nine months, back in 1929. And you,* Laila had asked,
> *do you feel slighted, Babi?* Babi had wiped his eyeglasses clean
> with the hem of his shirt. *To me, it's nonsense and very danger-
> ous nonsense at that all this talk of I'm Tajik and you're Pashtun
> and he's Hazara and she's Uzbek. We're all Afghans, and that's all
> that should matter. But when one group rules over the others for
> so long . . . There is contempt. Rivalry. There is. There always has
> been.* Maybe so. But Laila never felt it in Tariq's house, where
> these matters never even came up. Her time with Tariq's family
> always felt natural to Laila, effortless, uncomplicated by differ-
> ences in tribe or language, or by the personal spites and grudges
> that infected the air at her own home.[3]

Hosseini himself does not identify as any one ethnicity. In a recent interview concerning his portrayal of ethnic identities in Afghanistan he

---

3. Hosseini, *Thousand Splendid Suns*, 116–17.

explained his position, "I'm not pure anything. There's a Pashtun part of me [and] a Tajik part of me."[4] In another interview, when asked if he considers himself Afghan or American, he responds by saying "I'm not sure whether those distinctions are all that useful."[5]

Much like Ibrahim, Yusuf, and Ahmed, Hosseini conceptualizes identity as relational and at the same time geographic because of the location of the relationships:

> Roots are everything, you're not defined by your individual persona and your behavior, you're also defined, not only by who your parents are but who your grandparents were, who your great grandparents were. So, it's that ancestry, that sense of belonging to a tradition or lineage is so central to your identity, to how people understand and view you. To lose that or have it suddenly interrupted is really a traumatic experience.[6]

Hosseini's novels have sold more than 38 million copies world-wide. He shares how his novels are in some sense his own story told through fictional characters. As a UNHCR representative, he encourages other refugees to begin writing their stories in order to inform the world of the plight of the refugee.

Conclusion

Researchers have argued that *Pashtunwali* is the chief identity marker for the Pashtun (see Ch. 2). I considered the possibility that Ibrahim, having both a Pashtun father and mother, was possibly holding back a more reified Pashtun identity so not to offend his roommates who are not fully Pashtun. I waited until one evening when we were alone and I asked him, "Ibrahim, what is *Pashtunwali*?" His initial response was, "Have you seen the movie *Lone Survivor*?" I had seen the film but I asked him to further explain:

> Kabul is different. It has changed, but if you go to the countryside it is the same. If you go to someone's house they will protect you. Even if you kill someone's brother and you go to their house, they will forgive you. It's called *nanawat*. People won't go though, because they have too much pride. Sometimes in the villages, people have long-time enemies, even for more than one hundred or two hundred years. So, if I go to a village

4. Trantor, "Remaking Home."
5. "Kite Runner Author Khaled Hosseini on Identity."
6. "Kite Runner Author Khaled Hosseini on Identity."

somebody could shoot me and if I ask, "Why did you shoot me?" He might say, "Your grandfather shot one of our family members." Tribes are doing this. I think maybe they have it here too, like in Texas and other places?

That sums it up well. Ibrahim sees the traditional Pashtun identity in the way some Americans would describe the backwoods of Texas or the *hollers* of West Virginia. I found Yusuf's reference to Texas as ironic considering approximately half of my extended family resides in the rural parts of this state. *Pashtunwali* means no more to Ibrahim than the Wild West means to me.

I set out to document the renegotiation of Pashtun identity for Yusuf, Ibrahim, and Ahmed. Instead I found three young men who were uninterested and at times, even opposed to conceptualizing identity within an ethnic framework. Much of the pain in their lives was interpreted as a result of ethnic divisions. Therefore, they would rather see themselves as Afghans. The public narrative of a National Afghan identity was deeply rooted in each of their stories. These young men believed it was time for Afghans to lay down their ethnic identities which were rooted in differences in exchange for a unified Afghanistan.

What drew these young men together was not an ethno-linguistic affinity but rather a mutual love for Kabul, Afghanistan, a shared sense of suffering, and collective refugee experience. What Ibrahim, Yusuf, and Ahmed may be experiencing is a reconceptualization of geographical space through the lens of relationships. It is not so much the city of Kabul that they are longing for; it is instead what Kabul symbolizes. Geographer Doreen Massey suggests that rather than thinking of space as flat, we should view it like a pin cushion where every pin represents a story:

> The specificities of space are a product of interrelations— connections and disconnections—and their (combinatory) effects. Neither societies nor places are seen as having any timeless authenticity. They are, and always have been, interconnected and dynamic.[7]

In other words, space is relational. Places like Kabul can be imagined or conceptualized through the meaningful relationships that constitute the city. The narrative identities of people in a space means that space is constantly under construction. While all three young men hope one day to return to Kabul, the truth is that they can never go back and expect it to be the same. That would require the relationships they left not to have changed. A return

7. Massey, *For Space*, 67.

to the same place, according to Massey, would deprive everyone back home of continuing forward in their story.[8]

As for their shared experience of suffering, much of their hardships are associated with ethnic identity. They were forced to flee Kabul because of the ethnically Pashtun Taliban. Ibrahim, Yusuf, and Ahmed all recall being treated poorly in the societies where they temporarily resettled despite the fact that they had a shared ethno-linguistic background with the people in their host society. Ethno-linguistic identity granted them no special privileges. This was particularly the case for Ibrahim. Being fully Pashtun meant nothing to the Taliban, and the hospitality from his Pashtun neighbors in Pakistan had a limit for those who came from the other side of the national boundary line in Afghanistan. Both Yusuf and Ibrahim had permanent effects reminding them of their hardship. Ibrahim was shot in the leg by a member of the Taliban while flying a kite on a rooftop and Yusuf has a permanent stammer in his speech that he attributes to the trauma of being a child refugee.

Finally, these three young men have a shared experience of transience. Upon returning to Afghanistan after the U.S. invasion, all three worked with the coalition and were forced to flee for a second time. Now they find themselves again as refugees in the United States longing for their home in Kabul. All three hope one day to return to Kabul to help educate the rural peoples about the dangers of ethnic and religious violence. Ibrahim shared how he hopes one day that the rural villages of Afghanistan will reflect Kabul, a city he describes as wonderfully cosmopolitan. For now, it is only an imagined public narrative considering a 2016 United Nations report documented 22,941 civilian deaths and 40,993 injured in Afghanistan from 2009 to 2016. In the meantime, Ibrahim, Yusuf, and Ahmed share in a virtual return to their homeland through singing, dancing, and regular interaction with their friends and family back home via computer mediated communication.

8. Massey, *For Space*.

8

Life History of Alan

THE NUMBER OF DISPLACED Afghans has fluctuated over the past forty years. Estimates have varied from as high as 6 million in the 1990s to the current estimate of 2.5 million. This chapter focuses on the life history of one of these displaced Afghans who left Afghanistan in 1992 for Pakistan. Although he eventually returned to Afghanistan following the overthrow of the Taliban, he once again was forced to flee the country and now resides in the United States with his wife and three children. I reserve analysis until the end of the chapter in order not to detract from Alan's story.

> I still remember the day when we left the house in Kabul. I was nine. Me, my mom, my siblings, and my aunt left the house and went to Jalalabad. We rode in buses. Eventually things got bad there too, and we had to leave for Pakistan. We left everything. I remember my father couldn't come with us because he was a soldier in the Afghan army. He was stuck between two political parties that wanted power. He was stuck in Kabul. I remember my mom and I were crying because we thought he was gone.

For Alan, the most difficult thing was not leaving the city but leaving without knowing what would happen to his father. They left in a hurry, and he did not get to say goodbye. After two years had passed without contact, Alan recalls making a decision that he had to stop thinking about his father because he assumed he was dead. He can still remember feeling disillusioned when he heard his father had arrived in the refugee camp where he, his mother, and his siblings were living.

> I was playing outside and one of my cousins came and said to me, "Hey, your father has come!" I was like, father? What is he talking about? When I saw him, he kissed me and then put me in his lap and he just patted my head. I was crying. He just kept patting my head. I remember that scene. He had shrapnel in his arm from a big bullet or a mortar, I'm not really sure. I just remember his arm was in a sling. He wasn't bleeding, but I

knew he was hurt. My father was able to escape from the mujahideen after the coup. Someone gave him a hiding place in
their home for two nights, and on the third night they drove
him somewhere near the Pakistani border and dropped him
off. He walked for seven days before he found us. After he came,
we started a new life in Pakistan. We bought a house because
we weren't going to be going back. I remember my dad started
a small shop selling fruits and vegetables. We had to start life
over. I remember that was a hard time.

Alan says that he remembers his father always remaining positive.
Alan knew it was hard, but he could not articulate how he was aware of the
difficulty. It did not seem to bother Alan's father that he went from being a
high-ranking officer in the Afghan army to a shop keeper. Alan remembers
trying to stay positive as well. He knew his dad wanted them to be happy in
Pakistan even though it was not their home.

Transnational Narratives through Film

Over time, Alan's dad was able to make enough money to buy a small home
for his family. It was not like their large home in Kabul, but it was comfortable. What Alan remembers most about the home was the television set. It
was his favorite pastime. Alan did not know it then, but the television would
be instrumental in preparing him for his future.

I loved American movies. In Pakistan, I used to watch the show
CHiPs. The one with the motorcycle cops. Every Sunday night
I would watch the drama from 9–10. I loved watching CHiPs. I
would watch it all by myself. I would watch all kinds of American movies. I was a teenager, and I thought these guys were so
cool. Chasing bad people, going fast on motorcycles, I can still
remember loving CHiPs.

Alan attended a refugee school in Pakistan that was set up by Germans
specifically for Pashtun speakers. Because of Alan's love for American television and movies, he quickly became proficient in English. According to
Alan, it was not long before he was one of the best English speakers in
the entire school. He recalls being asked by his teachers to sit up front
and volunteer to demonstrate his English ability when foreign diplomats
would visit the school. He jokes that it had little to do with the school, but
he didn't say anything because he liked the attention. He remembers one

visiting foreigner who had a connection with the school taking his picture
as the model refugee student.

Returning to Kabul

Alan graduated from high school in Pakistan. Nearly ten years had passed
since leaving Kabul. He remembers thinking that his family would probably
never return to Afghanistan because, since their departure, the Taliban had
taken power in Kabul. Alan had a particular disdain for the Taliban despite
the fact that they were primarily Pashtun.

> When we left, the mujahideen had power, but they lost it to the
> Taliban. The Taliban had power for like seven years. It's like a
> big political game in Afghanistan. It's a game with Pakistan. The
> Taliban came from the Pakistani ISI. They are like the American
> CIA. It's the same thing, but in Pakistan they call it the ISI. They
> sent the Taliban to take power from the mujahideen. The Tali-
> ban are bad people because they are killing people for no reason.
> They cut people's heads off for no reason.

Alan says that 9/11 was a turning point in his life. Not so much the event
itself but the subsequent invasion of Afghanistan. Alan, for the first time in
ten years, had a sense of hope that he might be able to return to Kabul. He
was glad to see the Taliban overthrown.

> That night when it [9/11] happened, I was at a wedding party.
> The band stopped playing and someone put on the radio and
> they announced how two big planes hit the towers in America.
> We were like, "What big towers?" We didn't know what they
> meant so we were like, "Whatever." It wasn't until the next
> morning when I turned on my TV to watch the news. I used
> to love watching the news, I still do. But, I turned on the news,
> and I saw the big plane hit the tower and boom. Then the other
> one came and boom. I was like, "What is going on over there?"
> I don't remember when they [America] attacked Afghanistan,
> but, I remember we were watching the American jets drop big
> bombs on the Taliban in Afghanistan and we were like, "Yeah!"
> We were happy. I remember seeing on TV when troops were
> dropped off by big Chinook helicopters. They were carrying big
> duffle bags and they had on uniforms. I was like, "Dude, that's
> good, I wish I was a soldier like that!"

Following the overthrow of the Taliban, a provisional government under Hamid Karzai was established in December of 2001. Alan's family returned to Kabul the following Spring in 2002.

> The Taliban was gone. Karzai was calling to everyone saying, "Who lives somewhere in a far country? It's time to come back! Welcome to our own house. Welcome to our own country! Come back so we can start working on building our own country!" So, since my father was in the army before and Karzai was trying to build back the army, we moved back. My father told me, "It's our country. We need to go back and start our country."

Although Alan spent almost a decade in Pakistan, leaving was not difficult. Most of Alan's friends were refugees who were also returning to Kabul. He remembers being excited to go back, though he did not know what to expect.

> After ten years of living in Pakistan, I was ready to go home. It took three days and three nights to drive from Pakistan to Kabul because the roads were destroyed. I was asleep when we first arrived in Kabul. I remember my father telling me, "Wake up, we're home!" When I opened my eyes, I couldn't believe it. The power poles had bullet holes all over. So many of the buildings were destroyed, trucks on the street were burned. It was like, everything is gone. We went back to our house, but the house was gone. It was hit by rockets. We still had a roof and some walls, but that was pretty much it. I remember we had a front door, and it was closed even though the house was missing walls. I can still remember my father opening the door and looking for something. It was his army hat. After 10 years, it was still there. It was sad. There was nothing left in the home. They took everything. It wasn't just us. The whole city was destroyed. Everyone came back to find nothing.

It was like starting a new life according to Alan. He recalls his father remaining positive and saying things like, "We have our property and most of our home. That's good, right?" Alan remembers thinking, "Yeah, that's good thing."

Alan helped his father rebuild their lives in Kabul. He remembers how his father used to bring plants and flowers to make the house beautiful again. Alan also recalls how they had to buy everything new. "New carpets. New dishes. New everything." Alan's father was given a promotion when he returned to active duty in the army but according to Alan, "The pay was like nothing but fortunately everything was cheap at that time."

Joining the Fight to Rebuild Afghanistan

Alan knew he would need to find a job quickly so he could help his father provide for the family. However, Alan's father wanted him to go to college so that he could get a good job. Alan thought college would be an unnecessary financial burden on the family.

> I told my dad that, "I don't need to go to college. It will be too much to support me in college and the rest of the family." I was like, "If I go to college it will cost you lots of money. You will have to give me money to go there every day. You will have to pay for books, pens, pencils, notebooks that all cost money." My dad was like, "It's okay, let me see what I can do. I want you to go to college." So, I was like, "Alright." I went to college to take the entry exam and put down all the wrong answers. I told my dad that I didn't want to go anyways. I wanted to work with him in the army, you know. I told him, "I want to work with you shoulder to shoulder."

Alan told his father that he wanted to apply to become a translator for the United States Army, but he needed three months to prepare himself. He asked his father to support him with $20 a month to pay for English conversation classes and a stockpile of American films. His father gave him enough money to purchase a used laptop as well. For three months Alan immersed himself in American movies. He watched the films with the closed captioning turned on. He kept a dictionary on hand in case there was a word he did not recognize. When a word appeared that he had never heard, he would look it up and make a note.

Alan prefers action films. *Rambo III* is a particular favorite because it takes place amidst the Afghan-Russian war. Though I had seen the film as a child, I did not recall the plot or any references to Afghanistan. However, after reviewing the film, I can see why it was so impactful for Alan. One scene in particular includes a Pashtun guide explaining the history of Afghanistan to Rambo:

> This is Afghanistan. Alexander the Great tried to conquer this country, then Genghis Khan, then the British, now Russia. But the Afghan people fight hard. They will never be defeated. An ancient enemy made a prayer about these people, do you wish to hear? [Rambo nods yes] Very good. It says: "God deliver us from the venom of the cobra, the teeth of the Tiger, and the vengeance of the Afghan." Do you understand what this means?

[Rambo replies] That you guys don't take any shit. Yes [the Pashtun guide says smiling], something like this![1]

Alan loved the idea of justice, and he also liked the idea of being in the military. He is not sure why it was so interesting to him, but he always remembers having a fascination with the American military since he was a boy.

After three months of intensive American film immersion, Alan had a chance to apply for a job that would place him alongside American soldiers. His father secured him a job interview with a company hiring Afghan interpreters to assist the U.S. military. Upon arriving, Alan was given a magazine that had articles in three languages: English, Dari, and Pashto. He was told to translate a variety of pages into the other two languages. Despite the fact that the majority of Alan's training was auditory, he passed the exam. He said it was easy.

> After I passed, they sent me to do biometrics. They took a picture of my eyes and took my finger prints. They said they wanted to make sure I wasn't linked with bad people. The American guy who interviewed me, I remember he had a tooth pick in his mouth, he spoke perfect Dari. He said he had been living in Afghanistan for two years. After my interview, they printed my badge, but they didn't give it to me. They said to go home and wait for the company to call.

Alan sat at home for two weeks waiting. He began to wonder if maybe he did not do as well as he originally thought.

> I was sitting at the house when they called me. I was like, "Hello." Some guy said, "Is this Alan?" I said "Yes, this is Alan." He said, "Alright bro, get ready and come tomorrow at 2 o'clock. We got you a job." I was like, "Alright, thank you!" When I hung up, I called my mom. "Mom, mom, I got a job!" I was so excited. My family was so excited. We were happy. Mom was really happy. But she didn't know that I was going to be going to Kandahar. At that time, I didn't know I was going to Kandahar.

Initially, Alan thought he was going to be working in Kabul. When he arrived, he met twenty-one other Afghan interpreters. They were all told to report to Camp Phoenix that afternoon, but no one knew anything else. After being patted down, they were brought onto the base and told they would be outfitted with U.S. military uniforms and gear. Alan suddenly felt scared.

---

1. MacDonald, *Rambo III*.

> I remember saying, "What is this guy talking about? We're not soldiers. Why do we need boots? Why do we need uniforms? We're not in the army . . . are we?" One of the soldiers who heard me talking said, "You guys are terps [slang for interpreters], you're here to do translation between the American army and Afghan army." I was like, "Oh, good, I thought you were sending us somewhere for fighting!"

Once he knew he was not going to be fighting, Alan started to enjoy getting geared up. He was issued two pairs of boots, two uniforms, a sleeping bag, and a pack.

> It felt cool getting the gear and the uniform. It was like when I saw that Chinook helicopter dropping off the soldiers on television back in Pakistan. They were all walking and carrying big duffle bags like the ones they were giving us.

He remembers thinking that the amount of gear seemed excessive because he was trying to figure out where he was going to keep this stuff back home. Suddenly, the lead soldier spoke up:

> "Does everyone have what they need?" We were like, "Yeah." Then he was like, "Line up! This bus will be taking you to a transit station, and from there you will be going to Kandahar." I was like, "What? Not me!" Everybody started asking questions like "Why are we going to Kandahar?" We were like, "It's like six hours away and it is almost dark!" If we got stopped carrying U.S. military gear in one of these provinces, it would be bad. We were thinking, "The Taliban is still around. They may not be in power, but they are still around. If they see us traveling in this bus, they may not do anything to us. But they can still call people and report that we are helping the U.S. Army."

Alan and the others were told not to worry. They were going to have a military escort, and all the travel routes were secure. Still, some of the guys talked about quitting. Alan remembers everyone being scared. He recalls talking with some of the guys who wanted to quit.

> I was like, "I am not quitting and neither should you." I was thinking, "I need to support my family and $500 a month is a lot of money. I also need to help my country. I've never supported my country. Now I have a chance, and I don't want to lose this chance."

One particular translator confided in Alan that he was afraid to die. Alan tried to convince him to stay by saying, "Death is in God's hands. When you are born, God already knows when and how you are going to die." Alan's pep talk didn't work. The translator he tried to encourage, along with four others, refused to load the bus to Kandahar.

Good Days Killing Bad Guys and Bad Days Losing Good Guys

Alan and the other interpreters who remained arrived in Kandahar just before midnight. He recalls that, initially, there was not much to do and he had a lot of free time. All the translators lived together on the military compound. Their sleeping quarters were separate from the other soldiers', but they had shared access to the other facilities.

> Everything was free. Free food. Free laundry. We were just chilling there for like two weeks with nothing to do. After like two weeks, a team came through that needed a linguist. One of the officers came to the linguist village and said to me and my buddy, "What's up guys! You ready!?" We were like, "Yes sir!" He was like, "Alright then follow me!" We took our duffle bags and put them in a Humvee and went on our first mission to translate.

Alan's first job was assisting the Afghan Army Apache helicopter crews understand U.S. military protocol. He enjoyed being a mediator between the two armies.

> It was a hard job, but I loved it. Two different armies working together, shoulder to shoulder, that's awesome. My job was to make a connection and build the relationship between two armies because we had the same target, support our country and kill bad people.

While Alan appreciated his mediating role between the two armies, when the opportunity to translate for a special forces team arose, he, along with his best friend Maheer, couldn't resist volunteering.

> Working with special forces was fun. Our mission was chasing bad people. That was our only mission. There were bad days and good days. Bad days because we would lose too many friends by IEDs [improvised explosive devices] and sometimes ambushes. Good days because we were killing so many bad people.

I asked Alan what he meant by "bad days." He offered two examples which he says were the worst days for him. One was the loss of a close friend named Anzar. At night, Alan would often hang out in Anzar's room

playing cards and eating traditional Afghan food. Anzar was a driver in
the Afghan National Army.

The night before he died, Anzar called me and was like, "Hey,
what are you doing? Come over and I will cook up something
good and we can eat together." I was like, "Alright." So, me and
another guy went over. Anzar put a cassette tape in the recorder
to play some music. I remember he was cooking okra. He cooked
okra good. It was delicious. We ate the okra and we were just
hanging out and talking, listening to music. Before we left that
night, I asked Anzar, "Aren't you going downtown tomorrow?"
He said he was, so I was like, "Pick me up a tape recorder when
you are there." He was like, "I got you, I got you."

The next morning, Anzar came by my room when I was
sleeping. He said, "Get up man!" I was like, "What?" He said,
"Man, help me with that form." [Alan, explains that a truck
broke down and Anzar needed help filling out a form for the
repair.] So, I went with him to his room and helped him with
the form. Then, I went back to my room and went back to sleep.
The thing is, I don't remember seeing his face. I don't even know
how I went to his room and then made it back to my room.
I never saw his face, we were just walking. I thought he went
to downtown. After three hours, I was still asleep. Someone
came and said, "Get up! Get up! Go to the TMC [troop medical
clinic]! An ANA [Afghan National Army] truck got hit by an
IED!" I was like, "What? How is this possible?" I was wearing
like shorts and I went to the TMC and I saw Anzar. I was like,
"What are you doing here?" His legs were gone, not *gone*, but,
like *kind of* gone. His arm, his teeth, his lips, like everything was
gone. I was like, "Where was he hit by an IED? I thought he was
going downtown?" But, they said, "The mission got cancelled
and he got reassigned to go to checkpoints." I was like "How did
that happen?" We put him on a stretcher. He was looking at me
and said, "Give me some water." I was like, "No, you can't drink
water." Then he was like [Alan makes a gasping noise], and then
I started crying dude. He was also crying. His whole face was
black. When we tied his legs and chest [to the stretcher] his arm
fell down so I put it on his chest and he was like, "Water?" I was
like "No." I was crying. We called a medevac, a Blackhawk to
come. We put him in a truck and took him to the LZ [landing
zone]. Four guys, we put him in the Blackhawk. He squeezed
my hand. When they flew into the sky, he passed away. When I
saw him, I knew he was in a bad situation and probably wouldn't
make it. When we got back, we called and they told us he passed

away in the air. Me and my friend who hung out with him the night before, we were crying all day. You know, the night before he called us and said come to my room, I will cook you guys something and play music. That was good, but the next day that happened. It was sad. I remember that [Alan pauses and is visually emotional. He uses the next phrase to suppress his emotions] but you know, *whatever*. It was sad thing.

Alan immediately transitioned into what he refers to as the second "bad day." This incident took place shortly after Anzar's death while Alan was translating for a special forces team.

We were traveling between provinces, and someone told the Taliban that we were doing a mission. The enemy was smart. We had a big truck, like seven tons, riding in the front. If this truck hit an IED, it wouldn't kill anyone, just destroy the truck. But they used a remote control IED. It was 6:30 or 6:45 in the morning. I was tired, so I was laying in the back of the truck. We were the [counts on his hand] fifth truck back. The big truck crossed the remote controlled IED and then the second. Then, the third truck, boom, big boom, man, big boom. I was like, "Whoa, shit!" I got up and looked, and there was smoke, everything was like [makes explosion noise and an outward hand movement like something exploded]. I was like "What the fuck is happening?" [Alan apologizes for swearing]. We had a medic in our truck, so I ran with the doctor. It was an Afghan National Army Ford Ranger truck. A four-man truck. There were two guys in the back and two in the seats. The TC [Track Commander or navigator], he was dead. The driver, he was stuck. The engine was gone and the floor was sitting right there [points to his lap]. He was shaking and screaming for help. We tried to help him get out from the truck but he was stuck. There was no way to help that guy. No way. The two guys in the back got thrown up and then onto the ground. The one guy's chin was torn. He survived but after a while he went crazy. They say it was because he hit the ground or something. The other guy, I think he was good. But the two guys in the front, the passenger, he was gone when the truck got hit by the IED. But the driver, he was stuck in the truck. The floor went up and cut him right here [points to waist], but he was still alive. He was like, "Help! Help!" But, we were like, "Dude we can't help him!" We thought, "How were we going to help that guy?" But we had to, you know. So, me, our medic, and two more guys, we just got him and pulled him off of the truck and everything was left [indicates that his lower half remained in the truck]. He stayed alive for like fifteen minutes. We gave him some water because he was like "Give me water. I don't have a chance." Those are two bad things that happened. Lots of small things happened, but nothing too serious. Like my friend got shot or my other friend got hit by an IED. Just small shraps [shrapnel], nothing too serious. I got hit twice by IEDs, but I was in a big tank so that's a small thing.

Alan quickly shifts into examples of "good days" after sharing these two stories.

The fun thing was chasing bad people. That was fun. Killing bad people like the Taliban, that was fun. I will tell you something funny. Not really funny because we got ambushed. But, one night we had a mission. It was cold. Like, if you sleep outside, it is so cold that your blanket gets ice on it. The sun was not up yet, but it was starting to get light. About two clicks away from where we were sleeping there was a mountain. In between us and the mountain there was a hill. The Taliban started shooting at us from there. My buddy, he kicked me. I was like, "What?" He was like, "Get up man! Get Up! Get up! We're getting shot at!" I tried to unzip my sleeping bag but I couldn't so I just ran with it on and hopped into a truck [Alan laughs as he demonstrates the process]. Another fun day was the day we got ambushed during Ramadan. It was right after the day was finished. Like as soon as we broke our fast and said Allahu-Akbar, the Taliban started shooting at us. I remember the ANA guys were cleaning the ditch by using K-9 dogs and mine detectors. I was eating a green apple. So delicious. I took one bite and I was looking at the K-9 and ANA guys cleaning the ditch when I heard [makes machine gun impression]. We were like, "Where is that shit coming from?" Then, someone was like, "Right there!" So, then we started, dude. The mountain was like this much [holds hand high in the air] when we started and like this much [lowers hand to the coffee table] when we were done. We destroyed everything, .50 Calibers, 240s, M-4s, M-16s, M-9s, AK-47s, RPGs, everything, man! Then we called a jet. The special forces guys are quick, man. After like five or ten minutes, the jet is in the sky. They have a jet tech or something like that. His job is to call the jet. If the jet is late, that pilot is going to get fired. It's like a special forces policy or something. The jet came and dropped like a big bomb, like 500-pound bomb on those guys and they were gone! Some other times we would get hit by an ambush, and we would get to kill Taliban. That's was fun. We killed a lot, but it was fun.

Throughout our interviews, Alan consistently constructs a "good guys" versus "bad guys" narrative particularly when referencing his military experience. Even his recollection of American films is recounted through a framework of "good guys" chasing "bad guys." However, concerning his references to political powers, he is less confident constructing an "us" versus "them" narrative.

Jihad in the Context of Global Narratives

Alan suggests there is a more significant political "game" that is being played throughout the region in the name of jihad. He is not entirely sure who is playing, what the teams are, or even which team is good or bad. According to Alan, "They all think they are doing jihad." I asked Alan if he would clarify what he meant by jihad:

> Jihad in the world today is not real jihad. Jihad from before, like a long time ago, that was jihad. What's going on now in places like Syria, that's not jihad, dude. That's killing people for no reason. The fighting in Iraq and the fighting in Syria, that's all religious fighting between the Shiites and the Sunnis. They both want power. It's the same thing in Afghanistan with the Taliban, they just want power. They are just using Islam and jihad for power. That's not fair. All those people doing this, I hope God is hearing us right now, those people are going to hell because they are killing people for no reason. In my holy book, the Holy Qur'an, it says if you kill innocent people, it doesn't matter who, Christians, Buddhists, Yahudis [Jews], Muslims, if they did nothing wrong to you and you kill them, then you took their blood and you will go to hell. The killing right now is all religious and political. It's like a game. We don't even know who is playing in the game right now. It's like they play on the other side of a screen and we can't see what's really going on. But, it's just a game. It's a big game, dude. Do you know about ISIS? I saw a video on Facebook how they captured like a thousand Iraqi soldiers. They put them in a line with like hundred people and they shot them. Why? It's the same in Syria. Bashar Al-Assad and the fighting in Syria, it's all about power. He wants to be President. How many thousands of people have died so he can stay as president? He has already been president for like seventeen years! Are you kidding me? Just give the power to someone

else, dude. It's the same in Afghanistan. The Taliban wants to
have power. Our President says like, "If you want some power,
just come and talk to us." But the Taliban is like, "Nope, first
you need to take all those foreign troops and get them out of
Afghanistan. Then we can talk." The President is like, "Nope,
because they [foreign troops] are helping him." The Taliban can't
help him. They are a small group. They are like 100,000 people.
That's nothing. They can't help the country. The other countries,
like America, they are big supporters of Afghanistan. America
is helping Afghanistan a lot. For example, all the ANA [Afghan
National Army], the big trucks, the big guns, and the uniforms,
you know who is paying for all of that? America. Other countries too, like Germany, they are helping. Without the help of
these other countries, they can't even pay their own Afghan
army. If these countries left Afghanistan, they won't be paying
anybody because we still have too much corruption in our government. You get special treatment if you know somebody or
you pay somebody. It's a corrupt system.

Alan's narrative of jihad is consistent with other participants in this study.
The Pashtun from both Pakistan and Afghanistan, both from cities and rural villages, regularly frame the region in terms of a political game where
religion is used to gain power.

I asked Alan if he would be willing to share more about his religion,
particularly where he learned about Islam.

I grew up in a Muslim family. My father used to take me to the
mosque. I learned about Islam from the mullah and studying
the holy book, the Qur'an. I've read through the Qur'an twice.
It says that God sent 124,000 Prophets to the world. We believe
that Adam was the first prophet and that Hawa [Eve] was the
first mother. We believe that Muhammad was the last prophet.
We believe in four different holy books: including the Bible. The
Taurat, Zabur, and the Injeel. We believe that when you die you
have to answer questions. We believe in heaven and hell.

Alan acknowledges differences within Islam, particularly between Shiites
and Sunnis. He distinguishes himself from the Shiite soldiers in Afghanistan because, according to Alan, the Shiites had more loopholes in their
religion. He gave the example of fasting.

Shiites, they have a different culture. Shiites say that if you
cross two bridges then you can eat. We don't believe that. So,
they would walk across the same bridge twice and then say,

"Hey! We don't have to fast now." I'm not against the Shiites, but they believe that.

Alan suggests that he and the other Sunni soldiers took fasting more seriously, but he quickly assures me that he does not think less of the Shiites. He recalls during one particular mission, he and the other Afghan soldiers fasted together for fifteen days despite the fact that they were hiking nearly twenty miles each day.

> It was hard but God gave us power. If you believe and don't cheat on your fast, God will give you the energy. You don't have to fast though. God says if you are a soldier, you can eat during the fast, but we didn't.

Throughout our discussions, Alan never mentions or alludes to any cognitive dissonance regarding the killing of fellow Muslims in Afghanistan. It is worth noting, however, that he never references the opposition as anything other than the "Taliban" or "bad guys."

Alan on being Pashtun

I asked Alan if it was helpful to the U.S. military that he was Pashtun and if it was difficult for him knowing that the "bad guys" were also Pashtun.

> Most of the Taliban are Pashtun. But don't think all Pashtun are the same. They are not. The Taliban is like a gang. They're uneducated, and they only think about money. That's why they are robbing people. They learn about Islam only from the Mullahs, and these people are coming from other places like Saudi Arabia. They are brainwashing the people. If you kill someone, they will take revenge. It's the culture. I love my culture, but there is some bad stuff in the culture.

Alan's emphasis on the diversity of Pashtun people is consistent with other interviews I conducted. There is an ongoing discussion and debate among Pashtun immigrants concerning the identity and origin and ongoing support of the Taliban. However, there are two areas that have almost unanimous support by the immigrant Pashtun community regardless of whether they are from Afghanistan or Pakistan, the city or rural villages: first, the Taliban is a fluid movement, and as a result, no one is sure who is actually a part of the Taliban. It is bigger than just the Pashtun, yet a majority of the adherents still claim to be Pashtun. Alan, as well as other participants, suggest that the term "Taliban" is used as a catchall term for anyone against the current governments of Afghanistan and Pakistan. Secondly, there is consistency in the belief that the Pakistani ISI has something to do with the creation and ongoing support of the Taliban.

The primary reason Alan suggests that not all Pashtun are alike is because the culture is constantly changing. When asked if there is any consistency that remains among the Pashtun or any parts of the culture that he thinks will remain unchanged, Alan suggests two things that will remain in Pashtun culture: the *jirga* system and the values of honor and respect.

Alan explains the *jirga* system as follows:

> The *jirga* is important. If two families are fighting, maybe they have been fighting for a long time, they have to go to a *jirga*. An elder that represents each person meets with the *jirga* and makes a decision. Once they make a decision, you cannot say nothing. You can't say that it's not a fair decision or nothing. Once the *jirga* decides, you have to follow their decision.

He says this was something the U.S. military had to learn about so they could get help from the village Pashtun when fighting the Taliban. He translated for *jirga* meetings between the U.S. Army and the local village leaders.

> Every month we would have a *jirga* with different villages. We would talk to them about help, not just one-sided help but how we can each help each other. For example, we would say, "Sure we can build you a mosque or a school or a clinic, but you have to help us too. What will you do for us?" They would say something like, "We can help you with security. If we see some bad people down here, we can tell you." That's how it works.

As previously mentioned, Alan believes that the Pashtun currently have and will continue to have a common understanding of hospitality and respect. Alan explains how the two are linked.

> If we are eating dinner, you have to stay and eat dinner with us. You're my guest. We may not have much, but let us give you what we have. At least show us that respect. Americans, they show people respect too, but it is different. No one ever say anything bad to me and they never didn't show me respect. But, for example, there was this guy, a fellow soldier, he had two hamburgers for himself. I was so hungry, but he did not offer me anything to eat. I thought maybe if tell him that I am hungry then he will share with me. And he looked at me and said, "Then go get something to eat." Then, he grabbed his second burger and put the wrapper back on it and set right next to him. He

didn't say, "Here, you can have this extra one." I was like, "Alright." He just sat there eating while I sat there hungry.

This story comes from the military food court in Afghanistan. While Alan still considered the soldier a friend, he recognizes that that they had different views of what friendship looks like. However, when they were out on missions, those differences went away. Since coming to America, Alan's belief that there is a fundamental difference in understanding when it comes to hospitality and respect is being continually reinforced by his experiences.

The Move to America: Loss of Close Relationships and Meaningful Work

Alan describes his relationships with fellow soldiers during his service as a kind of brotherhood. In his recollection of events, it was clear that he believes that he belonged. The relationships he developed with both U.S. and Afghan soldiers were meaningful and gave him a *sense of being through belonging*. It is clear that the role Alan had in the military gave him a sense of purpose and hope for the future of Afghanistan.

Though Alan loved his job, his country, and being close with the soldiers, once rumors began circulating concerning his involvement with the U.S. Army, he felt he had to apply for a special immigrant visa to come to America. As soon as his visa request was approved, Alan resigned as an interpreter. In less than 72 hours he, along with his wife and three children, had to say goodbye to their families and Afghanistan. The day before he left, Alan's mother pulled him aside.

> I asked her to forgive me if there's anything I had ever done to offend her. She assured me that I had done nothing and told me that I was the best among my brothers. She didn't cry when she heard I was leaving. She was sad, but she had been praying that I would receive a visa to the United States. But the day we left she was crying. I was like "No, mom, stop crying." Then, we started crying together. We were all crying, everybody. We were crying until we were sitting in the plane. Even my father! I swear to God my father never cried in his life but when he walked with us to the last terminal. He could not go in with us. When we were walking in I turned around one last time, and I saw him cleaning his eyes with his handkerchief. I was crying. I was really crying. [Alan is fighting back tears]. My mom she is still crying when she is calling. I'm like, "Mom, stop. Don't cry, we're happy." But she is still crying. Mostly about my oldest son. He

used to sleep with her in her room. My sister back home says, "Mom is crying every day." She tries to hide it, but my sister says she can tell because her eyes are always red.

Alan is confident that his mom and dad want him to be here but says he sometimes wonders if he made the right decision. He misses being home. Back in Kabul he lived in a three-story compound type home with eighteen family members. Here, it is a two-bedroom apartment with his wife and kids. His mother Skype calls almost nightly to speak with Alan and his family. It seems the continual connection back home is causing Alan some emotional distress. He is consistently reminded of how much his mother misses them and how much he misses Afghanistan. Despite missing home, he feels as though he has to succeed in America in order to keep a promise he made to his mom before leaving:

> I made a promise to my mom and dad. I said, "When I go to America, first for my children, I am going to make sure they get an education. Then, I am going to send money so that you guys can go to Hajj." I hope God can help me with this wish. It's going to cost $10,000, for both of them. I love them so much. I am praying to God that my kids will see how much I love my mom and my dad, and they will love me the same way. I believe that they will do the same things for me. We have a saying that says something like, "If you do good to your mom and dad, your sons will do the same things for you."

Only time will tell if Alan's promise continues to be a motivating factor for him to succeed. Alan is not able to send any money back home yet. In fact, he has had to ask his father to borrow money in order to pay all his bills. His current job as a pizza delivery man is insufficient, but he hopes to find another job. It may be incredibly difficult for Alan to adjust if he continues to hold himself responsible to fulfilling a seemingly impossible task.

Reshaping Boundaries of Identity in America

Alan, like many others, is experiencing a dynamic relationship between his ethnic, national, and religious identifications. His experiences with both Americans and non-Pashtun Muslims continues to reshape his understanding of the boundary lines of identity. Alan explains how he is beginning to notice overlaps between Pashtun culture and other Muslim peoples.

> When we are at the bus stop, me, my wife and kids, everyone passes by. They just stare at us. No one offers us a ride, they

just stare. Why do they have to stare? Why can't they just stop and say, "Hey, do you need a ride?" But nobody stops. If we see someone who needs a ride, we ask them if we can take them. It is not like that in America. One time we were standing outside the bank near the bus stop, and this guy stopped and made a U-turn so that he could come back and ask if he could give us a ride. He rolled down his window and said *as-salaam-alaikum*. At first, I thought he was from Afghanistan, but he was from Iraq. He asked if he could give us a ride and all four of us piled into the backseat of his van. I think maybe Muslim people try their best to help each other.

Alan's ascription of hospitality and respect to the broader community of Muslims rather than just the Pashtun may be an indication of his current struggle in adjusting to his imagined America and his current experience.

Prior to coming to America, Alan felt strongly connected to American culture through movies and also his experiences with the American soldiers with whom he spent the majority of his time and fellowship. He, like many soldiers, is struggling to reproduce the relationships developed in war in daily American life. He has only been visited by one soldier with whom he served in Afghanistan. Other soldiers have stayed in touch with him through an occasional social media post. Some have even sent Alan gift cards to help him get established. Aside from that, Alan's experiences over the past three years have not produced any American friendships comparable to the ones he had in Afghanistan.

There is certainly the potential for an identity crisis if Alan's identity continues to be framed through religious narratives, particularly if he begins questioning his previous experiences with Muslim "bad guys" in Afghanistan. It is entirely possible that Alan will begin to struggle with the "good guys" versus "bad guys" dichotomy that he developed in Afghanistan. This may be particularly difficult for Alan considering his regular communication back home where there is an ongoing withdrawal of American troops despite the increasing violence in Afghanistan. In addition, Alan may struggle with the recent reduction in immigrant visas to the United States. He had hoped to try and bring his sister to the United States, but based on recent reductions, this will likely be impossible.

Alan is also beginning to experience a fluidity between the boundaries of Sunni and Shia Islam. In telling his story, Alan on more than one occasion upheld a boundary between himself and the Shiite soldiers in their religious expressions, though he would quickly suggest that he had nothing against them personally. However, now that Alan is in America, the boundaries between Afghan Shiites and Sunnis is almost non-existent. They attend the same mosque, they break the Ramadan fast together, and they celebrate Eid together. The men hang out late into the night and talk about their struggles together. During one of our interviews, Alan's wife informed him that she was going to take some food to another Afghan neighbor. I asked if the neighbor was also Pashtun. He replied,

> No, she is a Hazara lady. She is here by herself with her two chil-
> dren. It's our culture you know. We need to look out for her. It's
> not good for a Muslim lady to be by herself. So we bring her
> food every time we make something.

The historic animosity between the Pashtun and Hazara did not appear to exist among the immigrant community from either Afghanistan or Pakistan. Pashtun wives from both Pakistan and Afghanistan would regularly bring food to this widow's home despite the fact that she was neither Pashtun nor a Sunni Muslim. The boundary lines appear to be dissolved or, at the very least, suspended.

The fragmented boundary lines were particularly apparent when the Hazara widow lost one of her children in a tragic accident. One of her sons, during a game of hide and seek, was tragically killed in a traffic accident. The collective mourning included multiple ethnic peoples from both Afghanistan and Pakistan. The tragedy brought a level of inter-ethnic cohesion among the South Asian Muslim community. This event seemed to represent a strong sense that their religious identity and community transcends all other identifications. While many of the attendees were South Asian (primarily from Pakistan, India, and Afghanistan), the imam goes to great lengths to stress that there should be no divisions in Islam. He has repeatedly preached against religious, ethnic, and nationalistic sectarianism in his Friday messages. That is not to say that divisions do not come up or that they are completely dissolved in this particular community, but rather the individuals have learned to have unity amidst diversity. Though in some ways their diversity is becoming increasingly less obvious particularly when their shared values are juxtaposed with their American context.

The boundary of identity for Alan and his immediate Muslim community, by and large, is being constructed around a regional religious affinity through a shared sense of collective suffering and marginalization. This shared sense is rooted both in events that happen in the United States as well as their countries of origin. Because of transnationalism and computer mediated communication, the ongoing violence and suffering in both Pakistan and Afghanistan are a regular a part of the Friday prayers at Alan's local mosque. It is not uncommon at this mosque for there to be an announcement of a family member abroad tragically dying, particularly at the hands of religious extremists. This broader Muslim identity that is tied to marginalization and collective suffering transcends the more nuanced boundary lines that were present in their countries of origin.

Conclusion

Alan finds himself in a similar situation his father did nearly twenty years ago. Alan, like his father, is starting completely over in a country that is not his home. He is working a seemingly meaningless job for very little money. He wants, more than anything else, for his children to be happy even though America is unfamiliar and does not feel like home. Ironically, Alan's oldest son, Maheer, is nine years old. This is same age as Alan when he first left Afghanistan. Alan, much like his father twenty years prior, does his best to maintain a positive attitude despite difficult past experiences and current struggles. He tries to provide a hopeful outlook for his children much like his dad did for him and his siblings.

Alan's primary concern is the well-being of his children. He continues to be hopeful that America will provide good opportunities for them despite what he often sees in the news. During our interviews, Alan's children would sometimes be present. In one of our discussions, Alan shared with me how his oldest son has been asking for a bike, so he can keep up with the other kids who ride around the apartments where they live. He also shared Maheer's response when he told him he would have to wait until they could afford a bike:

> He was like, "Thank you father." He was happy. So, for about a week he didn't say nothing about the bike. Then, he came to me and said, "Do we have any money yet?" I said, "No, not yet." Maheer was like, "Okay, when you do get the money, just get the cheap bike not the expensive one."

Alan has to keep from crying as he explains how he wishes his son did not think about how much a bike will cost, but he is also thankful that Maheer does not demand the most expensive one either.

While there are uncanny similarities between Alan's and Maheer's refugee experiences, there are some significant differences between the two that may become problematic. Alan's resettlement was a collective experience in which the loss was collectively grieved with extended family members as a permanent situation with little hope or plan to return. In contrast, Maheer's experience is only with his immediate family and includes a regular reminder of separation through daily virtual visits with extended family members who remain in Kabul. This may be a significant factor in Maheer's resettlement process. At the very least, this will be an area in which Alan and Maheer will not be able to fully relate to one another in their experiences.

Additionally, consideration should be given to the fact that although Pakistan as a host society was not fully welcoming of the Pashtun refugee community, it hardly seems comparable to the current negative attitudes in America toward Muslim immigrants. According to 2017 study by the Pew Research Center, Americans are evenly divided over views of Islam and Muslim immigration.[2] Finally, while Alan's love for news and American media helped Alan to transition into becoming an American ally in Afghanistan, it may have an opposite effect in the U.S. given the current negativity of Muslim and Pashtun public narratives in mainstream media (see chapters 5 and 6).

Throughout our interviews, Alan never mentions the United States as being a player in the political game of the region. It seems inevitable, however, that Alan's love for media will eventually lead him to the increasing number of documentaries, films, and news reports about Afghanistan that portray America as, not only a player, but the primary orchestrator of the political game Alan despises.[3]

2. Mohamed et al., "U.S. Muslims Concerned About Their Place in Society."

3. Coombs et al., "CNN Encore Presentation"; Greenwald, "Rethink Afghanistan."

9

Life History of Miriam

THIS CHAPTER EXPLORES THE life history of Miriam Wazir, a 28-year-old Pashtun woman who, along with her family, immigrated to the United States as a refugee when she was seventeen. She is originally from a small village located in the Federally Administered Tribal Area (FATA) of Pakistan. The chapter is primarily Miriam's story followed by an analysis of her transnational identity formation.

> I was born in a small mud house in Pakistan in March, 1990. That's the date that I have in my passport, but I don't really know. We don't keep records like this in our village. I feel like I was born when I was seven years old, before that I don't remember much. They say when my brother Niaz was born, the family, especially my father's mother, was so happy because he was a boy. When I was born, she was okay, she was not really excited, she was not really happy or sad.

Miriam is not concerned by her paternal grandmother's indifference towards her birth and partiality toward her brother. While she had great respect for her grandmother, she knew her opinion was insignificant in comparison to how her maternal grandfather, Ahmad Wazir, viewed her. Miriam says she had favor with Ahmad Wazir, a man she describes as one of the most powerful and honorable men in all of the tribal areas of Pakistan.

Miriam's Grandfather: Ahmad Wazir

Throughout Miriam's life, she and her siblings heard the story of how Ahmad Wazir became renowned in the region by taking revenge against the people who ravaged his family when he was an infant.

> My grandfather was only two years old when it happened. One day his older brother took the goats onto the mountain to find food but he never came home. The people on the other side of

the mountain killed him and cut him into little pieces. After that, they went to my grandfather's house and killed his father. They also took his older sister, she was only thirteen, and forced her to marry an older man. They say that she was such a pretty young girl, and that the guy they forced her to marry was like sixty! He used to beat her up because she was too young and not strong enough to do the work he wanted her to do.

Miriam explains that these people would have killed her grandfather Ahmad too, but his mother hid him under some clothes the day his father was murdered and his sister was taken. Once the people left the house, Ahmad's mother took him and fled to another house and asked them to hide her and the child.

These people came looking for my grandfather, but they could never find him. His mom would go from house to house so they could not find her. She did this until she made it all the way to a village. She asked if someone in that village would take them in and protect them and they did.

When Ahmad turned eighteen, his mother and the men in the village told him about what these people did to his family. They explained that it was his responsibility to avenge the death of his father and brother and to find his sister. Miriam shares how Ahmad first set out to find his sister and reunite her with their mother.

The first man she was married to had died, and now she was living with another family in Afghanistan. He asked the Afghani people if she could go with him to visit her mother, but they were like, "No! We don't trust you because we don't even know if you're her real brother." You see his sister didn't recognize my grandfather because it had been so many years since she was taken. He was a baby the last time she saw him. His sister was crying a lot, so they eventually said she could go with him. My grandfather told us he was walking for almost an hour when he looked back and saw them coming after him. They had changed their minds because her husband didn't think my grandfather would bring her back. His sister tore her clothes and started screaming and crying in front of everyone. She was on the ground yelling to him, "Look at me! Look at what they did to me!" My grandfather was so mad that he made a promise not to sleep until he killed every person that did this to his sister.

When he was unable to retrieve his sister, Ahmad committed to avenge his family honor before returning back to his mother and the village. He walked for days before arriving at the home of the family who was responsible for what happened sixteen years prior. According to Miriam, he wasted no time fulfilling his vow:

> When he finally got to their place, he saw one guy outside and he killed him right away. Then, he went into the house and killed everyone else. *Everyone*. He thought, "They did this thing to me, so I'm going to do the same thing to them." He took revenge. Whatever they did to his family, he did the same thing to this other family. Some people say, and sometimes even I feel like, it was mean of him to do such a thing. But then, I feel like, if you grow up with this story about how this other family did this to your family just so that they can have more land, then I can understand why he did it.

Miriam wonders what might have happened in the story if Ahmad was allowed to bring his sister home. The thought of not being recognized by your own sibling and seeing how ashamed she was helps Miriam understand her grandfather's actions even though she may disagree.

Miriam also understands that there was an expectation on her grandfather to take revenge. She explains that if it wasn't for her grandfather's willingness, the responsibility would have fallen to one of his sons. In other words, her grandfather's actions freed his immediate family and future generations from a significant cultural burden, not only taking revenge, but by eliminating the possibility of a retaliation.

> He took the revenge, and it's finished because that family doesn't have anyone left, everybody [signals wiping motion with both her hands]. If he didn't take care of everyone, then, someone could come from that family, even 100 years later, and take revenge against my mother's family. That's why my mother's family is so proud of their father. My mother's brothers say, "How can we not be proud of our father because he did not leave any mess for us, he took care of everyone for us." My mother still shares this story with us all the time. I think she's proud of him too. She thinks he did a good thing. I'm thinking, I'm not so sure [she says this almost in a whisper, despite the fact that it is only my wife and I with her in the house].

Even though Miriam struggles to see the merit of his actions, she can see how the cultural context limited her grandfather's options. The honor associated with revenge in Pashtun culture is difficult for Miriam to accept. Even more difficult for Miriam is a system of retribution that is trans-generational.

> I guess my grandfather had to take revenge. There was no way
> for him to let it go because he was Pashtun. The Pashtun can
> never let revenge go that easily. What I don't like about revenge
> is that after 100 years it is a completely new generation. They
> may not have anything to do with the old generation that made
> the problem. They may not even know what happened 100 years
> ago. But that doesn't matter, still people will take revenge. It
> keeps going for generation after generation. I wish the Pashtun
> could change this tradition.

Ironically, Ahmad Wazir's actions as a younger man granted him a mediatory role in his older age. Miriam remembers how he would often be called
to settle disputes between people. She describes his influence and wisdom
in arbitration as almost a supernatural gift:

> When people have a *big* problem, they would ask my grandfa-
> ther to come and fix it. You see, most believe that, "if he talks,
> our problem will be solved in less than a minute." They would
> call other people, but no one could bring agreements between
> people like he could. After he got a little older, he wouldn't go as
> often because it was hard for him to travel. Sometimes he would
> send his older son as his representative. But for some problems,
> people would be like, "No, we want him to come." They would
> send a car for him, and he would be gone for a few hours.

Miriam knew that when their grandfather returned that he had successfully negotiated whatever problem he was sent to solve. His ability to bring
reconciliation between people was something that Miriam highly valued.

Inherited Honor through Ahmad Wazir

Ahmad Wazir's act of revenge as a younger man and his wisdom in his later
years afforded Miriam and her family a fair amount of prestige. She recalls
how people would treat her and her siblings differently because of their
grandfather.

> When we would go anywhere, or when people come from the
> mountains, we could just say his name, and people would be like,
> "Oh okay! So, you guys are his granddaughters." Like in the ma-
> drassa, when I went to the Islamic school, almost every single girl
> and even the teachers had heard about him. The men like talking
> about him and telling his story. So, it makes you feel like people
> know him, and sometimes that's a good thing [laughing].

Miriam admits that while she was not entirely comfortable with her grandfather's actions, she appreciated the position of honor that he afforded her and her siblings. Miriam's mother also benefited from Ahmad Wazir's position among people. It was not unusual for her mother to be asked to perform special prayers on behalf of others when they were in need of a blessing from God.

Miriam had favor with her grandfather, and that made her feel special among all her cousins. She explains that most of her female cousins were scared of their grandfather because of the revenge story and what she describes as an unfailing stern demeanor. The rules of gender segregation also made it difficult for any of the female cousins to get to know their grandfather. However, Miriam says these cultural boundaries did not apply to her and her sister and that Miriam was second only to Ahmad Wazir's oldest son:

> When he was in the main part of the house, none of the cousins would go in the house. Only his oldest son would come and sit with him. The cousins would just stand outside and wait for him to go back to his room. He would always tell the girls, "Remember that I make the rules, and I don't want you girls around men. No one should break that rule ever!" So, none of the girl cousins were allowed to sit with him. Except for me and my younger sister.

Miriam's and her sister's freedom to sit and talk with their grandfather created some jealousy among the cousins. I asked Miriam why she had the freedom to break the gender segregation rule with her grandfather:

> Well, I think it was because I liked to argue with him and ask him tough questions. I remember I would ask him things like, "Do you love your youngest son or oldest son more?" He would say, "Miriam, what kind of question is that? Why would you compare my oldest son to my youngest? You know that no one knows my youngest son, and my oldest son is known by all the people." And I said to him, "Oh, that's not nice of you. I think you should support your youngest son more." I would challenge his answers, and so I think he liked talking to me. I know I liked having conversations with him. I really loved my grandfather. I used to be scared of him like everyone else until I got to know him.

Ahmad Wazir died recently. Miriam claims he was at least ninety-five years old and may have lived longer than anyone else in the tribal areas. She says she does not recall a time in her life where her grandfather did not have a profound impact on her family. His influence on the family continues today despite his death. It is not uncommon in Miriam's home for her mother or one of the children to reference Ahmad Wazir in order to reinforce the honorable position their family held back in Pakistan. No matter who is telling the story, if Miriam is present, she finds a way to remind everyone of his partiality towards her.

Miriam's Parents Fazal and Nazima

As Miriam continues her story, she explains how throughout her life, she has had to negotiate between different expressions of Pashtun culture displayed by multiple extended family members. While she suggests there are commonalities among all Pashtun people, she articulates at least two types of Pashtun peoples and categorizes them in a geographical framework of mountain people and hill people. Her father Fazal comes from the hill people and her mother Nazima comes from the mountain people. Miriam also spends a considerable amount of time developing a narrative structure around what she commonly calls "my dad's people" and "my mom's people." It is imperative to understand the history of these meaningful relationships and their ongoing influence in Miriam's narrative identity.

Miriam explains how Pashtun culture expects for first cousins to marry, especially in the tribal villages. However, there were extenuating circumstances that left both her parents without a first cousin to marry. The murder of Ahmad Wazir's brother and the sending of his sister to Afghanistan meant that her mother Nazima had no first cousins to marry in the mountains. Miriam's father Fazal, had first cousins but she explains that he was not allowed to marry them because of a foster relationship created through breast milk.

> My father was supposed to marry his cousins, but when he was young his mom was sick. So, his aunts fed him with milk and they became like his mom. He could not marry their daughters because they all were like his sisters. That's why they had to look for a wife for him somewhere else.

Miriam does not explain why these first cousins became like sisters to her father after their mothers nursed him, but she knows it is related to Islam. According to the Qur'an:

> You are forbidden to take as wives your mothers, daughters, sisters, paternal and maternal aunts, the daughters of brothers and daughters of sisters, your milk-mothers and milk-sisters, your wives' mothers, the stepdaughters in your care—those born of women with whom you have consummated marriage, if you have not consummated the marriage, then you will not

be blamed–wives of your begotten sons, two sisters simultaneously—with the exception of what is past: God is most forgiving
and merciful. (Sura 4:23)

This passage is further explained by Aisha in *Hadith Sahih Bukhari* saying,

Prohibited to you (for marriage) are: your foster-mothers (who
suckled you) (4.23). Marriage is prohibited between persons
having a foster suckling relationship corresponding to a blood
relationship which renders marriage unlawful.[1]

It should be noted that in this particular situation, despite the importance of
the Pashtun marriages between first cousins in order to strengthen and preserve family lineage and wealth, Islamic tradition took precedence in Fazal's
family. This is something that, according to Miriam, rarely happens among
the mountain people. She suggests that when there is a conflict between Islam
and the Pashtun culture, the mountain people almost always give more importance to their culture. As for the hill people, Miriam says it depends on the
situation. However, when it comes to the treatment of women, she suggests
that it does not matter if it is the mountain people or hill people, Pashtun
traditions regarding women are more important than the teachings of Islam.
Miriam addresses this, in more depth, further into her story.

Nazima's People (Mountain People)

Miriam's parents' marriage was arranged by her father's uncle who oper-
ated a timber mill in the mountain regions. One of the mountains where he
did business was owned by Ahmad Wazir. She shares how uncommon it is
for the mountain people to give their daughters to people from outside the
region, making her parents' arrangement unique:

When my dad's uncle saw my mother [Nazima], he said, "I want
that girl for my nephew." They say that she was young and very
pretty. My grandmother agreed right away because she could
tell that the uncle was from a modern family. She didn't even
know the family, but she knew that they weren't from the mountains. My grandmother knew my mom would have a better life
with my father's family. My grandfather said no at first. But then
my father's uncle reminded him that they were good friends,
and that he should be willing to do anything for friendship. My
grandfather eventually agreed.

1. Sahih al-Bukhari, Book 67 Wedlock, Marriage (Nikaah) Hadith 20. https://sun-
nah.com/bukhari/67.

Miriam's grandmother was not originally from the mountains. She was raised in what Miriam refers to as a modern family in North Waziristan. Miriam suspects that her grandmother's experience of leaving a modern family and moving to the mountains may be the reason she was so quick to agree to the marriage despite not knowing the people.

> My grandmother's life after moving to the mountains was really difficult. It used to make us so sad when she would share her story. She would tell us how difficult it was to live in the mountain culture. Not just the culture but the people were difficult too. They were really mean to her. They use to say that she was bringing bad luck to everyone because she washed clothes with soap. In the mountains, they only wash their clothes with mud. She told us that they would not let her clean the house either. If she cleaned the house, they would say things like, "Oh my God! She is bringing the bad luck to our house!" I have never heard of anything like this in Islam, but they believed these things.

Things for Miriam's grandmother became even more problematic when Ahmad Wazir took a second wife. The new wife was from the mountains and, according to Miriam, she would often try to sabotage her grandmothers' relationship with the rest of the family.

The strained relationship between Miriam's grandmother and the rest of the family provided the space for her to raise her children with limited influence from others. Because of this, Miriam says it would be difficult for anyone to guess that her mother comes from the mountains.

> My grandmother raised her children to be more modern. If you met my mother's step-sisters, you wouldn't believe that they were raised in the same family. You will see a big difference in the way they talk and the way they do things. I say that my mother is from the mountains because her father is from mountains. But really, my mom is more like the people in North Waziristan than the mountain people.

Miriam recognizes that she views the mountain culture negatively. Her criticisms come from her grandmother's and mother's stories as well as some of her own experiences while visiting the mountains. One of the most difficult things about mountain culture for Miriam is the lack of freedom for women.

> In our village women have more power and respect than they do in the mountains. The mountain people will not even let a woman talk in front of a man or walk in front of a man. I don't know

how they are able to live like that! But I know they probably say the same things about us. They probably think we are wrong to speak in front of a man. So, we have this thing in common. We think they are wrong and they think we are wrong. They think we are too free, and we think their life is [long pause], I would say miserable. But for them, maybe it's not. I just can't imagine living that life every day.

Miriam is keenly aware that her views of women's rights may not be shared by all the women in the mountains. This struggle concerning women and freedom is something that Miriam further develops later in her story, particularly after she moves to America. For now, it is sufficient to say that since childhood, Miriam has struggled to find a balanced position on women's rights that is both culturally and religiously acceptable.

In addition to the culture, Miriam shares how daily living in the mountains is physically challenging for women. During her visits as a child, she would participate in some of the daily routines like gathering firewood or gardening. She admits that it was fun for a few days but can't imagine doing it daily to survive. One of her fondest and most frustrating memories is the day she tried to prove to her grandmother and cousins that she was capable of meeting the demands of mountain life:

> When my cousins were going to get water, I was like, "Wait! I'm going with you." I grabbed a big pot for the water and as I was leaving my grandmother shouted, "Don't take it Miriam! You are going to break it." But I didn't care, I knew she couldn't stop me. Oh, this story makes me mad. I put just a little water in the pot and started walking back up the mountain. I was so happy because I thought for sure I was going to make it. But, when I was this close [gestures a short space with her index finger and thumb] the thing fell from my head. I was like, "Aah! No!" My grandmother was like, "I told you Miriam! I knew you would break my pot [laughing]!"

Miriam says that she feels really close to her mother's family now but that was not always the case. Most of her village life was spent with her father Fazal's side of the family. In fact, Miriam and one of her sisters were promised from a very young age to marry their first cousins on their father's side. Prior to moving to the United States, it was Fazal's family that was the most influential in Miriam's life.

Fazal's People

When Fazal was fourteen years old, he left Pakistan in search of work. He joined the mass migration of young Pashtun males traveling to the Middle East to find work in the late 1960s. He got a job applying pitch to the walls in the harbor. It was a miserable job, he recalls the skin on his face blistering and peeling from the chemicals he was applying. Fazal sent nearly all of his earnings back to Pakistan to support his family. He did not return to Pakistan until his uncle informed him that he had arranged a marriage for him.

Fazal returned to marry Nazima, however, he did not stay for long. In order to continue earning money as a migrant worker, Fazal left his pregnant wife in the care of his younger brother Manan. While Fazal would make annual visits to his family, by and large, Miriam and her siblings were raised by their uncle Manan.

> Our father was not there much when we lived in the village. Sometimes he was in another country or in another part of Pakistan. He was always working. We wouldn't see him for a year or two, and then he would show up and stay for a couple months. The longest he ever stayed was six months. The funny thing is, we never really had a connection with him as a father. We thought, "Oh, he is here today, but he will be going again soon." We would be happy for a few days but then we knew that he would be going back. I think that is why we were so close to our uncle. Manan was always around. Since our father was not there much, he was the one making decisions for us.

The absence of Fazal made it difficult for Miriam, particularly when it came to decisions regarding her education. She describes her father as more progressive than her uncle and that meant that when her father was present she had privileges that her uncle would quickly revoke as soon as her father left.

> I asked my father during one of his visits if I could go to an English medium school. He said yes and he took me and my cousin to the school to sign up. I had so much fun at that school. I loved the teachers and the other students. I was so energetic and smart at that time. The only problem was that it was a school for boys. In the villages, not a lot of people allow girls to go to boys' school but my father thought since we were still young we could go. There were like 300 boys and 10 of us girls in the school. Since we were young, the boys and girls were in class together. I went there for like three years, and then one day my uncle called the principal and told him to send me and my cousin back home. When we got home my uncle told us we couldn't go to school

anymore because we were getting too tall. Once you are twelve, you can't go to school anymore, and you have to start wearing the *burqa* [a garment that covers the entire body, often blue in color]. I was only eight years old but, since I was tall for my age, my uncle thought the boys might think I was older. When my father came later that year, he took me back to the school and said I could stay until I was twelve.

When Miriam's father left the country again, her uncle removed her from the boy's school for the second time. This time it was permanent. Manan enrolled Miriam and her cousin in an all-girls Islamic madrassa.

Miriam recalls her initial feelings about the school being quite negative. She wanted to learn about a variety of subjects, and she wanted to study English. The primary curriculum at the madrassa was religious. There were some non-religious subjects taught, but they were limited by a lack of qualified female teachers and strict policies concerning gender segregation. The most difficult thing for Miriam was the demanding schedule.

> The Islamic school was hard because we were there all day. We started at seven in the morning and finished at five in the evening. We would have to memorize large amounts of religious texts in order to pass our exams. It's not like here where they give you one question and then a few choices for the answer. You had to memorize a whole book, and then you would write like two or three paragraphs for each answer. I wasn't sleeping because I was studying so much. I thought I was going crazy. When I started Islamic school, I was not really into it, but I think going made me a different person. I would say a better person. After a while, I did not care about anything except school. I thought that school is the only thing I need to concentrate on or worry about. The madrassa became my life.

Miriam studied in the madrassa for eight years. Despite her initial concerns, by the end, her attitude about the madrassa had completely changed. She made close friendships with the other girls in the program and developed a love for Islamic studies. Her father was not very happy that she was attending an Islamic school, but he never interfered. He was primarily concerned about the limitations of the madrassa curriculum.

Seeking Asylum in America

Prior to 9/11, Fazal was able to obtain a work visa and a job in the United States. Miriam explains that her father would regularly tell her and her

siblings over the phone that he was trying to bring them to America but
they never took him seriously. Even when they had to travel to Islamabad
for interviews at the American Embassy, it never occurred to Miriam that
she might one day leave Pakistan.

> I think the reason my father wanted us to come here is because
> he saw all the people talking about education. For some rea-
> son, he always wanted us to get a good education. He knew
> that would not happen in our village. He would say things like,
> "Be ready! I submitted your papers." But, we never took him
> seriously. We never thought we would actually go to America.
> Then, in 2008 we had an interview in Islamabad, and they were
> like, "Congratulations, you guys are going to USA!" Before that,
> we had a lot of other interviews, but they would never say any-
> thing to us. They would just send us home. When they told us
> congratulations, for some reason, we weren't happy. All of us
> felt sad. We thought, "Oh my God! What is happening?" But
> then I started to get excited because I thought we had like three
> months to get ready. I had one month left in Islamic school, and
> I was glad that I would be there to graduate. But then, the next
> morning, my father called and told us we were leaving in three
> days. He thought that something could happen if we waited, so
> we had to leave as soon as possible.

Miriam was initially devastated because she would miss her graduation from
the madrassa. In three days, Miriam had to say goodbye to all of her friends
and family. Two of the days were spent traveling to and from the mountains
to attend a wedding and say goodbye to Nazima's extended family.

They returned to the village and spent their last day packing and saying goodbye to their family in Manan's home. Miriam recalls all the men
being concerned about the girls moving to America. She recalls her uncle
Manan being particularly concerned saying,

> When these girls go to America they will change. The minute
> you go to America you forget about Islam and your culture.
> They will be doing things they shouldn't. They will change their
> clothes, and they will marry whoever they want. Now they are
> supposed to marry their cousins. After a few years they will be
> like, "No, we don't want to marry them." You won't pray any-
> more. You won't fast anymore. When you go there you will be-
> come right away like them, completely changed.

Despite her uncle's warnings and opposition, the next day Miriam and her
family boarded a plane for New York.

Moving to America

Miriam remembers having mixed emotions as they boarded the plane for the United States. While their father Fazal had been traveling the globe since he was fourteen, his wife and children had never traveled outside of the Afghan-Pakistan border region.

> You just can't imagine living your whole life in a village never being outside, never being around any man that you do not know and then the next day we came. For the most part, I was scared. I was leaving my friends and my family. Coming out from the airplane, when I saw my father, I couldn't open my eyes, my tears were just running. We stayed in New York with my father's friend but only for a day because we wanted to go to the place we were going to be living.

At this point, Miriam had no context for where she was or where she was going. She had no idea where her father lived in relation to New York. After several hours in the car she started to wonder if they were heading back to Pakistan.

The culture shock for Miriam was overwhelming. She had hoped that once they arrived in their new home and unpacked, things would get better. However, the new home was not what she was expecting.

> When we came to the house, there were people working on fixing the bathroom, so we hid downstairs. We stayed there all day. When the people left, we went upstairs and tried to get to the open roof, but we couldn't. When we got to the top of the house, all we found were small rooms filled with old stuff [the attic]. I was like, "Oh my God, what are we going to do now?" In Pakistan, we are used to big open houses. This house was way too small for us [the home is about 2,000 square feet]. After a few days, we started cleaning the house. In Pakistan, we never, especially me, did any work like this. When I started my Islamic school, my aunt or my mom they would make tea for me. I never did anything myself. And here, I had become a house cleaner. I remember thinking, I don't want this kind of life.

In less than a month, Miriam and her siblings were enrolled in a public school. Because she didn't speak any English, Miriam was placed in the ninth grade in her new school and enrolled in English as a Second Language classes (ESL).

High School Freshman at Seventeen Years Old

Miriam remembers feeling uncomfortable being the only seventeen-year-old freshman in high school and having no idea what anyone was saying. However, more than the age gap and language barrier, she remembers the cultural differences overwhelming her the most:

> When I would sit in the class, I would just be looking at the teacher's mouth and think, "Okay, what is she saying?" I had no idea because I didn't know any English. When they first took us to school, I was like, "What is this? What am I going to do here?" I had never been to this kind of school in my whole life. It was completely shocking for me! I had never seen people dress that way. Where I grew up, I wore the *burqa* all my life, and I was coming here with no *burqa*, sitting with boys, girls were wearing shorts, and I thought, "This is not going to work for me." For two years I never talked to anyone. I was twelve when I started wearing the *burqa*, and I was seventeen when I came here. Still when I go back I wear the *burqa*. Every single day that I went to that school I was like, "Today is my last day here, I am not coming back because I'm going back to Pakistan." But I never really did. Then, day by day it got better. I remember thinking, "I am just making myself miserable by planning to go back to Pakistan." So, I stopped telling myself that I was going to leave school.

Not only did Miriam resolve to stay in school, she decided that she would strive to maintain her cultural traditions despite the fact that she felt isolated in doing so. Miriam wanted to prove her uncle wrong. She had no intention of allowing America to change her.

> At that time, I was new to the country, and I was so into my own culture that I was like, "There is no way I'm going to change a single thing for anyone." When I went to school, I would wear my traditional clothes like the shalwar kameez. I was the only one dressed like this in the whole school. I knew that since I was wearing these clothes in front of 2,000 kids who had never seen clothes like this before that they would say mean things about me. But I thought, even if someone does say something to me, I'm not going to change it. I knew that once I dealt with these people, I could deal with anyone. Maybe they said things behind my back, but I don't know for sure because I never really paid attention or cared.

Miriam was determined to maintain her Pashtun culture and Muslim faith in America. She would often come home from school and spend a significant amount of time and energy reinforcing these identities by watching You-Tube videos of Pashtun weddings, parties, funerals, and music videos. She would also read literature posted on Pashtun websites and forums. She even found a new interest in Pashtun proverbs and folklore.

In some ways, Miriam was more interested in being Pashtun in the United States than she was before leaving her village in Pakistan. The same is true concerning her religious faith. Miriam was able to maintain connections with some of her Islamic teachers back in Pakistan by phone. Because of gender segregation, she had more direct access to the imam by phone in America then she had in her village back home. Now that she was living in America, she had more questions about Islam. The perception of being the only Muslim in her school deepened her religious faith.

> We fast the same way we did in Pakistan, but here I feel like its little better because you know back in Pakistan everybody is doing it but here you feel like the only one. We are the only ones fasting in our whole neighborhood. That makes me feel like I am doing something different than everyone else, and that feels good. I don't know if people back home would be able to do it, but we do. The whole time we have been here, I have never really changed the way I dress or how I practice Islam.

Miriam shares that she did not make many friends during high school. She admits that it was her commitment to dress differently and unwillingness to socialize that is likely to blame. She is thankful that some of the high school teachers went out of their way to help her to adjust and step out of her plan to remain isolated.

Miriam shares about one teacher in particular that helped her to adjust by simply asking Miriam to share her story:

> I became close with the teachers, especially this one teacher who taught ESL. Not just me, but like every student who was from a foreign country loved her class. After a tiring day, I would go to her class, and it felt like, "Yes! I'm home!" That's the kind of teacher she was. I would tell her my story about how we came here. She loved to listen to my story.

It was in ESL class that Miriam started to experience a sense of belonging. Being around other students who came from different places and hearing their stories gave Miriam a sense that she was not alone in her struggle to adjust. Sharing her story and having a teacher that was genuinely interested in hearing it also had a profound and positive impact in Miriam's adjustment.

According to Miriam, all of her teachers were nice and very helpful throughout high school. However, it was the teachers who took interest in her past experiences in Pakistan that seemed to have a lasting impact on her. For example, she recalls an art teacher who went out of his way to introduce some of Miriam's cultural experiences to her classmates. While his tactics were initially uncomfortable for Miriam, she appreciated his attempts:

> One time he showed a picture of Afghani people and said, "These are Miriam's cousins." The kids in the picture did not have nice clothes, and I was like, "Oh my God, why would he say this to these kids." Once, he asked me about the main difference between school in Pakistan and America. I told him that kids in Pakistan had a lot more respect for teachers because they carry a stick. The next morning, he brought in a long stick and when kids started talking, he hit the table and yelled, "Don't talk! I have a stick. Back in Miriam's country the teachers beat students when they do something wrong."

Miriam was initially embarrassed by the teacher's antics. She struggled to understand why he was asking her things about her culture and then making fun of them in front of the class. However, she also noticed that some of the kids in that class began asking her questions about her culture. This was the first time that other students began to take an interest in Miriam's story. The teacher explained to her that he thought maybe other kids were afraid to ask her questions because she might be offended. His strategy was to break the ice for other students to feel free to inquire further about Miriam's experiences.

Miriam graduated high school with honors. Her grades were such that she earned a state scholarship and admittance into a state university. However, the slow Green Card process meant that she had to pay out-of-state tuition and was ineligible to receive the awarded scholarship, making even community college unaffordable. Federal and state financial aid is not available for refugees with asylum status in the state where she resides.

Green Card Denied

Miriam did not understand what could possibly be taking so long for her to receive her Green Card. Other immigrant families that had arrived after her family had all received their legal residency within a year. It was not until their fifth year of living in the United States that Miriam's father received a letter explaining that their application for Green Cards was denied, and that they would have asylum status until further notice.

Miriam is no longer anticipating a Green Card and has resolved to move forward regardless if she ever becomes a permanent resident. That is not to say that the process has not taken a toll on Miriam's emotional well-being. The multiple interviews by Homeland Security, the continual stream of paperwork, and the process of waiting with no end in sight has caused Miriam to reconsider her initial thoughts regarding life in America.

> I think when we were in Pakistan, we thought America is one rich place. We thought that Americans never had to work. We thought that everything just comes to your house. Whatever you want, you can get it easily. I think that the way we imagined America was not even close to what it is really like. I feel like we have to go through so much for every single small thing. There is so much paperwork required for everything that we try to do. It makes us feel so tired.

Miriam's description of feeling tired might be better understood as hopelessness. Throughout our interviews, Miriam tends to vacillate between hopelessness and perseverance. She is keenly aware of how bad the situation is, but she often quickly counterbalances her negative thinking with something hopeful.

Initially it was the thought of getting an education that gave Miriam a sense of hope and the desire to persevere. However, she eventually concluded that the burden of caring for the entire extended family back in Pakistan and paying the full price for out of state tuition was simply too expensive.

> I wanted to go to school but since I didn't have a Green Card, it was too much money. Now, I look at my books and I feel shy around them. I feel like, you know, at one time, these books were my life, but now I don't even touch them. This is the saddest thing. I think I will regret this for all my life. But, sometimes I feel like, I know that I am 28 years old but maybe, *Inshalla* when I have time, I might go back to Islamic school. I want that time back in my life. Studying in the madrassa was the happiest time in my life.

If Miriam had been a permanent resident, her financial aid package would have exceeded the tuition bill. However, after seeing the cost of an American education, she accepted the fact that her dream of going to college would never be realized.

Transnational Family Dynamics in Pakistan

Miriam's family was struggling financially and could no longer continue sending the same amount of money back home to Pakistan. The decrease in monthly remittances quickly soured the relationship between Fazal and his brothers. It was at this point that Fazal's brothers demanded that he send both Miriam and her sister back to Pakistan to marry their first-cousins they had been promised to since they were young children.

> They decided our engagement to our cousins when we were young. The thing is, my father never even made the arrangement. It was my grandparents who said it when we were young. But it's part of the culture, and the woman doesn't really have a choice. It could be much worse. Sometimes they will make a young girl marry an older guy. The girl might be only like fourteen or fifteen years old, and the guy could be like forty years old. She has to live with him whether she likes him or not. They don't have a lot of respect for women in Pashtun culture. They don't give them a right to say what they want in life. If a woman wants to do anything they have to check with the men. The men might be like, "No, you can't do that thing because it is against our culture." They should give the ladies a little more say [long pause]. I mean, I'm not saying they should give us like full freedom to do whatever we want. I'm against that kind of freedom. But I think little more freedom would be good.

Miriam was willing to return to Pakistan and marry her cousin out of a desire to obey her parents. Her sister on the other hand was not. She never liked the arrangement with her cousin, and she had hoped that coming to America meant that she would not have to marry him. She pleaded with her mother and father to break off the engagement. Miriam shares how her father tried to discuss her sister's engagement with his brother however, it didn't go well.

> My uncle told my father that if she didn't marry his son then she couldn't marry anyone else. He said, "If she even thinks about marrying another guy then we will kill him." I think that's wrong and they shouldn't act this way, but that's what he said.

Miriam was also unhappy about her arrangement to her cousin but never considered asking to break the engagement. She believed that her feelings about marriage were less important than preserving family peace and unity.

However, seeing the response of her uncle towards her sister gave Miriam serious concerns about moving forward in marrying her cousin.

She had observed the discord with her future in-laws continually escalate since moving to America. Miriam began to wonder if she might be treated badly due to the problems between her father and his brothers. She feared that they would use her as a means to control her family in America and did not want to be used as leverage against her parents and siblings.

> I went to my father, and I was like, "Dad, you know I have never said anything to you about marrying my cousin Hamid, but I don't think I can do it. They will try to use me to take everything from you." I told him, "You know that everything I have done until now has been what's best for the whole family, not just me. But now, I can see that the family is not going to get better. Every single day they do things that makes our families worse with each other. Marrying Hamid isn't going to make that better, so I can't do it. I can't marry Hamid." He was like, "If you don't want to marry him, it's your life, you don't have to." I think if I was still in Pakistan I couldn't have done that. Not just Pakistan. Even one year ago here in America, I would have never said that to my father. So, I told my cousin, even now it makes me feel so bad, but I told him, "Hamid, I don't think it is going to work. You can marry whoever you want because I don't want, when I marry you, for your family not to treat me well." I think my father was surprised.

After annulling Miriam's and her sister's engagements, her father was immediately taken to a *jirga* by his brothers. Fazal was unable to obtain the necessary travel documents to go to Pakistan and attend the *jirga* meeting. He was ordered to pay money to his brothers and to equally distribute the properties he owned in Pakistan. His brothers were also given rights to any properties or wealth Fazal accumulates in America as well.

Miriam's father attempted to make an arrangement for her with another Pashtun American immigrant once the engagement to her cousin was broken. The terms of the engagement were quickly agreed upon by both families, and the wedding date was set. Then, three days later, everything was abruptly called off by the other family. Through a mutual friend in Pakistan, Miriam's future father in-law heard about her annulled engagement with her cousin and was advised not to pursue the marriage because her former fiancé would likely seek revenge against his son if they ever visited Pakistan. Miriam and her sister remain unmarried and are regularly reminded by their first cousins that they have no other options.

Nazima Returns to Pakistan

Miriam's mother, Nazima, returned to Pakistan to visit her ailing father. She promised to return after six months but did not. It has been more than three years. It is unlikely that Nazima will ever be allowed to return to the United States because she overstayed her six-month travel visa. Miriam and her siblings regularly take turns visiting their mother so that she always has one of her children with her in Pakistan. Since returning to Pakistan, Nazima has arranged marriages for Miriam's siblings who were not promised to cousins on their father's side, with their cousins on her side of the family.

As much as Miriam would like to marry someone on her mother's side, she has accepted that it is not possible. Now that her siblings are regularly visiting their spouses and mother in Pakistan, peace with Fazal's brothers is essential. Fazal wants Nazima to return to the United States, but thus far she has given no indication that she will. Even if Nazima was permitted to return to the United States, Miriam is not sure that she would because she seems happier in Pakistan. Miriam can understand why she left and does not blame her for returning home.

> We miss her, and I know my dad wants her to come back, but, I am happy that she is with her family. They are around her all the time. When she was here she was mostly alone. I was at work, and my brother and sisters were in school, so she was by herself all day long. She couldn't speak English, she couldn't go outside, and she couldn't drive so she would just stay inside and wait for us to come home. Then, when we would come, she would cook for us and make tea for us. She would be so excited when it was time for us to come home. She would sit in the kitchen, and we would just sit with her for a few minutes and then be like, "Okay Mom, we are going to watch YouTube." Then, she was alone again. I feel like, I wish I could bring that time back. It hurts me every time I think about it. If I could go back and spend more time with her I would, but I know that time isn't going to come back, and I don't think she is ever going to return.

Miriam says she wants that time back, but she also realizes that she continues to have the same struggle finding time to connect with her father as well. She rarely sees him, and when she does, it is usually only for a short time. During times when they are both home, Miriam says it is normally entertainment preferences that divide the family into separate rooms:

> When I visit Pakistan, I feel bad about the way I treat my father
> in America. I feel like I am doing the same thing to him that I
> did to my mom. When he's home, he is just sitting alone in his
> room watching the computer. The problem is he likes watch-
> ing the computer but not what we like to watch. He watches the
> news from back home all the time. We don't disturb him because
> he doesn't like us to ask him questions when he is watching the
> news. So, the rest of us sit upstairs and watch TV without him.

Miriam attributes the breakdown in her immediate family's unity to the
influence of American culture. While there are many things which she
values about the culture, the lack of family values is something she wishes
would change:

> I feel like, in America, families never have time for each other.
> Especially when it comes to older people. When older people
> come in to my work, they want to talk to me for a long time.
> They don't want to let me go because they are lonely, and they
> need someone to talk to. They want to tell me their story. They
> need people to listen to their stories, but they don't have anyone.
> Many of them are living alone in nursing homes. That makes me
> sad. Sometimes people come to the store where I work to get a
> card for their grandmother's birthday who lives in the nearby
> nursing home. I want to tell them, "Your grandmother doesn't
> need a card, she needs your time. She needs your attention but
> she is living alone." I wish that was different.

Miriam regularly encounters aging Americans because she has been
working for three years in the pharmacy and greeting card section of a
grocery store.

Miriam's Role as a Financial Provider

Miriam shares how she never imagined herself getting a job, but the American cultural expectation to work eventually wore her down: "Back in our
country, we never worked. But here, if you don't have a job, you feel lazy
and bad about yourself because everyone else is working and you are not."
Though Miriam initially resisted the idea of finding a job, her work experience has been mostly positive. When she started working, she was overwhelmed and couldn't sleep because of the steep learning curve. However, it
was not long before Miriam felt confident in her new role as a grocery store
employee. She says it was the patience and kindness of the customers and
coworkers that helped her to adjust. She has been recognized as "employee

of the month" three times in the past three years. Overall, she feels that the customers are incredibly kind to her. There were, however, two notable exceptions when Miriam's Muslim faith was perceived as problematic.

> My favorite part of work is talking with the customers because they are all so nice. Well, not all of them, but most of them were really kind to me. There was this one man who was not so nice, and I think it was because of my headscarf. He was an older guy who was looking for a birthday card. I went up to him and said, "Hello sir, how are you doing?" He didn't say anything back to me, but I didn't think anything of it because sometimes people just don't like to talk. But when he went to the front of the store, he told the cashier, "I just can't stand these people." After he left, the lady came to me looking concerned and said, "Did that guy say something to you?" I said, "No. Why?" That's when she told me what he had said about me. She also told me how sorry she was that he said something like that about me. It's a good thing he did not say it to me. I think if he had said it to me, it would have been more upsetting.
>
> There was another person who said something mean, but again, I thank God that I didn't hear it. This one lady told the manager, "The girl wearing a scarf on her head needs to go back to her own country!" They told me how she said some other mean stuff about me. For some reason, this lady's comments really hurt my feelings. My feelings were so hurt that I immediately got a headache. I thought my head was about to blow up or something. But then I decided, you know, in three years working here, only one or two persons have said mean things to me. Sometimes I say mean things about people if I don't like them. And the good thing is they didn't say it to my face, they said it to someone else. The girl who told me what happened, she said that she told the lady, "I don't know why you would say something about Miriam. She's the sweetest girl in our whole store." That made me feel better.

Miriam has developed such a good relationship with the store managers that she is able to return to Pakistan once a year for six months with a job waiting for her when she returns. She sees it as a privilege to spend time listening to the older customers even though at times she feels like she is not able to get all of her work completed.

Working full time has had an impact on Miriam's family relationships both in America and in Pakistan. For the first time, she recognizes how her father has spent most of his life working hard so that no one else had to. This realization has, in turn, created some frustration toward family members back home who continue to demand financial remittances.

> When we lived in Pakistan we used to tell our dad to send us money, and he would. We never thought about how hard he worked to get the money he was sending. We thought he had money because he was living in America. People always call us and ask us to send them money like we have an endless supply. My uncles and our cousins call all the time, and it makes us so mad. They have no idea how hard we work. We don't even see each other anymore because we work so much. Sometimes I feel like, why don't these people do something themselves? They don't know anything about making money because they have never had to work for money. Before I started working, I spent money without thinking because, if I needed more, I can just ask my father. I bought whatever I wanted. But then when I started working, I realized that it feels bad when you spend the money you worked so hard to get. Now I think about what I am buying, whether I really need it or if I just want it.

Most of Miriam's paychecks are spent on a combination of household necessities, trips for her siblings back to Pakistan, and money for her extended family back home.

The continual demands of extended family back in Pakistan means long working hours for Miriam and others in the family. Between conflicting work schedules and regular returns to Pakistan, it's rare for Miriam's family to have time together. Miriam feels her family is divided between America and Pakistan and is falling apart in both places.

Regardless of how hard she works, she can't seem to get ahead. While she is incredibly grateful for her experiences in America, she often wonders if her life is really better as a result of immigrating. She knows she has more freedom here as a woman. However, she is also keenly aware that her freedom is primarily expressed through working hard so that her family back in Pakistan does not have to. Almost all of her friends back in Islamic school have married and are now raising children. They, too, are primarily supported by the remittances sent from family members working abroad. This may lead Miriam to contemplate who has more freedom—her or the people she works so hard to support.

Analysis of Miriam's Narrative Identity

It would be difficult to overstate the impact of transnationalism on Miriam's identity formation. A significant part of Miriam's life in Pakistan entailed the difficulty of navigating the complex transnational relationship between her uncle, father, and mother. While her father's remittances financially provided for his entire extended family, it was her uncle who acted as the primary caretaker for Miriam and her siblings. She describes in her story how she hardly knew her father growing up and that she always considered her uncle as a father figure because they lived in his home. At one point in her story, Miriam voices regret for taking her uncle's side in conflicts involving her mother and father. Prior to moving, Miriam defined "us" as her uncle's people, a category that was often reinforced at the expense of making her mother's family "them". However, following the weddings of Miriam's siblings to their cousins on their mother's side, the "us" and "them" boundaries have essentially reversed. If it were not for the financial ties that Fazal's brothers were awarded in the *jirga*, Miriam suspects she would never hear from her uncle's people.

While Miriam's "us" and "them" framework is dynamic, her position throughout the story as a mediator remains rather static. In Pakistan and in the United States she narrates herself at the intersection of contentious family relationships that span across two countries. That role remains consistent for Miriam. She, more than anyone else in the family, is responsible to maintain regular contact with all extended family back in Pakistan, including her uncle's people which is a difficult task. Miriam's extended and immediate families have unofficially nominated her as the bridge builder between the two cultures which often compete and conflict with one another. Miriam is the one who best understands both languages and cultures, and she can skillfully navigate in either setting. She is, therefore, responsible to integrate her family, ensuring that they are capable of operating in both societies seamlessly and that there is family peace despite the recent events of broken engagements and lawsuits. While Miriam's regular interaction with the extended family has afforded her a great deal of influence in their daily lives in Pakistan, the same is true of their influence on her life in America.

Problematic Social Media Posts

In addition to maintaining peace between extended family members, Miriam must regularly communicate and demonstrate how she and her siblings maintain their cultural and religious traditions to skeptical family members back in Pakistan. She does this through computer mediated communication and social media. Since it is culturally taboo for her to have an online profile, she uses her brother's account. All but four of her brother's 88 Facebook friends are extended family members and friends back in Pakistan. Miriam regularly makes posts on his wall affirming his Pashtun identity and commitment to Islam. Miriam arrived in the United States knowing that her extended family back in Pakistan expected her to abandon her religion and culture. At times, it seems Miriam is on a quest to prove them wrong. She posts pictures of a wonderful *Eid* celebration in the mosque despite the fact that she personally thought the celebration was significantly lacking compared to the ones in Pakistan. Miriam's Facebook posts depict more of a socially desirable identity then the actual one that is embodied offline. She is constantly reminded of her uncle's words prior to leaving Pakistan, "The minute you go to America you forget about Islam and your culture." She knows that her family back home is watching and waiting to see how America changes her and her siblings. For Miriam, this is a significant motivator for her and her siblings to maintain their Islamic faith and culture.

In addition, Facebook poses a continual problem for Miriam's family concerning financial remittances. The desire to show people back home that they are thriving in America rather than struggling to make ends meet increases the financial demands of extended family members. This leaves Miriam with the difficult decision to either let people know about their financial hardship (which would likely be embarrassing) or continue sending more money than they can afford. The latter is the only viable option because of the overwhelming pressure to maintain an honorable position with family members in Pakistan.

Conclusion through the Lens of the Taliban

Miriam's use of Ahmad Wazir as the preface to her life history is intriguing considering he was able to transcend boundaries and garner respect from both the mountain and hill people. While Miriam describes the boundaries between these two peoples as related to education and modernity, a careful analysis of her story reveals that these boundaries could be rearticulated as the mountain people's preference for traditional Pashtun culture over the teachings of Islam. Miriam frames the mountain people within a context of folklore and backwards cultural practices that she suggests have no basis in Islam. This is not surprising considering Miriam views education in Pakistan primarily through the lens of the Islamic madrassa. She also equates modernity with women's rights, particularly the right to an Islamic education. She suggests that the mountain women are deprived of education because the men value Pashtun culture more than the teachings of Islam.

The conflict between culture and religion is further developed by Miriam when she blames Pashtun culture for her arranged marriage and the problems that her uncle's people have caused following the dissolution of the engagement. Miriam uses the boundary between Pashtun culture and Islam in her story as a means of explaining and justifying ways in which she and her family have changed. The competing ideologies of Pashtun culture and Islam for Miriam are most clearly articulated in a story she shares regarding the identity and role of the Taliban in her village:

> We call them the peace community, but some call them Taliban. They have helped a lot of people. Especially in 2001 when everyone was coming over the border from Afghanistan during the war. We could not tell who were good people and who were bad people, and things got really bad in our village. It was like every single morning we would find out about somebody who was killed during the nighttime. Every day we would go to the market for shopping, and there would be someone dead. Sometimes they would even cut people's heads off.
>
> Before they [Taliban] came, we were afraid to go to the market because everyone would be carrying guns like it was part of men's fashion. But, after they came, no one was allowed to take their gun to the market. Even the mountain people would hide their guns before they would come into the village. When the peace community was visiting, there were no more problems.
>
> They would even stand up for women! If a woman needs help, she can call the peace community, and they can come and help her. I once heard that there was going to be a forced marriage, and they came to that house and said, "If that girl doesn't want to marry that guy you can't force her to do it because Islam doesn't say you can do that to her!"
>
> They keep people from giving more importance to the culture than to Islam. Even if there is a problem with families, you can call them, and they will come and listen to both sides and decide who is right and who is wrong based on Islam not the culture. This is not a *jirga*. Most of the time I think the *jirga* people do the right thing but sometimes, even they give more importance to the culture. But the peace community will stand up for what Islam says. They say what the right thing to do is based on what Islam says, not the culture. But you know, that is how it used to be. These days there are so many bad people in

Pakistan. We don't really know anymore who is really part of the peace community.

It is no coincidence that the specific Pashtun traditions addressed by the Taliban in her brief description are the same issues that have plagued her and her family since moving to the United States. Associating forced marriages, the threat of revenge killings, and cultural *jirga* rulings as incompatible with Islam enables Miriam to maintain both a Pashtun and Muslim identity in the United States despite the opinions back home that may suggest otherwise. Miriam's suggestion that her family in Pakistan is ascribing more power to Pashtun traditions than Islam is questionable considering there is much debate among Islamic scholars regarding forced marriages, revenge killings, and inheritance rights.

Miriam's appeal to Islam over Pashtun culture when there is a conflict makes her connection with Ahmad Wazir particularly intriguing. The event that earned him, and Miriam by association, an honorable position among both the mountain and hill peoples was a revenge killing, something that she now believes is antithetical to the teachings of Islam. However, it was the un-Islamic forced marriage of her grandfather's sister to a much older man that somewhat justified the revenge for Miriam. This vacillation concerning the morality of Ahmad Wazir's actions in light of Pashtun traditions and the teachings of Islam is a reoccurring theme throughout Miriam's story. She continually strives to do what she believes is right and good in light of the relationships and the context. She recognizes that whatever she does will be interpreted through the lenses of competing ideologies espoused by a variety of strained but significant relationships across two countries. This is a heavy burden for Miriam. However, from childhood she has learned how to navigate contentious relationships in various contexts. When Miriam's internal desires are in conflict with the broader expectations of her extended family, she redefines Islam as a means of validating her position and realigning her allegiances.

Despite the hardship, Miriam maintains a positive attitude about her life in America and her life in Pakistan. She demonstrates an amazing ability to remain optimistic even though America is nothing like she imagined it would be. One reason for Miriam's adaptability is that she is nothing like she thought she would be either. She never imagined that she would attend a mixed gendered high school, learn English, and graduate with honors. Even when her hopes for a Green Card and going to college ended, she found a new sense of purpose through working and providing an income source for her family both in America and back in Pakistan. Throughout her story, it becomes apparent that Miriam strives to see the others through a lens of charity even if they do not offer her the same courtesy. Neverthe-less, her boldness and independence has earned her a privileged position amongst her family and friends. Thinking back to the preface of Miriam's story concerning Ahmad Wazir, I can't help but wonder if her narration of the partiality shown to her by grandfather might be Miriam's way of establishing herself as a peacemaker who bridges the gap between multiple peoples by attaining honor in both spaces.

10

Concluding with a Reflexive Challenge to People Group Identity

GIVEN THE SHIFT IN ethnography towards greater reflexivity, this chapter discusses some of my previous experiences and assumptions concerning identity and how they have changed in light of the past six years of research. Prior to conducting this study, my wife and I spent six years in a mission organization where we were trained to separate the world's population into ethno-linguistic People Groups or People Group Identity. For nearly twenty years, People Group thinking has shaped my views of culture, peoples, and theology. However, walking alongside my research participants over the past six years has challenged my confidence in the validity of the People Group paradigm.

I originally set out in this project to study the acculturation patterns of Pashtun immigrants. However, it soon became apparent that in some cases, I was more interested in Pashtun identity than some of my research participants. In fact, almost all the Pashtun immigrants I interviewed would contrast their Pashtun identity in opposition to some other expression of Pashtun culture. Most seemed to view being Pashtun alongside multiple other overlapping sociocultural identifications rather than having a strong reified ethnic identity. These identifications have dynamic meanings and levels of importance depending on the sociocultural and relational context. Thus, I am not convinced that simply considering an individual's interaction, integration, or rejection of sociocultural boundaries implies a substantive sense of identity or non-identity with any particular group. In light of this conclusion, this final chapter explores the advent of People Group thinking and challenges the biblical weight I assigned it nearly two decades ago.

The 1974 Lausanne Congress

People Group thinking, as it is understood among evangelical missiologists, was first articulated by Ralph Winter at the 1974 Lausanne Congress. Prior to addressing Lausanne participants, Ralph Winter circulated a paper addressing the common misconception that since the gospel was present in nearly every nation, the Great Commission had been fulfilled. His primary aim was to demonstrate that the geographical spread of the gospel did not imply that all cultural sub-groups within nations had access to it. Winter coined the term "people blindness" to explain why these sub-groups were going unnoticed:

> Blindness to the existence of separate *peoples* within *countries*; a blindness I might add, which seems more prevalent in the U.S. and among U.S. missionaries than anywhere else. The Bible rightly translated could have made this plain to us. The nations to which Jesus often referred were mainly ethnic groups within the single political structure of the Roman government.[1]

These sub-groups, according to Winter, could be due to cultural, linguistic, or even generational distance that often leads to barriers of effective evangelism. Winter does distinguish between generational and cultural barriers suggesting that age differences are only temporary while cultural differences are possibly permanent. Winter argued that these cultural distinctions would require new congregations and a special kind of evangelism that would remove sociocultural stumbling blocks or barriers to the gospel.

Winter's categories of evangelism are as follows: E-1 (same culture and language), E-2 (similar culture and language), and E-3 (different culture and language). The basis of distinction between E-1 and E-2 is the need for forming a new congregation based on cultural differences between groups. The need for distinct congregations requires the need for outside or special evangelism. Winter's underlying assumption is that the cultural differences, and in some cases, historical animosity between near neighbor groups may prevent the gospel from spreading between them. Therefore, he suggests that E-3 evangelists from the outside may be more effective than their near neighbor E-2 evangelist in reaching a cultural group that has no Christian witness.

Much of Winter's argument was based on Acts 1:8: "But you shall receive power when the Holy Spirit has come upon you; and you will be my witnesses in Jerusalem [E-1] and in all Judea [E-1] and Samaria [E-2], and to the end of the earth [E-3]" (RSV). Winter argued that the preceding

---

1. Winter, "Highest Priority," 221.

passage was not a geographical mandate, but rather that Jesus is "taking into account cultural distance as the primary factor."[2] However, most New Testament scholars argue the passage is both geographical and ethnic.[3] There is significant debate concerning the geographic scope of the phrase "ends of the earth." However, the ethnic denotation of the phrase is clearly laid out in Luke's use of Isaiah 49:6: "For so the Lord has commanded us, saying, 'I have made you a light for the Gentiles, that you may bring salvation to the ends of the earth'" (Acts 13:47, ESV). The ethnic category so far as Luke is concerned, is broadly defined as Gentiles rather than People Groups. The ethnic emphasis is on the universal scope of salvation that includes Gentiles rather than a proof text for categorizing identity based on cultural boundaries. Furthermore, it is debatable that Acts 1:8 is an appropriate passage to develop such a doctrine given a number of New Testament scholars see this passage as simply as an outline of the book of Acts.[4]

A selection of people responded to Winter's pre-conference paper. Some took issue with Winter's new model of evangelism, particularly the need for new congregations and a special kind of outside evangelism. It seems there was significant pushback concerning Winter's unapologetic views of cultural determinism. Jacob Loewen, for example, was concerned with Winter's suggestion of using outside workers to evangelize near neighbors that may have prejudice towards one another:

> I find the prejudice reason for using E-3 over against E-2 very questionable, because Christ, Paul plainly tells us, has torn down the walls of separation (Eph. 2:13–16), and in Christ there is no distinction between Jews or Gentiles, slave or free man, etc. (Col. 3:10–11). Thus when a person of E-3 distance must evangelize in a situation where prejudice keeps the church of E-2 distance from doing the job, I fear that the converts are really being taught to accept an inferior kind of Christianity—a Christianity that is not strong enough to break down the walls of prejudice. I have serious question [sic] whether this kind of Christianity is worth "selling."[5]

Loewen also stated anthropological concerns with Winter's underlying assumptions of the impenetrability of cultural boundaries by citing two examples of cultural diffusion between enemy tribes in the use of

2. Winter, "Highest Priority," 219.

3. Bock, Acts; Bruce, Commentary Acts; Keener, Acts Exegetical Commentary; Köstenberger and O'Brien, Salvation to the Ends of the Earth; Larkin, Acts.

4. Melbourne, "Acts 1: 8 re-examined," 1–19.

5. Loewen, "Response to Dr. Ralph Winter's Paper," 248.

hallucinogenic drugs and anti-witch medicine. His point was that very few cultures in the twentieth century live in isolation and many of their cultural traits are diffused from neighboring cultural contact. Loewen's argument that cultural practices are not bound but rather are passed back and forth among near neighboring cultures begged the question as to why the gospel would differ? In other words, Winter's suggestion that the gospel would not overcome cultural boundaries while drugs and witchcraft did was questionable. Loewen argued that as one culture or group experiences the gospel and is transformed by the gospel, the boundaries of culture will burst, and the gospel will overflow into surrounding groups rather than being contained or isolated.

Phillip Hogan's response applauded Winter's assessment of the cultural scope of missions as opposed to a geographical one. He further acknowledged the pragmatic nature of the new model for evangelism. However, for Hogan, pragmatism alone was insufficient considering the potential repercussion of further dividing the body of Christ:

> Must we forever remain divided on the basis of culture, language, or color? Is it not possible to believe that newly-won Christians can be so obsessed with the object of their new love that the expulsive power of this new affection will overcome human dividing lines?[6]

Hogan concludes his response by reminding the Lausanne gatherers of the need to depend ultimately on the Holy Spirit rather than human strategies. He specifically references Winter's proof text, Acts 1:8, and emphasizes that if the Holy Spirit does not work powerfully on the believer's behalf then no human strategy, no matter how well planned, will be effective.

Pablo Pérez stated similar concerns about forming churches around cultural distinctions saying,

> This may be pragmatically defensible, and even temporarily tolerated, but it will also tend to perpetuate adverse existing conditions and prejudices simply because they can be labeled as culturally determined . . . even the implied thought behind this reasoning will tend to absolutize culture.[7]

He concludes his argument, much like Hogan and Loewen, by reminding the Lausanne Congress of the radical nature of the church and its ability to effect change in culture. While he acknowledges the importance of culture and affirms the need for cultural sensitivity, Pérez refused to

---

6. Hogan, "Response to Dr. Ralph Winter's Paper," 243.

7. Pérez, "Response to Dr. Ralph Winter's Paper," 256–57.

accept cultural determinism as the basis for evangelistic strategies. Rather, he argues that the Holy Spirit is the only determinant in evangelism and cultural barriers or distances are not obstacles for Him.

Winter, in his Lausanne presentation, responds to Hogan, Pérez, and Loewen. He graciously reminded Hogan that the Holy Spirit and careful strategizing need not be mutually exclusive. Winter essentially dismisses Pérez, as a mono-cultural evangelist, and therefore, unable to speak to the need for cross-cultural evangelism:

> Dr. Pérez has helpfully stressed the fact that the gospel changes human cultures; it does not merely yield to them. He, of course, is speaking within a culture as an E-1 evangelist. This is the proper attitude. But if Dr. Pérez were to go to a foreign country to a new situation, he would then be in a different situation, and would have to be very respectful of the culture and not fight against it as he knows how to do within his own culture.[8]

In addressing Loewen's concerns, Winter suggests something quite strange, "As an anthropologist, he [Loewen] seems almost to say that witnessing to totally strange people [E-3] is so difficult that it ought not be attempted."[9] In reading Loewen's response, it is difficult to understand how Winter came to such a conclusion. Certainly, Loewen is keenly aware of the difficulties associated with E-3 evangelism and does write about the limitations from an anthropological perspective. However, he clearly states the value of E-3 evangelism in his response to Winter saying, "As God has used E-3 in the past, I am convinced he will also use it in the future."[10]

During the presentation, Winter emphatically rejected the idea that this new form of evangelism was a form of segregating of churches. Rather, he viewed it as a symphony with various cultures playing their own instruments from the same score—the Bible. He is arguing for unity in diversity, a clear shift from the cultural imperialism of mission history. He is not arguing for segregation but rather the "equal acceptability of cultural traditions" which he suggests was the norm for the New Testament Church and the apostle Paul. Winter sees this most clearly in Paul's letter to the churches in Galatia,

> Paul's letter to the Galatians . . . shows us how determined he was to allow the Galatian Christians to follow a different Christian life-style. Thus, while we do not have any record of his

---

8. Winter, "Highest Priority," 227.

9. Winter, "Highest Priority," 227.

10. Loewen, "Response to Dr. Ralph Winter's Paper," 248.

[Paul] forcing people to meet separately, we do encounter all of Paul's holy boldness set in opposition to anyone who would try to preserve a single normative pattern of Christian life through a cultural imperialism that would prevent people from employing their own language and culture as a vehicle for worship and witness. . . . It is a clear-cut apostolic policy against forcing Christians of one life-style to be proselytized to the cultural patterns of another. This is not a peripheral matter in the New Testament. True circumcision is of the heart. True baptism is of the heart. It is a matter of faith, not works, or customs, or rites. In Christ there is freedom and liberty in this regard— people must be free either to retain or abandon their native language and life-style. . . . In my opinion, this question about evangelistic strategy in the forming of separate congregations must be considered an area of Christian liberty, and is to be decided purely on the basis of whether or not it allows the gospel to be presented effectively to more people–that is, whether it is evangelistically strategic.[11]

Perhaps it is Winter's conflation of a normative or prescribed Christian life-style with patterns of worship that cause so much confusion. Winter's reading of Galatians concerning Paul's refusal to force Gentile believers to observe patterns of the Jewish law for salvation is widely accepted. However, it is a far leap to conclude that the apostle would have therefore been in favor of separate congregations based on linguistic and cultural differences or affinities. Nevertheless, the 1974 Lausanne Congress was a watershed moment for missiology with Winter's new model for evangelism being the most influential paradigm shift in missiological thinking. Despite the significant pushback from the respondents, this new model would quickly become the analytical framework to measure and mobilize the Church for Great Commission work among People Groups.

Popularizing the Model

Following the 1974 presentation at Lausanne, Winter released a pamphlet titled *The New Macedonia: A Revolutionary New Era in Mission Begins.* The pamphlet was a combination of the paper circulated prior to the Lausanne meeting and the paper presented at the conference. Winter's comments addressing the concerns of Hogan, Loewen, and Pérez were not included. Winter's colleague and Dean Emeritus of Fuller Seminary School of World Mission, Donald McGavran, wrote the introduction.

---

11. Winter, "Highest Priority," 237–40.

Within this introduction, he outlines a strategy utilizing Winter's new categories of evangelism. McGavran begins by addressing "old era" concerns of Western paternalism stating,

> To continue harping on that old message is wrong in this new era when suddenly we are conscious of the two point seven billion who are living and dying without Christ and who *cannot be reached by near neighbor evangelism* [emphasis added].[12]

McGavran argued that the Church was entering a new era in which mature churches in every country needed to recruit missionaries to,

> Deculturalize themselves and enculture themselves in the segment of population concerned, learn the language thoroughly, and then father new congregations which are soundly Christian, filled with the Holy Spirit, obedient to the Bible *and loyal to the good in their own culture* [emphasis added].[13]

He defines segment populations as "a country, a ward of our great city, a tribe, a caste, an income bracket, the intelligentsia, the illiterate, the community whose men drive taxis in our metropolis, the landowners, [and] landless laborers."[14] McGavran concludes the introduction with a strong statement of support for Winter's ideas presented at Lausanne,

> Christians must not delude themselves with the comfortable assumption that existing churches using near neighbor evangelism will complete the task. They will not. They cannot. This is the hard, unshakable core of what Dr. Winter told Lausanne. . . . Nothing said at Lausanne had more meaning for the expansion of Christianity between now [1975] and the year 2000.[15]

Though Winter had stated from the beginning that his strategy for evangelism was not promoting enforced segregation of congregations, McGavran's statement regarding the need for churches to remain "loyal to the good in their own culture" seems to suggest otherwise. It was not until 1982 that a Lausanne strategy group gathered together to define the concept of People Groups:

> A People Group is 'a significantly large grouping of individuals who perceive themselves to have a common affinity for one another because of their shared language, religion, ethnicity, residence,

12. Winter, *New Macedonia*, 3.
13. Winter, *New Macedonia*, 3.
14. Winter, *New Macedonia*, 3.
15. Winter, *New Macedonia*, 5.

occupation, class or caste, situation, etc., or combinations of these.' For evangelistic purposes it is 'the largest group within which the gospel can spread as a church planting movement without encountering barriers of understanding or acceptance.'[16]

A combination of these definitions would quickly become the language that most missiologists, churches, and mission organizations used and continue to use in strategizing mission activity. For example, the International Mission Board (IMB) Global Research website defines People Groups as follows:

> Ethnolinguistic group with a common self-identity that is shared by the various members. . . . Usually there is a common self-name and a sense of common identity of individuals identified with the group. A common history, customs, family and clan identities, as well as marriage rules and practices, age-grades and other obligation covenants, and inheritance patterns and rules are some of the common ethnic factors defining or distinguishing a people.[17]

Organizations such as the Joshua Project and Finishing the Task simplify the definition to the latter part of the Lausanne Chicago definition stating, "The largest group within which the gospel can spread as a church planting movement without encountering barriers of understanding or acceptance."

Winter's and Bruce Koch's article *Finishing the Task*, featured in the third and fourth editions of *Perspectives on the World Christian Movement*, is likely more well-known than his 1974 Lausanne presentation or pamphlet. It is here that the People Group model is popularized and takes its current shape that is often referenced in missiological and church settings. The article outlines "four useful ways of looking at the idea of people groups: blocs of peoples, ethnolinguistic peoples, sociopeoples, and unimax peoples."[18] These four ways of viewing People Groups are defined as follows:

1. Blocs of peoples are a limited number of summary categories into which we can place peoples in order to analyze them

2. An ethnolinguistic people is an ethnic group distinguished by its self-identity with traditions of common descent, history, customs, and language

---

16. Winter and Koch, "Finishing the Task," 536.

17. Peoplegroups.org.

18. Winter and Koch, "Finishing the Task," 534.

3. A sociopeople is a relatively small association of peers who have an affinity for one another based upon a shared interest, activity or occupation

4. A unimax people is the maximum sized group sufficiently unified to be the target of a single people movement to Christ, where 'unified' refers to the fact that there are no significant barriers of either understanding or acceptance to stop the spread of the gospel.[19]

While this expansion of the 1974 presentation is a step in the right direction, it still problematic in that it is built upon a fundamentally flawed foundation of nineteenth century cultural determinism.

Missiology not Shifting

In addition to the aforementioned concerns voiced at Lausanne, evangelical social scientists have urged caution regarding the use of the People Group model since its inception. Paul Hiebert, for example, was particularly troubled with Winter and McGavern's use of outdated theories in social science:

> The church growth and people groups movements are in danger of social reductionism. . . . The concept of people groups fits tribal societies at best, like those social anthropologists used as the basis for their studies. But peasant and urban societies cannot be cut up into distinct, bounded people groups without seriously distorting the picture.[20]

For Hiebert, the People Group model is too simplistic to address the dynamic nature of culture and societies and is prone to cultural relativism that often leads to missionaries seeking to preserve cultures at all cost. Hiebert warned that such an approach "leads us to emphasize human differences, to justify ethnic pride, and ultimately to sanction segregation and ethnic cleansing.[21]

Robert Priest also has concerns with some of the ideas spawned from McGavran's Church Growth School. He views the homogeneous unit principle, People Groups, and indigeneity as "crude categories."[22] Priest further suggests that these categories are rooted in a territorialized past that is hardly

---

19. Winter and Koch, "Finishing the Task," 535.
20. Hiebert, "Social Sciences and Missions," 193.
21. Hiebert, "Social Sciences and Missions," 207.
22. Priest, "Afterword," 191.

representative of current trends of migration. He attributes these outdated
paradigms to McGavran's intentional disengagement from anthropology:

> While anthropology was pioneering sophisticated new ways of
> understanding ethnicity and ethnic boundaries, McGavran's
> disciples were not encouraged to interact with, and draw on,
> such new conceptual tools. His school of missiology cut itself off
> from the best thinking and research on the nature of social class
> and of racial and ethnic boundaries. It treated "boundaries" as
> natural and automatic by-products of difference (which could
> include differences of phenotype, language, culture, wealth),
> with assumed homogeneity within a given unit. There was little
> effort to carefully unpack the exact nature of social identities and
> boundaries that exist. Boundaries of hatred and prejudice were
> treated as equivalent to boundaries of language and culture.[23]

When social scientists made significant shifts away from essentialism
toward constructivism in the mid-twentieth century, missiology did not
follow suit. Michael Rynkiewich suggests that mission studies and anthropology once had a mutually beneficial relationship that has since "stag-
nated and now is waning."[24] Rynkiewich suggests that missiology adopted
a modernist approach from anthropology after WWII and never looked
back. While this disentanglement of missiology from anthropology is not
a recent phenomenon, Priest suggests that "at no time in the last sixty
years has the outlook for missiological engagement with anthropology
looked more dismal."[25]

     In addition to debatable theories and conceptual tools for studying
culture, missiological paradigms for conceptualizing identity are equally
lacking. Identity is presented as culturally or socially determined and observable through behaviors driven by values and beliefs. Craig Ott sum-
marizes the influence of essentialist anthropology in missiological concepts
of identity saying,

> Under the influence of nineteenth-century European Roman-
> ticism and nationalism, the concept of culture developed as a
> distinct and essential feature of human identity. This essentialist
> understanding of culture claims that cultures are well-defined
> entities, more or less self-contained, bounded social systems,

---

23. Priest, "Afterword," 186.

24. Rynkiewich, "Do We Need a Postmodern Anthropology for Mission," 151.

25. Priest, "Value of Anthropology for Missiological Engagements," 29–30.

clearly differentiated from one another, the culture defined a person's identity, values, and behavior.[26]

Ott further argues that this nineteenth century essentialist understandings of anthropology heavily influenced Winter's People Group model and many of the subsequent strategies as well.

While the People Group model appears to be outdated, and in many cases no longer applicable, it may be the case that what these contemporary patterns reveal is that these groups were far less bounded and culturally determined than originally thought. Based on the previous chapters, I would argue that the variety of new narratives introduced by global flows of people, ideas, and technologies has simply revealed what has always been true—individuals are simultaneously shaping and being shaped by culture as opposed to the unidirectional model of cultural determinism so often perpetuated in nineteenth-century anthropology and much of current missiology.

The affinities used to define People Groups are categories of practice which are intrinsic to all of social life.[27] The People Group model wrongfully conflates these categories of practice into categories of analysis and, eventually, categories of identity. For example, a person may be observed negotiating categories of practice such as religion, politics, and culture etc., then, in turn, be presented as having a substantive religious, national, or ethnic identity. The categories used for analysis in identity politics may not be accepted categories of an individual's identity. In fact, individuals may not classify themselves at all. One should not assume that categorical identity is intrinsic, shared, or desired.

The People Group model gives culture a misleading ontological or metaphysical status. In doing so, "culture becomes a kind of ghetto or prison: you are this kind of human being, born in this community, this tradition, this religion."[28] Presenting individuals as a reflection of sociocultural entities overemphasizes culture and collective identity and deemphasizes the individual capacity to create, sustain, and even transform culture. In essence, missiology needs a shift from looking at group identity to looking at individual identifications and the cognitive interpretive process of group making. Cultural groups are not ontological realities but rather epistemological realities; not things in the world, but rather ways in which to see the world. It should not be assumed that a cultural boundary signaling an affinity or difference is necessarily a person's identity.

26. Ott, "Globalization and Contextualization," 49–50.

27. Brubaker, *Ethnicity Without Groups*.

28. Rapport, "Liberal Treatment of Difference," 706.

Missiological classification of People Groups, much like identity politics, is driven by the need for an interpretive and analytical framework in order to measure progress and mobilize. In that sense, the People Group model is incredibly effective. No other model is more widely accepted and used to measure progress in completing the Great Commission. However, acknowledging the effectiveness of the model as an analytical tool is not an affirmation of its validity. Even the use of the model for the sake of analysis and measurement has created problems. The larger concern however is that the People Group model has moved beyond an analytical framework for mobilization to a theological one that informs missiological strategies.

From Analytical Tool to the Biblical Model

Despite the fact that there is reasonable concern regarding the validity and the sufficiency of the People Group model, it is rarely questioned. One reason, as mentioned above, is the disconnect of missiology from the social sciences. However, another more pressing reason for the unexamined support of People Group thinking is the ascribed biblical validity of the model. Robertson McQuilken warned about the temptation to read People Group classification and the ensuing strategies back into the Bible. He sees these models as "legitimate for tactical purposes" but cautions giving them scriptural authority.[29] In reference to the confusion often associated with enumerating and classifying People Groups, McQuilken states:

> We might dissipate some of the confusion if we stuck with biblical definitions of the task of the church and clearly identified as extra-biblical but pragmatically defensible other definitions, goals, and programs. For the sake of pointing toward a solution, let me suggest a simple statement of biblical definitions as I see them: the initial evangelistic task of the church is to see that every person on earth hears the gospel with understanding and that a congregation of regenerated people is established in every community.[30]

McQuilken's suggestion sounds reminiscent of the original responses given to Winter more than twenty years prior. He recognizes the pragmatic value of the model yet questions the validity of giving biblical weight to extra biblical categories.

29. McQuilken, "Use and Misuse of the Social Sciences," 182.
30. McQuilken, "Use and Misuse of the Social Sciences," 181.

Despite McQuilken's clear call for caution, the model continues to be readily accepted as biblical and is, therefore, given an intrinsic value that will not likely change for many years. For example, Rick Warren, pastor of the mega-church Saddleback, recently stated in an interview with Christianity Today, "Twice Revelation says that around the throne in heaven will be people from every language, every nation, and every tribe. I take this literally. Yet there are still 3,400 unengaged tribes because they're very small."[31] John Piper sees the ethno-linguistic categorization of People Groups as biblically based as well. He argues that the "people group focus governed Paul's missionary practice."[32] He, too, sees Revelation 5:9–10 as the "decisive text" that describes the missionary strategy. Piper differentiates, however, between the sociological and cultural affinities of the 1982 Lausanne definition developed in Chicago, stating,

> The *biblical* concept of 'peoples' or 'nations' cannot be stretched to include individuals grouped on the basis of things like occupation or residence or handicaps. These are sociological groupings that are very relevant for evangelistic strategy but do not figure into defining the biblical meaning of 'peoples' or 'nations.'[33]

Piper underestimates the influence of the sociological and overlooks the biblical examples of socio-political nations throughout scripture (i.e., Egypt, Assyria, Babylon, and Rome). Much like McGavran and Winter, Piper gives culture a misleading ontological status and discounts the influence and rise of nationalism.

The Apostle Paul ascribes to multiple identifications in Scripture: a Jew (Romans 9:3, 4) and a Benjamite (Philippians 3:5), a Roman citizen (Acts 22:22–29), born in Tarsus (Acts 22:3), and a citizen of heaven (Philippians 3:20). Paul had the ability to utilize or suspend these identifications and take on others so that he might save some (1 Corinthians 9:20–22). It seems unlikely that the Apostle viewed the world in light of People Groups especially considering he did not see himself in such narrow terms. However, according to Piper,

> Paul's conception of the missionary task is not merely to win more and more individual people to Christ (which he could have done very efficiently in these familiar regions), but the reaching of more and more peoples or nations. His focus was

---

31. Morgan, "Rick Warren's Final Frontier," 36.

32. Piper, "Supremacy of God among 'All the Nations,'" 20.

33. Piper, "Supremacy of God among 'All the Nations,'" 16.

not primarily on new geographic areas. Rather, he was gripped
by the vision of unreached peoples.[34]

Piper argues at length that the New Testament phrase *panta ta ethne* was understood by Paul as "people groups rather than Gentile individuals."[35] Further,
he cites Romans 15:9–21 as one of many proof texts to demonstrate Paul's
emphasis on People Groups rather than a geographical framework.

In contrast to Piper, David Bosch uses Romans 15:9–21 to show Paul's
regional/geographic understanding of the mission. "Paul thinks regionally,
not ethnically; he chooses cities that have a representative character."[36] Bosch
further argues that it is "misleading" to suggests that Paul was interested in
'nations' rather than individual 'gentiles.'[37] For Bosch, the geographic focus
of the New Testament is meant to reveal the theological and missiological scope of Christ's salvation. Bosch sees Matthew's use of *panta ta ethne*
through the lens of God's universal mission rather than a statement about
sociocultural groupings. "It is clear, then that Matthew was simply trying to
say that Jesus was no longer sent only to Israel but had, in fact, become the
savior of all humankind including the Jews."[38]

The unity of the Church is paramount for Bosch. He explains that human barriers of separation are transcended by our participation in the death
and resurrection of Christ through baptism and realized through the Lord's
Supper. He believes that the unity of the body of Christ is what constitutes
its being:

> The unity of the church—no, the church itself—is called in
> question when groups of Christians segregate themselves on
> the basis of such dubious distinctions as race, ethnicity, sex, or
> social status. God in Christ has accepted us unconditionally;
> we have to do likewise in regard to one another. Segregation of
> the church destroys its internal life and denies its grounding in
> the substitutionary death of Christ.[39]

For Bosch, the idea of separate local congregations due to sociocultural
differences would be inconceivable in Paul's thinking. He argues that what
Paul envisioned Jews and Gentiles transformed into the people of God
without distinction.

34. Piper, "Supremacy of God among 'All the Nations,'" 21.
35. Piper, "Supremacy of God among 'All the Nations,'" 19.
36. Bosch, *Transforming Mission*, 130.
37. Bosch, *Transforming Mission*, 130.
38. Bosch, *Transforming Mission*, 64.
39. Bosch, *Transforming Mission*, 167.

John Zizioulas also argues that New Testament Christian assemblies were identified through particular cities rather than sociocultural groupings. He too suggests that there is no evidence of multiple congregations based on ethnic distinctions within a singular locality within the early church:

> From a study especially of the Pauline letters we are led to the conclusion that almost without exception the word εκκλεσια is used in the singular when applied to a city, whereas its use in the plural is always connected with geographic areas larger than a city. If this is not to be regarded as a mere accident, it becomes significant to ask: why does Paul *never* use the term Church in plural when referring to a city? Given the concreteness with which the word εκκλεσια is used in Paul's writings, where it normally means the actual assembly of the faithful (see e.g., 1 Cor.10–14), the conclusion is almost inevitable that there was only one such assembly which was named εκκλεσια. In other words, we must conclude that the earliest form of local Church we know of is that of the *Church of a city*, and that the concrete form of this city Church is the assembly that comprises *all* the Christians of that geographical area. Christianity seems to have appeared first as a city Church and if we read rightly the existing sources, it must have remained such until at least the middle of the second century.[40]

It is worth noting that all but one of the Apostle's epistles are addressed to the people of God in a geographical city: to the saints at Philippi (Philippians 1:1), church of God in Corinth (1 Corinthians 1:2), churches of Galatia (Galatians 1:1), saints in Ephesus (Ephesians 1:1), those in Rome loved by God (1:7), and the brothers in Christ at Colossae (Colossians 1:2).

Certainly the argument of a singular City Church will be met with oppositional claims of the early Church meeting in homes: και οικον εκκλεσια or house churches.[41] Concerning this phrase, Zizioulas argues that "If this term meant in fact the formation of an εκκλεσια on the basis of the unit of the *family*, then we are confronted with a definition of the local Church in a non-geographic sense; we are in fact faced with a *sociological* conception of 'locality'" [emphasis original].[42] While the sociological conception of locality fits well with Winter's People Group model as well as McGavern's Homogeneous Unit Principle, according to Zizioulas, no such sociological concept is found in the New Testament,

---

40. Zizioulas, *Being as Communion*, 248.

41. Simson, *Houses that Change the World*.

42. Zizioulas, *Being as Communion*, 249.

The term και οικον εκκλεσια in the New Testament does not point to a family-centered gathering but rather to the assembly of all the faithful of a city who meet as *guests of a particular house* (see Rom. 16:23, cf. the archeological evidence of churches named after house-owners in Rome, etc.) One could even claim that there seems to have been no more than one such "household Church" in each city at that time. . . . There is not a single case where the term "household Church" would appear more than once with reference to the same city in the same text.[43]

Zizioulas further argues that there are two basic ecclesiological principles that give the Church its meaning,

a. *The catholic* [universal] *nature of the eucharist.* This means that each eucharist assembly should include all the members of the Church of a particular place, with no distinction whatsoever with regard to ages, professions, sexes, races, languages, etc.

b. *The geographical nature of the eucharist,* which means that the eucharist assembly—and through it the Church—is always a community of *some place* (e.g., the Church of Thessalonika, of Corinth, etc. in the Pauline letters.[44]

The geographical nature of the Church, located in cities, was the normative pattern of worship at least until the middle of the second century.[45]

Simon Chan makes a similar assessment concerning the universal nature of Christianity and the sacrament of the eucharist as a means of demonstrating and preserving the unity of believers in the early Church,

In the eucharist the church manifests its essential being as the one body of Christ. The sharing of one bread and cup is a poignant way of manifesting its unity. The early Christians maintained the sense of unity of the church by gathering at one place in each town, and even when it was necessary to have more than one congregation meeting in large cities and towns, each congregation would send a piece of the consecrated bread to other congregations in the city as a sign of their unity.[46]

43. Zizioulas, *Being as Communion,* 249.

44. Zizioulas, *Being as Communion,* 247.

45. It should be noted that household churches are mentioned in letters to City Churches (see for example Rom 16:5 and Col 4:15) and that household churches may be complimentary aspects of the same reality rather than being one and the same. This is certainly the case as Christianity expands beyond the city.

46. Chan, *Liturgical Theology,* 144.

It might be argued that the People Group model is in direct opposition to these preceding principles. There are serious concerns with reading People Groups back into the Bible as a means of parsing humanity and forming separate congregations within a single geographical location.

Allowing sociocultural identifications to reify a strong sense of identity and, therefore, the need for separate congregations is counterintuitive to Paul's considerable efforts in the New Testament to suggest that the gospel transcends such categories. Vladimir Lossky puts it succinctly saying, "There is no Church of the Jews or of the Greeks, of the Barbarians or the Scythians, just as there is no Church of the slaves or the free men, of men or of women."[47] Lossky contends that secular anthropology has little value for the church because "the anthropological realities of our everyday experience are deformed by sin and correspond little to the pure norms of the new creation which is being realized in the Church."[48]

Zizioulas echoes Lossky's concerns regarding churches based upon social identifications saying,

> A eucharist which discriminates between races, sexes, ages, professions, social classes etc. violates not certain ethical principles but its eschatological nature. For this reason such a eucharist is not a "bad"—i.e. morally deficient—eucharist but no eucharist at all.[49]

In other words, congregations meeting on the basis of shared affinities should not be regarded as the Church because they fail to demonstrate the eschatological nature of the Church where divisions are transcended by the people of God rather than reinforced. This is not an argument suggesting that people with shared affinities cannot or should not meet together but that they should not consider their meeting Church lest Church be reduced to a social club and fail to bear witness to its universal scope. Much of Lossky's and Zizioulas's arguments come from the Orthodox understanding of the mysterious nature of the eucharist as an event that is not bound by space or time. In that sense, participating in the eucharist is a present reality as well as a historical and eschatological one. The eucharist is a moment of connection for the Church and the believer with the saints of past, present, and future. This moment gives the Church and the believer a sense that they are part of something bigger than themselves and the locality of their church. They are in some sense

---

47. Lossky, *In the Image and Likeness of God*, 184.
48. Lossky, *In the Image and Likeness of God*, 185.
49. Zizioulas, *Being as Communion*, 255.

participating in the Church of all tribes, tongues, peoples, and nations in all times and in all places (Revelation 5:9).

Concerning Revelation 5:9, what Piper considers to be the decisive text for People Group thinking, the fourfold phrase "every tribe, tongue, people and nation" is far more likely a reference to Daniel showing the universality of God's redemption rather than a classification model for people in the twenty first century. G.K. Beale, in discussing John's use of the phrase suggests, "The general consensus is that this phrase is to be traced back to the almost identical expression repeated in Daniel. There the wording refers generally to the inhabitants of the world."[50]

Similarly, Richard Bauckham states,

> In Revelation, four is the number of the world, seven is the number of completeness. The sevenfold use of the fourfold phrase indicates that reference is being made to all the nations of the world. In the symbolic world of Revelation, there could hardly be a more emphatic indication of universalism.[51]

If this is the case, then we must conclude that Winter's People Group thinking did not come from the Bible but rather was read into the Bible. As was stated in the first chapter of this study, "We begin to conceptualize matters of identity at the very time in history when they become a problem."[52] For Winter, the problem in 1974 was people blindness and the solution was People Group identity.

Eventually the effects of globalization led Winter to conclude that People Groups are far less cohesive than he originally had suggested:

> Beware of taking ethnolinguistic lists too seriously, however. They are a good place to begin strategizing church planting efforts, but cross-cultural workers should be prepared for surprising discoveries when confronted by the cultural realities on the field. . . . Another reason to be cautious when applying people group thinking is the reality that powerful forces such as urbanization, migration, assimilation, and globalization are changing the composition and identity of people groups all the time. The complexities of the world's peoples cannot be neatly reduced to distinct, non-overlapping, bounded sets of individuals with permanent impermeable boundaries. Members of any community have complex relationships and may have multiple

50. Beale, *Book of Revelation*, 359.

51. Bauckham, *Climax of Prophecy*, 326.

52. Erikson, *Childhood and Society*, 282.

identities and allegiances. Those identities and allegiances are subject to change over time.[53]

If People Group identity is dynamic, multiple, and highly contextual, it is debatable as to its usefulness or validity as an analytical tool. What globalization revealed was the fundamentally flawed assumption of cultural or ethnic identity.

Identity or Identification

The consistent need for the above qualifying terms in discussions of ethnic identity is an industry standard according to Brubaker, something he cleverly terms "clichéd constructivism."[54] He argues that the term identity "tends to mean too much (when understood in a strong sense), too little (when understood in a weak sense), or nothing at all (because of its sheer ambiguity)."[55] Because of the elasticity and ambiguity of the term "identity," he opts for the term identification, noting it as an active term forcing the researcher to specify individuals doing the identifying. Henry Hale echoes Brubaker's use of the term identification saying,

> It would therefore be more productive not to talk about someone acquiring a 'new identity' or about a new identity being created but instead to refer to the formation of a 'new identification.' Because the term itself implies a process, one can easily refer to identifications that are strong and weak, thick and thin, waxing and waning, and so on, without introducing confusion because identification does not imply that any particular threshold level of thickness is necessary for a self-categorization to be called an 'identification.' . . . people have multiple identifications, multiple dimensions of identity, but not multiple identities.[56]

Hale further argues that some may wrongfully associate the constructivist use of multiple identities with mental illness. However, the term identification, "calls attention to complex (and often ambivalent) *processes*, while the term 'identity,' designating a *condition* rather than a *process*, implies too easy to fit between the individual and the social."[57]

---

53. Winter and Koch, "Finishing the Task," 537.
54. Brubaker, *Ethnicity without Groups*, 38.
55. Brubaker, *Ethnicity without Groups*, 28.
56. Hale, "Explaining Ethnicity," 480.
57. Brubaker, *Ethnicity without Groups*, 44.

Richard Jenkins sees ethnicity as an "ongoing *process* of ethnic identification" as well.[58] Identification does not presuppose a bounded group based
on an internal sameness. Whereas "[Identification is] intrinsic to social life;
'identity' in the strong sense is not."[59] Identification allows one to identify
oneself—to locate oneself in a narrative in time and space, both contextually and relationally. How an individual identifies oneself and is identified by
others may vary greatly depending on these factors. This work of identifying
oneself should not be equated with identity. If this occurs, we run the risk of
overgeneralizing, imposing, and potentially exaggerating categorical belonging. Therein lies the primary problem with the People Group thinking.

Not only is ethnic identity overemphasized in the People Group model,
but national identification and political boundaries are too easily dismissed.
Winter describes national identities as a "cookie cutter" approach, suggesting
geopolitical boundaries that divide a People Group into different nations will
not change the fact that they are still from the same dough.[60] This static view
of culture underestimates the ability of an individual to select identifications
for personal gain and to make sense of the world. It may be the case in the
twenty-first century that nationalism becomes the overarching collective
identification for individuals rather than ethnicity—a concept elucidated
in Benedict Anderson's 1984 publication, *Imagined Communities*. Certainly
that seems to be the case in the United States as opposed to the multicultural-
ism of postcolonial Europe. The public narrative of nationalism may have a
greater influence than the narrative of the tribe. This does not necessarily
imply that identification with the tribe will cease, but it may. In essence, classifying or assigning identity based on categories of practice is too simplistic
and, therefore, an ineffective means of parsing the global population.

Deemphasizing categories is not to say the categories do not exist or
are not important. According to Brubaker:

> Categories structure and order the world for us. We use catego-
> ries to parse the flow of experience into discriminable and inter-
> pretable objects, attributes, and events . . . they thereby make the
> natural and social worlds intelligible, interpretable, communi-
> cable, and transformable. Without categories, the world would
> be a "blooming, buzzing confusion"; experience and action as
> we know them would be impossible.[61]

---

58. Jenkins, *Rethinking Ethnicity*, 15.
59. Brubaker, *Ethnicity without Groups*, 41.
60. Winter and Koch, "Finishing the Task," 537.
61. Brubaker, *Ethnicity without Groups*, 71.

The problem is not categories, but rather the depersonalization of individuals for the sake of categories that may or may not be important to individuals. Too often People Group thinking bypasses the individual for the sake of an imagined collective. Individuals are thus reduced to mechanistic byproducts of external sociocultural factors. According to Cohen, ignoring the individual "has probably rendered our accounts of other societies inaccurate in important respects, since they must be revealed as generalisations from only partially perceived, at worst misperceived, elements of those societies."[62] He further argues that ascribing analytical collectivities to groups is a "crude means of categorization."[63] This categorization is often achieved through exaggeration of similarities and differences and seeking the lowest common denominator to express collective identity. Individuals are mostly absent or presented as byproducts of cultural and social power structures. These reductive models fail to represent individual self-awareness.

Many missiologists continue to make the generalizations that anthropology and sociology have made in the past. People Group classification is especially problematic when we consider that the categories imposed have little or no legitimacy in the researcher's life. Cohen describes such methods as top-down approaches to ethnography in which individuals are derived "from the social structures to which they belong: class, nationality, state, ethnic group, tribe, kinship group, gender, religion, caste, generation, and so on."[64] He further suggests that researchers consider whether or not we have appreciated attitudes being imputed to us based on a categorization. Most researchers would be uncomfortable with the notion of studying sociocultural factors in order to demonstrate their individual sense of self. Scholars often go to great lengths in representing themselves in such a precise manner in order to avoid being misrepresented, misunderstood, or categorized. Nevertheless, some insist on classifying groups based on categories they would never personally accept.

In assessing my own experience, I must consider how Christians, particularly southern evangelicals, are often portrayed. I find these representations to be inadequate at best and, at worst, wholly inaccurate caricatures. The same could be said about classifying People Groups. It would be an interesting experiment to ask Western missiologists to classify themselves into a People Group. I have experimented with this recently at conferences. The response is often a puzzled look rather than a strong sense of collective identity with any particular group.

62. Cohen, *Self Consciousness*, 5.
63. Cohen, *Self Consciousness*, 5.
64. Cohen, *Self Consciousness*, 6.

It could be argued that missiology has swung the pendulum too far from its imperialistic past, to a postcolonial model of an unexamined idealization of culture and preserving communal societies at the sake of individuals. While Winter's ideas certainly avoid accusations of exporting Western culture and individualism, they may also be seen as externally ascribed collectivism and cultural determinism. Classifications based on collective identity are often reductive caricatures of individuals who, depending on the context, may or may not identify with the group externally ascribed. Gil-White argues that classification of groups is based on naturalism's biological categories of kinds of species in evolutionary theory.[65] This makes sense, considering that Carl Linnaeus's early taxonomy charts classified people according to observable differences in skin color. This sort of classification may be suitable for plants and animals but is hardly sufficient for describing complex human beings navigating a variety of sociocultural narratives alongside multifaceted relationships that often span the globe.

65. Gil-White, "Are Ethnic Groups Biological," 515–36.

Conclusion

WHILE MORE RECENT COGNITIVE approaches that center identity in the individual limit cultural determinism, this too may be swinging the pendulum too far. Emphasis on the cognitive negotiation of sociocultural artifacts may result in a misleading dichotomy between individual and collective identity. While this shift moves the discussion of identity away from static and deterministic models of the past, there is a risk of psychologizing culture to the point that groups are irrelevant at best, or non-existent at worst.

Current interdisciplinary approaches using a narrative framework offer a more balanced and nuanced approach to identity that privileges the individual without discounting the influence of the collective. Narrative identity demonstrates the relationship between individuals and communities rather than placing them in opposition (see chapter 4). However, the narrative approach is not without problems. One particular problem, demonstrated in this research, is the influence of transnational practices through computer mediated communication. Future research should address the influence of the increasing number of new narratives made available through the internet, particularly social media (see chapter 3). A particular problem for the Pashtun is that many of these public narratives are overwhelmingly negative and often associated with violent acts of terrorism (see chapter 5).

While virtual space may remove the previous constraining boundaries of locality, it does not necessitate an individual identity over or against a collective one. It is imperative to acknowledge the potential for an individual to find their sense of self in relationship with others through a shared adoration of a particular narrative identity.

This concept of narrative identity is demonstrated in the life history of Sayyid Qutb (see chapter 6). Qutb struggled throughout his life to reconcile the competing narratives of secular modernism and quranic traditionalism. As a young man, he decided to abandon the Islamic traditions of his village upbringing for a vision of a secular Egypt rooted in Western education. However, Qutb became disenchanted with this vision when he saw there was no room in the Egyptian imagination for his Muslim brothers across the national boundary in Palestine. Since Qutb was not able to find a suitable narrative within the Egyptian sociocultural stock of stories, he resurrected one from the seventh century. Qutb found a new sense of belonging by transcending time and space and rooting himself in the shared beliefs of the companions of Muhammad. He considered himself in relationship to this Muslim community through faith that superseded all the identities that had become fractured in his life. Not only was there no longer a need for a national, ethnic, tribal, or familial identity for Qutb, he believed these groupings contained elements of *shirk* (a grave sin of adding partners to God) because the groupings were not based upon shared beliefs or the Shari'ah (Islamic Law).

Qutb attempted to reconcile his past experiences with his imprisonment into a cohesive story that gave meaning to his suffering as well as hope that others may join him in his cause. In other words, *Milestones* is the embodiment of Sayyid Qutb's narrative identity where he attempts to regain a sense of self that is only dependent upon Islam and the Muslim community as he imagined it. Being a powerful storyteller, Qutb re-invents a so-called unique quranic generation as a historical collectivity that embodied his beliefs and gave meaning to his suffering. Exploring Qutb's narrative framework for a global *ummah* (Muslim community) has significant implications for understanding the process of identity formation at the intersection of personal, global, and sociocultural narratives.

The concept of narrative identity is further demonstrated in the lives of three young refugees who were drawn together not by a shared ethnic identity but rather a mutual love for Afghanistan, particularly the city of Kabul (see chapter 7). These young men were uninterested and at times, even opposed to conceptualizing identity within an ethnic framework. Much of the pain in their lives was interpreted as a result of ethnic divisions. Therefore, they would rather see themselves as Afghans. The public narrative of a national Afghan identity was deeply rooted in each of their stories. These young men believed it was time for Afghans to lay down their ethnic identities which were rooted in differences in exchange for a unified Afghanistan. Each of these young men was forced to flee Kabul as children and again as young adults. They have effectively reconceptualized geographical space through the lens of their relationships together and the ones they maintain back home through social media. It is not so much the city of Kabul that they are longing for; it is instead what Kabul symbolizes—a place that they imagine as wonderfully cosmopolitan rather than a city in ruins due to identity politics.

There is also a reconceptualization of ethnic boundary lines demonstrated in the life history interview with Alan (see chapter 8). Alan, like the other participants, experiences a dynamic relationship between his ethnic, national, and religious identifications. His experiences with both Americans and non-Pashtun Muslims continue to reshape his understanding of the boundary lines of identity. The boundary of identity for Alan and his immediate Muslim community, by and large, is being constructed around a regional religious affinity through a shared sense of collective suffering and marginalization. This is rooted both in events that happen in the United States as well as their countries of origin. Because of transnationalism and regular access to events back home through social media, the ongoing violence and suffering in both Pakistan and Afghanistan is a regular focus of the Friday prayers at Alan's mosque. This broader Muslim identity that is tied to marginalization and collective suffering transcends the more nuanced boundary lines that were present in their countries of origin.

Regular communication back home is impacting the lives of these refugees both positively and negatively. This is most clearly seen in the life history interview with Miriam (see chapter 9). Her extended and immediate families have unofficially nominated her as the bridge builder between the two cultures which often compete and conflict with one another. She carries the heavy burden of her actions being interpreted through the lenses of competing ideologies espoused by a variety of strained but significant relationships across two countries. When Miriam's internal desires conflict with the broader expectations of her extended family, she tends to align her actions with Islam as a means of validating her positions that may be rejected by her family in Pakistan. In other words, when Miriam's Pashtun family in Pakistan disagrees with her, she tends to allege that they are upholding a cultural identity over a religious one. Tension and fluidity between ethnic, religious, and national identity were present with all the research participants.

This research documents the interaction of *close relationships* in the mutual constitution of a narrative identity through the life history of Sayyid Qutb and the lives of Pashtun refugees living in the United States. While it is often narratives that are the medium through which a sense of self is constructed, stories alone do not have the power to give identity. Rather it is the framework to cultivate *close relationships* that take on an ontological significance by mutually constituting one another's identity. More simply stated, I find my sense of being in this person and this person finds their sense of being in me. What draws us together is a shared love of a particular narrative identity that gives us a sense of where we've come from, what our purpose is, where we belong, and where we are going. This framework for identity formation will move us away from classifying people based on observable categories towards understanding the role of shared narratives that form the basis for relationships of ontological significance.

Bibliography

Abdul-Rauf, Feisal. *What's Right with Islam is What's Right with America*. San Francisco: Harper One, 2004.

Ackerman, Gary. "Time Square Bomber Suspect Faisal Shahzad." *Washington Post*, May 4 2010. http://www.washingtonpost.com/wp-dyn/content/discussion/2010/05/04/DI2010050402210.html.

Adeney, Miriam. *Daughters of Islam: Building Bridges with Muslim Women*. Downers Grove, IL: InterVarsity, 2002.

Agar, Michael H. *The Professional Stranger: An Informal Introduction to Ethnography*. New York: Emerald, 1980.

Ahmed, Akbar S. *Millennium and Charisma among Pathans: A Critical Essay in Social Anthropology*. London: Routledge and Kegan Paul, 1976.

———. *Pukhtun Economy and Society: Traditional Structure and Economic Development in a Tribal Society*. London: Routledge and Kegan Paul, 1980.

———. "Religious Presence and Symbolism in Pukhtun Society." In *Islam in Tribal Societies: From Atlas to the Indus*, edited by A. S. Ahmed and D. Hart, 310–30. London: Routledge and Kegan Paul, 1984.

Ahmed, Akbar S., and James B. Mynors. "Fowlmere: Roundheads, Rambo and Rivalry in an English Village Today." *Anthropology Today* 10 (1994) 3–8.

Ahmed, Amineh. *Sorrow and Joy among Muslim Women*. New York: Cambridge University Press, 2006.

Ahmed, Saifuddin, and Jörg Matthes. "Media Representation of Muslims and Islam from 2000 to 2015: A Meta-Analysis." *International Communication Gazette* 79 (2016) 219–44.

Alinejad, Donya. "Mapping Homelands through Virtual Spaces: Transnational Embodiment and Iranian Diaspora Bloggers." *Global Networks* 11 (2001) 43–62.

Alonso, Andoni, and Pedro J. Oiarzabal, eds. *Diasporas in the New Media Age: Identity, Politics, and Community*. Reno: University of Nevada Press, 2010.

Alsultany, Evelyn. *Arabs and Muslims in the Media: Race and Representation After 9/11*. New York: New York University Press, 2012.

Altheide, David, L. "The News Media, the Problem Frame, and the Production of Fear." *The Sociological Quarterly* 38(1997) 647–68.

Anderson, Benedict. *Imagined Communities: Reflections on the Origin and Spread of Nationalism*. London: Verso, 1983.

Appadurai, Arjun. *Modernity at Large: Cultural Dimensions of Globalization*. Minneapolis: University of Minnesota Press, 1996.

Arjana, Sophia R. *Muslims in the Western Imagination*. New York: Oxford University Press, 2015.

Augustine. *Confessions*. Translated by R.S. Pine-Coffin. London: Penguin, 1961.

Babar, Majeed, and Kirk Semple. "In Brooklyn, Pashtuns March Against the Taliban." *New York Times*, May 15, 2009. https://cityroom.blogs.nytimes.com/2009/05/15/in-brooklyn-pashtuns-march-against-the-taliban/.

Banerjee, Mukulika. *The Pathan Unarmed: Opposition and Memory in the North West Frontier*. Santa Fe, NM: School of American Research Press, 2000.

Banerjee, Padmini, and Myna German. "Migration and Transculturation in the Digital Age: A Framework for Studying the "Space Between.""" *Journal of International and Global Studies* 2(2010) 23–35.

Barrow, Isaac. *The Usefulness of Mathematical Learning Explained and Demonstrated: Being Mathematical Lectures Read in the Publik Schools at The University of Cambridge*. Translated by Rev. J. Kirkby. London: St Paul Church Yard, 1734.

Barth, Fredrik, ed. *Ethnic Groups and Boundaries: The Social Organization of Cultural Difference*. Long Grove, IL: Waveland, 1998.

Bartlotti, Leonard N. "Negotiating Pakhto: Proverbs, Islam and the Construction of Identity among Pashtuns." PhD diss., Oxford Centre for Mission Studies, 2000.

Bauböck, Rainer. "Towards a Political Theory of Migrant Transnationalism." *International Migration Review* 37 (2003) 700–723.

Bauckham, Richard. *The Climax of Prophecy: Studies on the Book of Revelation*. Edinburgh: T. & T. Clark, 1993.

Baum, Geraldine. "Failed Times Square Bomber Faisal Shahzad gets Life in Prison." *Los Angeles Times*, October 5, 2010. https://www.latimes.com/archives/la-xpm-2010-oct-05-la-na-times-square-bomber-20101005-story.html.

Beale, G. K. *The Book of Revelation: A Commentary on the Greek Text*. Grand Rapids: Eerdmans, 1999.

Beck, Glenn. "The Glenn Beck Program." *Media Matters for America*, December 10, 2010. https://www.mediamatters.org/video/2010/12/06/beck-thinks-10-percent-of-muslims-are-terrorist/174061.

Benitez, Jose. "Transnational Dimensions of the Digital Divide among Salvadoran Immigrants in the Washington DC Metropolitan Area." *Global Networks* 6 (2006) 181–99.

Bernal, Victoria. "Diaspora, Cyberspace and Political Imagination: the Eritrean Diaspora Online." *Global Networks* 6 (2006) 161–79.

Bernays, Edward. *Propaganda*. Edited by M. C. Miller. Brooklyn: Ig, 2005.

Berry, John W. "Immigration, Acculturation, and Adaptation." *Applied Psychology* 46 (1997) 5–34.

———. "Acculturation: Living Successfully in Two Cultures." *International Journal of Intercultural Relations* 29 (2005) 697–712.

Berry, John W., and David L. Sam. "Accuracy in Scientific Discourse." *Scandinavian Journal of Psychology* 44 (2003) 65–68.

Blauner, Bob. "Problems of Editing "First-Person" Sociology." *Qualitative Sociology* 10 (1987) 46–64.

Bock, Darrell L. *Acts*. Baker Exegetical Commentary on the New Testament. Grand Rapids: Baker, 2007.

Bosch, David J. *Transforming Mission: Paradigm Shifts in Theology of Mission*. Maryknoll, NY: Orbis, 1991.

Boyd, Dana, and Nicole Ellison. "Social Network Sites: Definition, History, and Scholarship." *Journal of Computer-Mediated Communication* 13 (2007) 210–30.

Brinkerhoff, Jennifer M. *Digital Diasporas: Identity and Transnational Engagement.* New York: Cambridge University Press, 2009.

Brubaker, Rogers. *Ethnicity Without Groups.* Cambridge, MA: Harvard University Press, 2004.

Brubaker, Rogers, and Frederick Cooper. "Beyond Identity." *Theory and Society* 29(2000) 1–47.

Bruce, F. F. *Commentary on the Book of the Acts: The English Text with Introduction, Exposition and Notes.* Grand Rapids: Eerdmans, 1955.

Bruner, Jerome. "Culture and Mind: Their fruitful Incommensurability." *Ethos Journal of the Society for Psychological Anthropology* 36 (2008) 29–45.

———. "The Narrative Construction of Reality." *Critical Inquiry* 18 (1991) 1–21.

———. "A Narrative Model of Self-Construction." *Annals of the New York Academy of Sciences* 818 (1997) 145–61.

Burde, Diane. *Schools for Conflict or Peace in Afghanistan.* New York: Columbia University Press, 2014.

Bush, George W. "Selected Speeches of President George W. Bush 2001–2008." *National Archives,* 2001. https://georgewbush-whitehouse.archives.gov.

Bustamante, Javier. "Tidelike Diasporas in Brazil: From Slavery to Orkut." In *Diasporas in the New Media Age: Identity, Politics, and Community,* edited by Adoni Alonso and Pedro J. Oiarzabal, 170–89. Reno: University of Nevada Press, 2010.

Calvert, John. *Sayyid Qutb and the Origins of Radical Islamism.* New York: Oxford University Press, 2013.

Campbell, David. "Cultural Governance and Pictorial Resistance: Reflections on the Imaging of War." *Review of International Studies* 29 (2003) 57–73.

Cavallaro, James, et al. "Living Under Drones: Death, Injury and Trauma to Civilians from US Drone Practices in Pakistan." *Stanford: International Human Rights and Conflict Resolution Clinic,* Stanford Law School; New York: NYU School of Law, Global Justice Clinic, 2012. https://law.stanford.edu/publications/living-under-drones-death-injury-and-trauma-to-civilians-from-us-drone-practices-in-pakistan/.

Chan, Simon. *Liturgical Theology: The Church as Worshiping Community.* Downers Grove, IL: InterVarsity, 2006.

Chapman University. "America's Top Fears 2016: Chapman University Survey of American Fears." https://blogs.chapman.edu/wilkinson/2016/10/11/americas-top-fears-2016/.

Churchill, Winston. *The Story of the Malakand Field Force: An Episode of Frontier War.* London: Thomas Nelson & Sons, 1916.

Clifford, James, and George E. Marcus, eds. *Writing Culture: The Poetics and Politics of Ethnography.* Berkeley: University of California Press, 1986.

Cole, Andra, and Knowles, Gary. *Lives in Context: The Art of Life History Research.* Walnut Creek, CA: AltaMira, 2001.

Cohen, Anthony P. *Self Consciousness: An Alternative Anthropology of Identity.* London: Routledge, 2002.

Combating Terrorism Center at West Point. "Declaration of Jihad against the Americans Occupying the Land of the Two Holiest Sites." https://ctc.usma.edu/harmony-program/declaration-of-jihad-against-the-americans-occupying-the-land-of-the-two-holiest-sites-original-language-2/.

Coombs, Tessa, et al. "CNN Encore Presentation: 'Soldiers of God.'" Aired September 29, 2001. http://transcripts.cnn.com/TRANSCRIPTS/0109/29/cp.00.html.

Coulson, Andrew. "Education and Indoctrination in the Muslim World: Is There a Problem? What Can We Do About It?" *Policy Analysis* 511 (2004) 1–36.

Cox, Daniel, et al. "What It Means to Be American; Attitudes towards Increasing Diversity in America Ten Years after 9/11." *Public Religion Research Institute,* 2011.

Council on American-Islamic Relations (CAIR). "CAIR Civil Rights Report 2017." https://ca.cair.com/sacval/publications/2017-cair-national-civil-rights-report/.

Curtis, Adam, dir. *Bitter Lake.* London: BBC Documentary, 2015.

Davies, Collin. *The Problem of the North-West Frontier, 1890–1908, with a Survey of Policy Since 1849.* London: Cambridge University Press, 1932.

Davis, Craig. "'A' Is for Allah, 'J' Is for Jihad." *World Policy Journal* 19 (2002) 90–94.

Department of Defense. "2015 Demographics: Profile of the Military Community." http://download.militaryonesource.mil/12038/MOS/Reports/2015-Demographics-Report.pdf.

DiMaggio, Paul. "Culture and Cognition." *Annual Review of Sociology* 23 (1997) 263–87.

Dixon, Travis L., and Charlotte L. Williams. "The Changing Misrepresentation of Race and Crime on Network and Cable News." *Journal of Communication* 65 (2015) 24–39.

Drake, Bruce, and Carrol Doherty. "Key Findings on How Americans View the U.S. in the World." *Pew Research Center,* May 5, 2016. https://www.pewresearch.org/fact-tank/2016/05/05/key-findings-on-how-americans-view-the-u-s-role-in-the-world/.

D'souza, Dinesh. *The Enemy at Home: The Cultural Left and its Responsibility for 9/11.* New York: Broadway, 2008.

Edwards, David. "Learning from the Swat Pathans: Political Leadership in Afghanistan, 1978–97." *American Ethnologist* 25 (1998) 712–28.

Elliott, Andrea, et al. "For Times Square Suspect, Long Roots of Discontent." *New York Times,* May 15, 2010. http://www.nytimes.com/2010/05/16/nyregion/16suspect.html.

Elmsie, G. R. *Notes on Some of the Characteristics of Crime and Criminals in the Peshawar Division of the Punjab, Illustrated by Selections from Judgements of the Sessions Court from 1872 to 1877.* Lahore: W. Ball, 1884.

Emerson, Robert, et al. *Writing Ethnographic Fieldnotes.* Chicago: University of Chicago Press, 2011.

Emerson, Steven. *American Jihad: The Terrorists Living among Us.* New York: Free, 2002.

Erikson, Erik H. *Childhood and Society.* New York: W. W. Norton, 1963.

———. *Gandhi's Truth: On the Origins of Militant Nonviolence.* New York: W. W. Norton, 1969.

———. *Identity: Youth and Crisis.* New York: W.W. Norton, 1968.

———. *Life History and the Historical Moment: Diverse Presentations.* New York: W. W. Norton, 1975.

———. *Young Man Luther: A Study in Psychoanalysis and History.* New York: W. W. Norton, 1958.

Esposito, John, and Dalia Mogahed. *Who Speaks for Islam? What a Billion Muslims Really Think.* New York: Gallup, 2007.

Euclid. *The Elements of Geometrie of the Most Ancient Philosopher Euclid of Megara*. Translated by Henry Billingsley. Imprinted at London: John Daye, 1570.

Faist, Thomas. "Diaspora and Transnationalism: What kind of Dance Partners?" In *Diaspora and Transnationalism: Concepts, Theories and Methods*, edited by R. Bauböck and T. Faist, 11–34. Amsterdam: Amsterdam University Press, 2010.

Fallwell, Jerry, Jr. "President Thanks Students for Support During Semester's Last Convocation." *Liberty Alumni News*, December 9, 2015. https://www.liberty.edu/news/2015/12/09/president-thanks-students-for-support-during-semesters-last-convocation/.

Fearon, James D. "What is Identity (As We Now Use The Word)." Department of Political Science, Stanford University, Stanford, CA. Unpublished Manuscript. http://www.web.stanford.edu/group/fearon-research/cgi-bin/wordpress/wp-content/uploads/2013/10/What-is-Identity-as-we-now-use-the-word-.pdf.

Filkins, Dexter. "A Nation Challenged: A New York Mosque; Afghans at Queens Mosque Split Over bin Laden." *New York Times*, September 19, 2001. http://www.nytimes.com/2001/09/19/nyregion/nation-challenged-new-york-mosque-afghans-queens-mosque-split-over-bin-laden.html.

Geertz, Clifford. *The Interpretation of Cultures: Selected Essays*. New York: Basic, 1973.

Geller, Pamela. *Stop the Islamization of America: A Practical Guide to the Resistance*. Los Angeles: WND, 2011.

George, Timothy. *Is the Father of Jesus the God of Muhammad?* Grand Rapids: Zondervan, 2002.

Gibbs, David N. "Afghanistan: The Soviet Invasion in Retrospect." *International Politics* 37(2000) 233–46.

Gil-White, Francisco J. "Are Ethnic Groups Biological "Species" to the Human Brain?" *Current Anthropology* 42 (2001) 515–36.

Glaser, Ida. *The Bible and Other Faiths: What Does the Lord Require of Us?* Carlisle, Cumbria: Langham, 2005.

Glassner, Barry. "Narrative Techniques of Fear Mongering." *Social Research: An International Quarterly* 71(2004) 819–26.

Glatzer, Bernt. "The Pashtun Tribal System." In *Contemporary Society: Tribal Studies*. *Contemporary Society: Tribal Studies*, edited by G. Pfeffer and D. K. Behera, 5:265–82. New Delhi: Concept, 2002.

Gleason, Philip. "Identifying Identity: A Semantic History." *The Journal of American History* 69 (1983)910–31.

Goldberg, Jonathan, and Madhavi Menon. "Queering History." *PMLA* 120 (2005) 1608–17.

Goodheart, Lawrence B. "The Odyssey of Malcolm X: An Eriksonian Interpretation." *Historian* 53 (1990) 47–62.

Gordon, Bruce. *Calvin*. New Haven, CT: Yale University Press, 2009.

Graham, Mark, and Shahram Khosravi. "Reordering Public and Private in Iranian Cyberspace: Identity, Politics, and Mobilization." *Identities: Global Studies in Culture and Power* 9 (2002) 219–46.

Greenwald, Robert. "Rethink Afghanistan." Culver City, CA: Brave New Films, 2009.

Greenway, H. D. S. "War with the Wrong Enemy." *New York Times*, May 16, 2011. http://www.nytimes.com/2011/05/17/opinion/17iht-edgreenway17.html.

Greenlee, David, ed. *Longing for Community: Church Ummah or Somewhere in Between?* Pasadena: William Carrey Library, 2013.

Guarnizo, Luis E., et al. "Assimilation and Transnationalism: Determinants of Transnational Political Action among Contemporary Migrants." *American Journal of Sociology* 108 (2003) 1211–48.

Hale, Henry E. "Explaining Ethnicity." *Comparative Political Studies* 37 (2004) 458–85.

Hall, Stuart. "Whose Heritage? Un-settling 'The Heritage', Re-imagining the Post-nation." *Third Text* 13 (1999) 3–13.

Hays, Tom. "Faisal Shahzad, Times Square Car Bomb Suspect, Pleads Guilty To 'Mass Destruction' Charge." *Huffington Post*, June 21, 2010. https://www.huffpost.com/entry/faisal-shahzad-times-squa_0_n_620107.

Herskovits, Melville. *Acculturation: The Study of Culture Contact.* New York: J. J. Augustin, 1938.

Hiebert, Paul G. "The Social Sciences and Missions: Applying the Message." In *Missiology and the Social Science: Contributions, Cautions and Conclusions,* edited by E. Rommen and G. Corwin, 184–213. Pasadena: William Carrey, 1996.

Hippolytus. *Apostolic Traditions of Hippolytus.* Translated by B. S. Easton. Ann Arbor: Cushing-Malloy, 1962.

Hogan, Phillip. "Response to Dr. Ralph Winter's Paper." In *Let the earth hear His Voice: Official Reference Volume, Papers and Responses/International Congress on World Evangelization, Lausanne, Switzerland,* edited by J. D. Douglas, 242–45. Minneapolis: World Wide, 1975.

Horsch, John. "The Rise and Fall of the Anabaptists of Muenster." *Mennonite Quarterly Review* 9(1935) 129–43.

———. "The Rise and Fall of the Anabaptists of Muenster Concluded." *Mennonite Quarterly Review* 9 (1935) 92–103.

Horsley, Richard A. "The Sicarii: Ancient Jewish 'Terrorists.'" *The Journal of Religion* 59 (1979) 435–58.

Hosseini, Khaled. *The Kite Runner.* New York: Riverhead, 2003.

———. "Kite Runner Author Khaled Hosseini on Identity." *BBC Culture,* October 21, 2014. http://www.bbc.com/culture/story/20140110-hosseini-roots-are-everything.

———. *A Thousand Splendid Suns.* London: Bloomsbury, 2008.

Issa-Salwe, Abdisalam M. "The Internet and the Somali Diaspora: The Web as a Means of Expression." *Bildhaan: An International Journal of Somali Studies* 6 (2008) 54–67.

Jabbour, Nabeel. "10 Reasons Muslims are Eager to Join ISIS." *Zwemer Center for Muslim Studies,* 2015. http://www.zwemercenter.com/sample -post-with-a-title/.

Jan, Muhammad Ayub. "Contested and Contextual Identities: Ethnicity, Religion and Identity among the Pakhtuns of Malakand, Pakistan." PhD diss., University of New York, 2010. http://etheses.whiterose.ac.uk/1179/1/Ayub_Jan_Thesis.pdf.

———. "Current Unrest and the Ensuing Debates about Identity among the Pakhtuns in Cultural and Virtual Spaces." Presented at The Dynamic of Change in Conflict Societies: Pakhtun Region in Perspective, Peshawar, Pakistan, November 14–15, 2011.

Jenkins, Richard. *Rethinking Ethnicity.* 2nd ed. London: Sage, 2008..

Jones, Robert P., et al. "Anxiety Nostalgia and Mistrust: Findings from the 2015 American Values Survey." *PRRI,* November 17, 2015. http://www.prri.org/research/survey-anxiety-nostalgia-and-mistrust-findings-from-the-2015-american-values-survey/.

Joshua Project. "What is a People Group." *Frontier Ventures.* https://joshuaproject.net/resources/articles/what_is_a_people_group.

Karon, Tony. "The Taliban and Afghanistan." *Time Magazine,* September 18, 2001. http://content.time.com/time/nation/article/0,8599,175372,00.html.

Katersky, Aaron. "Faisal Shahzad: 'War with Muslims has just Begun.'" *ABC World News,* October 5, 2010. https://abcnews.go.com/Blotter/times-square-bomber-faisal-shahzad-sentenced-life/story?id=11802740.

Kaye, John W. *The War in Afghanistan.* Vol. 1. 3rd ed. London: W. H. Allen, 1874.

Kaylan, Melik. "Immigration, Terror and Assimilation." *Forbes Magazine.* May 6, 2010. http://www.forbes.com/2010/05/06/times-square-bomber-immigration-opinions-columnists-melik-kaylan-assimilation.html.

Keener, Craig S. *Acts. An Exegetical Commentary: Introduction and 1:1–2:47.* Grand Rapids: Baker, 2012.

Kidd, Thomas S. *American Christians and Islam: Evangelical Culture and Muslims from the Colonial Period to the Age of Terrorism.* Princeton: Princeton University Press, 2009.

Kolmer, Christian. "Terror and Fear Shape the Image of Islam." Presented at the International Agenda Setting Conference, September 22–24, 2016, Vienna. http://us.mediatenor.com/en/library/newsletters/798/terror-and-fear-shape-the-image-of-islam#.

Köstenberger, Andreas J., and Peter T. O'Brien. *Salvation to the Ends of the Earth: A Biblical Theology of Mission.* Downers Grove, IL: InterVarsity, 2001.

Kraft, Kathryn A. *Searching for Heaven in the Real World: A Sociological Discussion of Conversion in the Arab World.* Oxford: Regnum, 2012.

Kumar, Deepa. *Islamophobia and the Politics of Empire.* Chicago: Haymarket, 2012.

Langness, Lewis. *The Life History in Anthropological Science.* Chicago: Holt Rinehart and Winston, 1965.

Larkin, William J. *Acts.* Downers Grove, IL: InterVarsity, 1995.

Lean, Nathan. *The Islamophobia Industry: How the Right Manufactures Fear of Muslims.* London: Pluto, 2012.

Letter to Baghdadi. "Letter to Dr. Ibrahim Awwad Al-Badri, alias 'Abu Bakr Al-Baghdadi' and To the Fighters and Followers of the Self-Declared 'Islamic State.'" http://lettertobaghdadi.com/14/english-v14.pdf.

Levitt, Peggy, and Nina Schiller. "Conceptualizing Simultaneity." In *Rethinking Migration: New Theoretical and Empirical Perspectives,* edited by A. Portes and J. DeWind, 181–218. New York: Berghahn, 2007.

Lima, Fernando H. "Transnational Families: Institutions of Transnational Social Space." In *New Transnational Social Spaces: International Migration and Transnational Companies in the Early Twenty-First Century,* edited by L. Pries, 77–93. New York: Routledge, 2001.

Lindholm, Charles. *Generosity and Jealousy: The Swat Pukhtun of Northern Pakistan.* New York: Columbia University Press, 1982.

Locke, John. *An Essay Concerning Human Understanding.* Edited by P. Nidditch. Oxford: Oxford University Press, 1975.

Loewen, Jacob A. "Response to Dr. Ralph Winter's Paper." In *Let the earth hear His Voice: Official Reference Volume, Papers and Responses/International Congress on World Evangelization, Lausanne, Switzerland,* edited by J. D. Douglas, 246–52. Minneapolis: World Wide, 1975.

Loewen, Joy. *Woman to Woman: Sharing Jesus with a Muslim Friend.* Grand Rapids: Chosen, 2010.

Lorenz, Hendrik. "Ancient Theories of Soul." In *The Stanford Encyclopedia of Philosophy* (SEP), edited by E. N. Zalta. Stanford, CA: Stanford University, 2009. https://plato.stanford.edu/entries/ancient-soul/#2.

Lossky, Vladmir. *In the Image and Likeness of God,* edited by J. Erickson and T. Bird. Crestwood, NY: St. Vladimir Seminary Press, 1974.

Loukili, Amina. "Moroccan Diaspora, Internet and National Imagination: Building a Community Online through the Internet Portal Yabiladi." Presented at the Nordic Africa Institute Nordic Africa Days, Uppsala, Sweden, October 5–7, 2007.

Lunn, John, and Ben Smith. "The AfPak Policy and the Pashtuns." Briefing paper presented to the United Kingdom Parliament. https://commonslibrary.parliament.uk/research-briefings/rp10-45/.

Luther, Martin. "On the Jews and their Lies." In *Luther's Works, Volume 47: The Christian in Society IV,* edited by H. T. Lehman and F. Sherman, 121–306. Philadelphia: Fortress, 1971.

MacDonald, Peter, dir. *Rambo III.* Boca Raton, FL: Tristar Pictures, 1988.

MacIntyre, Alasdair. *After Virtue: A Study in Moral Theory.* 3rd ed. Notre Dame: Notre Dame Press, 2007.

Malet, Antoni. "Changing Notions of Proportionality in Pre-Modern Mathematics." *Asclepio* 42 (1990) 183–211.

Marcus, George E. "Ethnography in/of the World System: The Emergence of Multi-Sited Ethnography." *Annual Review of Anthropology* 24 (1995) 95–117.

Martin, Raymond, and John Barresi. *The Rise and Fall of Soul and Self: An Intellectual History of Personal Identity.* New York: Columbia University Press, 2006.

Massey, Doreen. *For Space.* London: Sage, 2008.

McCarthy, Andrew. *The Grand Jihad: How Islam and the Left Sabotage America.* Jackson, TN: Encounter, 2012.

Mcgirk, Tim. "The Pashtun: Deep Loyalties, Ancient Hatreds." *Time Magazine,* November 19, 2001. http://content.time.com/time/subscriber/article/0,33009,1001273,00.html.

McQuilken, Robertson. "Use and Misuse of the Social Sciences: Interpreting the Biblical Text." In *Missiology and the Social Science: Contributions, Cautions and Conclusions,* edited by E. Rommen and G. Corwin, 165–83. Pasadena: William Carrey, 1996.

Medearis, Carl. *Muslims Christians and Jesus.* Bloomington, MN: Bethany House, 2008.

Melbourne, Bertram L. "Acts 1: 8 Re-examined: is Acts 8 its Fulfillment?" *The Journal of Religious Thought* 57 (2001) 1–19.

Mohamed, Besheer, et al. "U.S. Muslims Concerned About Their Place in Society, but Continue to Believe in the American Dream." *Pew Research Center,* July 26, 2017. https://www.pewforum.org/2017/07/26/findings-from-pew-research-centers-2017-survey-of-us-muslims/.

Morgan, Tomothy C. "Rick Warren's Final Frontier." *Christianity Today* 57 (2013) 34–37.

Morton, Thomas. *A treatise of the three-fold state of man, or An anatomie of the soule: Wherein is handled, 1 His created holinesse in his innocencie. 2 His sinfulnesse since the fall of Adam. 3 His renewed holinesse in his regeneration.* Imprinted in London: R. Robinson, 1596.

Murthy, Dhiraj. "Digital Ethnography: An Examination of the Use of New Technologies for Social Research." *Sociology* 42 (2008) 837–55.

Newsweek Staff Writer. "Pashtuns May Bring The Afghan War Home To America." *Newsweek*, September 23, 2009. http://www.newsweek.com/pashtuns-may-bring-afghan-war-home-america-79325.

Nichols, Robert. *A History of Pashtun Migration*. New York: Oxford University Press, 2008.

Nobel Foundation. "The Nobel Prize in Literature 1953." *Nobelprize.org*. http://www.nobelprize.org/nobel_prizes/literature/laureates/1953/.

North Carolina Pastors Network. "Pastors Support President's Travel Ban." https://ncpastors.net/2017/05/20/pastors-support-presidents-travel-ban/.

One Anonymous. "9/11: Did We Learn Anything? Not So Much." *Global Missiology* 3 (2017) 1–4.

Ott, Craig. "Globalization and Contextualization: Reframing the Task of Contextualization in the Twenty-First Century." Missiology 43 (2015) 43–58.

Parshall, Phil. *The Cross and the Crescent: Understanding the Muslim Heart and Mind*. Downers Grove, IL: InterVarsity, 2002.

Peoplegroups.org. "What is a People Group." *International Mission Board*. http://peoplegroups.org/understand/313.aspx.

Pérez-Latre, Francisco Javier, et al. "Social Networks, Media, and Audiences: A Literature Review." *Comunicación y Sociedad* 24 (2011) 63–74.

Pérez, Pablo M. "Response to Dr. Ralph Winter's Paper." In *Let the earth hear His Voice: Official Reference Volume, Papers and Responses/International Congress on World Evangelization, Lausanne, Switzerland*, edited by J. D. Douglas, 255–58. Minneapolis: World Wide Publications, 1975.

Phinney, Jean S., et al. "Ethnic Identity, Immigration, and Well-Being: An Interactional Perspective." *Journal of Social Issues* 57 (2001) 493–510.

Piper, John. "Should Christians Be Encouraged to Arm Themselves?" *Desiring God*, December 22, 2015. https://www.desiringgod.org/articles/should-christians-be-encouraged-to-arm-themselves.

———. "The Supremacy of God among 'All the Nations.'" *International Journal of Frontier Missions* 13 (1996) 15–26.

Piper, John, and Wayne Grudem. *50 Crucial Questions an Overview of Central Concerns about Manhood and Womanhood*. Wheaton, IL: Crossway, 2016.

Portes, Alejandro, et al. "The Study of Transnationalism: Pitfalls and Promise of an Emergent Research Field." *Ethnic and Racial Studies* 22 (1999) 217–37.

Postman, Neil. *Amusing Ourselves to Death: Public Discourse in the Age of Show Business*. New York: Penguin, 2006.

Poushter, Jacob. "In Nations with Significant Muslim Populations, Much Disdain for ISIS." *Pew Research Center Fact Tank*, November 17, 2015. https://www.pewresearch.org/fact-tank/2015/11/17/in-nations-with-significant-muslim-populations-much-disdain-for-isis/.

Powell, J. W. *Introduction to the Study of Indian Languages, with Words, Phrases, and Sentences to be Collected*. 2nd ed. Washington, DC: U.S. Government Printing Office, 1880.

Priest, Robert J. "Afterword: Concluding Missiological Reflection." In *Power and Identity in the Global Church: Six Contemporary Cases*, edited by B. Howell and E. Zehner, 185–92. Pasadena, CA: William Carey, 2009.

———. "The Value of Anthropology for Missiological Engagements with Context: The Case of Witch Accusations." *Missiology* 43 (2015)27–42.

Qureshi, Nabeel. *Answering Jihad*. Grand Rapids: Zondervan, 2016.

Qutb, Sayyid. "The America I have Seen: In the scale of Human Values." *CIA Library*. https://www.cia.gov/library/abbottabad-compound/3F/3F56ACA473044436B4C 1740F65D5C3B6_Sayyid_Qutb_-_The_America_I_Have_Seen.pdf.

———. *A Child from the Village*. Translated by J. Calvert and W. Shephard. Syracuse: Syracuse University Press, 2004.

———. *Milestones*. Cedar Rapids: Mother Mosque Foundation, 2003.

Rapport, Nigel. "The Narrative as Fieldwork Technique: A Processual Ethnography for a World in Motion." In *Constructing the Field: Ethnographic Fieldwork in a Contemporary World*, edited by V. Amit, 71–95. London: Routledge, 1999.

———. "The Liberal Treatment of Difference: An Untimely Meditation on Culture and Civilization." *Current Anthropology* 52 (2011) 687–710.

Rashid, Ahmed. "Pashtuns want an Image Change." *BBC News*, December 5, 2006. http://news.bbc.co.uk/2/hi/south_asia/6198382.stm.

———. "The Taliban: Exporting Extremism." *Foreign Affairs* 78 (1999) 22–35.

Redfield, Robert, et al. "Memorandum for the Study of Acculturation." *American Anthropologist* 38 (1936) 149–52.

Reisacher, Evelyne A. *Joyful Witness in the Muslim World: Sharing the Gospel in Everyday Encounters*. Grand Rapids: Baker, 2016.

Ricoeur, Paul. "Narrative Identity." *Philosophy Today* 35 (1991) 73–81.

———. *Memory, History, Forgetting*. Translated by K. Blamey and D. Pellauer. Chicago: University of Chicago Press, 2004.

Ronald Reagan Presidential Library. "Remarks Following a Meeting with Afghan Resistance Leaders and Members of Congress." *Reagan Library*, November 12, 1987. https://www.reaganlibrary.gov/archives/speech/remarks-following-meeting -afghan-resistance-leaders-and-members-congress.

Rose, H. A. *A Glossary of the Tribes and Castes of the Punjab and North-West Frontier Province: Based on the Census Report for the Punjab*. Vol. 3. Lahore: Civil and Military Gazette, 1914.

Rudmin, Floyd W., and Vali Ahmadzadeh. "Psychometric Critique of Acculturation Psychology: The Case of Iranian Migrants in Norway." *Scandinavian Journal of Psychology* 42 (2001) 41–56.

Rudmin, Floyd W. "Critical History of the Acculturation Psychology of Assimilation, Separation, Integration, and Marginalization." *Review of General Psychology* 7 (2003) 3–37.

Rynkiewich, Michael A. "Do We Need a Postmodern Anthropology for Mission in a Postcolonial World?" *Mission Studies* 28 (2011) 151–69.

Said, Edward. *Orientalism*. London: Routledge & Kegan Paul, 1997.

Saunders, Nicholas. *The Supper of Our Lord Set Foorth in Six Bookes: According to the Truth of the Gospell, and the Faith of the Catholike Churche*. Imprinted in Louanii: John Fowler, 1565.

Schiller, Nina G., et al. "From Immigrant to Transmigrant: Theorizing Transnational Migration." *Anthropological Quarterly* 68 (1995) 48–63.

———. "Towards a Definition of Transnationalism." *Annals of the New York Academy of Sciences* 645 (1992) 9–14.

Schwartz, Seth, et al. "The Role of Identity in Acculturation among Immigrant People: Theoretical Propositions, Empirical Questions, and Applied Recommendations." *Human Development* 49 (2006) 1–30.

Shah, Syed Wiqar Ali. *Ethnicity, Islam and Nationalism: Muslim Politics in the North-West Frontier Province 1937–1947.* New York: Oxford University Press, 1999.

Shepard, Stephen. "Poll: Majority of Voters Back Trump Travel Ban." *Politico,* July 5, 2017. https://www.politico.com/story/2017/07/05/trump-travel-ban-poll-voters-240215.

Shenk, David W. *Journeys of the Muslim Nation and the Christian Church: Exploring the Mission of Two Communities.* Scottdale: Herald, 2003.

Simson, Wolfgang. *Houses that Change the World: The Return of the House Church.* Emmelsbüll, Germany: C&P, 1999.

Skeen, Andrew. *Passing it On: Fighting the Pushtun on Afghanistan's Frontier.* Edited by L. W. Grau & R. H. Baer. Fort Leavenworth, KS: Foreign Military Studies, 2010.

Smietana, Bob. "Research: 1 in 3 Americans Worry About Sharia Law Being Applied in America." *Lifeway Newsroom,* February 11, 2015. https://blog.lifeway.com/newsroom/2015/02/11/research-1-in-3-americans-worry-about-sharia-law-being-applied-in-america/.

Smith, Gregory. "Most White Evangelicals Approve of Trump Travel Prohibition and Express Concerns about Extremism." *Pew Research Center Fact Tank,* February 27, 2017. https://www.pewresearch.org/fact-tank/2017/02/27/most-white-evangelicals-approve-of-trump-travel-prohibition-and-express-concerns-about-extremism/.

Smith, Michael, and Luis Guarnizo, eds. *Transnationalism from Below.* Vol. 6. New Brunswick, NJ: Transaction, 1998.

Smucker, Phillip. "To many Pashtuns, bin Laden is a Muslim Brother." *Christian Science Monitor* October 15, 2001. https://www.csmonitor.com/2001/1015/p7s1-wosc.html.

Snow, Nancy, and Philip M. Taylor. "The Revival of the Propaganda State: US Propaganda at Home and Abroad Since 9/11." *International Communication Gazette* 68 (2006) 389–407.

Sökefeld, Martin. "Alevism Online: Re-imagining a Community in Virtual Space." *Diaspora: A Journal of Transnational Studies* 11 (2002) 5–38.

———. "Debating Self, Identity, and Culture in Anthropology." *Current Anthropology* 40 (1999) 417–48.

Sommers, Margaret R. "The Narrative Constitution of Identity: A Relational and Network Approach." *Theory and Society* 23 (1994) 605–49.

Spain, James W. *The Pathan Borderland.* The Hague: Mouton, 1963.

———. *Pathans of the Latter Day. Karachi.* Pakistan: Oxford University Press, 1995.

Spencer, Robert. *Stealth Jihad: How Radical Islam Is Subverting America without Guns or Bombs.* Washington, DC: Regnery, 2008.

Spiro, Melford. "The Acculturation of American Ethnic Groups." *American Anthropologist* 57 (1955) 1240–52.

Spradley, James P. *The Ethnographic Interview.* Long Grove, IL: Waveland, 2016.

Stone, Matthew. *Reaching the Heart and Mind of Muslims.* Charleston, SC: Create Space, 2012.

Sutton, Constance, and Susan Makiesky-Barrow. "Migration and West Indian Racial and Ethnic Consciousness." *Center for Migration Studies Special Issues* 7 (1989) 86–107.

Thomas, William I., and Florian Znaniecki. *The Polish Peasant in Europe and America.* 5 vols. New York: Alfred A. Knopf, 1918–1921.

Tilghman, Andrew. "DoD: Most Insider Attacks Involve Pashtuns." *Marine Corps Times,* September 10, 2012. http://www.marinecorpstimes.com/news/2012/09/military-afghanistan-pashtuns-insider-attacks-091012w.

Trantor, Kristen. "Remaking Home." *The Sydney Morning Herald,* June 1, 2013. https://www.smh.com.au/lifestyle/remaking-home-20130527-2n60z.html.

Two Anonymous. "Essentialism and Islam." *Global Missiology* 3 (2017) 1–8.

Tynes, Robert. "Nation-building and the Diaspora on Leonenet: A Case of Sierra Leone in Cyberspace." *New Media and Society* 9 (2007) 497–518.

United States Agency for International Development (USAID). "Mission to Pakistan and Afghanistan: Project Assistance Completion Report Education Sector Support Project (306–0202)." Order No. PD-ABJ-201-90043. https://pdf.usaid.gov/pdf_docs/PDABJ201.pdf.

UNAMA. "Afghanistan: Record Level of Civilian Casualties Sustained in the First Half of 2016." *United Nations Assistance Mission in Afghanistan,* July 25, 2016. https://unama.unmissions.org/afghanistan-record-level-civilian-casualties-sustained-first-half-2016-un-report.

Van den Bos, Matthijs, and Liza Nell. "Territorial Bounds to Virtual Space: Transnational Online and Offline Networks of Iranian and Turkish–Kurdish Immigrants in the Netherlands." *Global Networks* 6 (2006) 201–20.

Williams, George H. *The Radical Reformation.* Philadelphia: Westminster, 1962.

Wilson, Lydia. "Understanding the Appeal of ISIS." *New England Journal of Public Policy* 29 (2017) Article 5.

Wilson, Michael. "Shahzad Gets Life Term for Times Square Bombing Attempt." *New York Times,* October 5, 2010. http://www.nytimes.com/2010/10/06/nyregion/06shahzad.html.

Wilson, Samuel M., and Leighton C. Peterson. "The Anthropology of Online Communities." *Annual Review of Anthropology* 31 (2002) 449–46.

Winter, Ralph D. "The Highest Priority: Cross-Cultural Evangelism." In *Let the earth hear His Voice*: *Official Reference Volume, Papers and Responses/International Congress on World Evangelization, Lausanne, Switzerland,* edited by J. D. Douglas, 213–41. Minneapolis: World Wide, 1975.

———. *The New Macedonia: A Revolutionary New Era in Missions Begins.* Pasadena: William Carrey, 1975.

Winter, Ralph D., and Bruce A. Koch. "Finishing the Task: The Unreached Peoples Challenge." In *Perspectives on the World Christian Movement,* edited by R. D. Winter and S. C. Hawthorne, 531–46. Pasadena: William Carrey, 2013.

Yousaf, Farooq. "Pakistan's Pashtun Profiling: Pakistan's Government is Labeling Pashtuns as Terror Suspects Based Solely on Ethnicity." *The Diplomat,* March 1, 2017. https://thediplomat.com/2017/03/pakistans-pashtun-profiling/.

Zaheer, Mohsin. "'I Am a Khan, I Am Not a Terrorist' Say Pashtuns in New York." *Feet in Two Worlds,* January 6, 2011. https://fi2w.org/i-am-a-khan-i-am-not-a-terrorist-say-pashtuns-in-new-york/.

Zhao, Shanyang, et al. "Identity Construction on Facebook: Digital Empowerment in Anchored Relationships." *Computers in Human Behavior* 24 (2008) 1816–36.

Zizioulas, John. *Being as Communion: Studies in Personhood and the Church.* Crestwood, NY: St. Vladimir Seminary Press, 1985.

Zwemer, Samuel M. *Islam and the Cross: Selections from the "Apostle to Islam."* Edited by R.S. Greenway. Philipsburg, NJ: P&R, 2002.

www.ingramcontent.com/pod-product-compliance
Lightning Source LLC
Chambersburg PA
CBHW070400270326
41926CB00014B/2636